ADVANCE PRAISE FOR

At Zero Tolerance

"Ronnie Casella's *At Zero Tolerance* provides a disquieting critique of the zero tolerance policies adopted by many public schools in the wake of the 1994 Gun-Free Schools Act passed by Congress after several fatal shootings at schools across the country. Casella uses historical and sociological data to sustain his arguments against zero tolerance policies; he claims that society should not merely clamp down on youths, but needs to address the behaviors and attitudes that ferment violence in American society. Casella's book will have wide appeal. It is a 'must' read for everyone concerned about the future of our nation's public schools."

Joan Burstyn, Professor of Education and History,
Department of Cultural Foundations of Education,
Syracuse University

"Ronnie Casella's fine ethnographic work—in both schools and prisons—is more than just a critique of zero tolerance. His contribution—as both anthropologist and as advocate—is to demonstrate the intimate social links between the deterioration of school systems, urban poverty, and the rise in the prison population. His work enables us to begin to understand how violence must be understood not just by examining the individual behavior but also the nitty-gritty human context in which it takes place. Casella also helps us to unpack 'context' in the broadest possible way—by getting at the historical underpinnings and the political meanings in our exploration of 'causes.' This book should be on the 'required reading list' of every school of education and department of anthropology."

John Devine, Chair, Academic Advisory Council,
National Campaign against Youth Violence

At Zero Tolerance

AC / SS
Adolescent
Cultures,
School
& Society

Joseph L. DeVitis & Linda Irwin-DeVitis
General Editors

Vol. 17

PETER LANG
New York • Washington, D.C./Baltimore • Bern
Frankfurt am Main • Berlin • Brussels • Vienna • Oxford

Ronnie Casella

At Zero Tolerance

Punishment, Prevention, and School Violence

PETER LANG
New York • Washington, D.C./Baltimore • Bern
Frankfurt am Main • Berlin • Brussels • Vienna • Oxford

Library of Congress Cataloging-in-Publication Data

Casella, Ronnie.
At zero tolerance: punishment, prevention,
and school violence / Ronnie Casella.
p. cm. — (Adolescent cultures, school, and society; vol. 17)
Includes bibliographical references (p.   ) and index.
1. School violence—United States—Prevention. 2. School violence—
Social aspects—United States. 3. School violence—Government policy—
United States. I. Title. II. Adolescent cultures, school & society; vol. 17.
LB3013.3 .C39   373.17'82'0973—dc21   00-020417
ISBN 0-8204-4996-2
ISSN 1091-1464

Die Deutsche Bibliothek-CIP-Einheitsaufnahme

Casella, Ronnie:
At zero tolerance: punishment, prevention,
and school violence / Ronnie Casella.
–New York; Washington, D.C./Baltimore; Bern;
Frankfurt am Main; Berlin; Brussels; Vienna; Oxford: Lang.
(Adolescent cultures, school and society; Vol. 17)
ISBN 0-8204-4996-2

Cover design by Lisa Dillon

The paper in this book meets the guidelines for permanence and durability
of the Committee on Production Guidelines for Book Longevity
of the Council of Library Resources.

© 2001 Peter Lang Publishing, Inc., New York

Printed in the United States of America

This book is dedicated to my mother and my father

Table of Contents

Acknowledgments

Expressions of appreciation should be succinct and heartfelt, and with that I would like to extend special thanks to a number of people who helped me with the research and writing of this book. The project, from the start, would have been impossible without those individuals who let me in buildings where they worked so I could study what turned out to be, in some cases, our shared interests. The principals of the schools and the warden of the prison discussed in this book deserve thanks for their trust and the time they spent with me. In addition, special thanks go to Jean at the New York high school, Mitch at the Connecticut high school, and Dee at the prison. Thanks as well to the head of security at the Connecticut high school, and the police officer at the New York high school. Warm thanks to Barbara who introduced me to the inmates whom I later interviewed and got to know during workshops at the prison. The inmates, especially Angel and Bob, gave up much of their time—and even chow time—to talk with me and to later correspond in letters. Students in the high schools interrupted their busy schedules to be interviewed and put up with my observations of them.

Several people read drafts of this manuscript and gave excellent suggestions for rewriting. Thanks to Joe DeVitis for his initial run-through and for planting the idea in me that I write this book. Maureen Gilroy gave feedback in writing and conversations and reminded me that what I say of adolescents in this book applies to younger children, as well. Joan Burstyn was especially helpful in providing suggestions about the historical aspects: No doubt my writing here is still wanting to her keen historical eye. Jack Gilroy pushed me to make my points stronger, to not hide justice behind academic rhetoric. Daniel Mulcahy provided feedback in the most informal of settings. Articles and conversations that brought with them new ideas came freely from Carole Shmurak. Larry Klein reminds me that political positions must be acted upon, in spite of risks. Tammy Cohen helped me with library research and was a master of finding just the right article or archive to force my thinking in new directions. In Central Connecticut State University—that provided a research grant and release time—I found a truly inspirational environment in which to write and teach. Finally, to the staff at Peter Lang Publishing, thanks for quick responses to questions and for excellent feedback.

Introduction
Background Notes

In the early 1990s I had the opportunity to teach high school for two years in Cali, Colombia. Before leaving, friends and family gave me their blessings, and one person worked hard to dissuade me from taking the job. "You're going to such a violent country," he told me. "Are you crazy!" Others had similar reactions. Then, after a month of teaching in Colombia, I learned a lesson about these perceptions of violence. As was customary, after several weeks of teaching the director of the school wanted to meet with new teachers from the United States to check in on how their work and stay was going. I arrived in her office, told her how much I enjoyed the first term, and the director, a Colombian woman who had hired me in New York City, told me that she had heard students praise me as well. She was genuinely pleased; I was happy to hear the positive feedback, but then she said something that baffled me. She told me, "And the students are no longer scared of you." I asked her, "Were they scared of *me*?" She nodded, knowingly, realizing that I could not see myself as a Colombian may. She explained, "When they heard that their teacher was from the United States, and especially from New York City, they thought the usual—that you would be mean. She said, "They think everybody from

New York has a gun, even the teachers."

For the first time, I felt myself classified as violent: I was from the United States, and worse yet, a New Yorker.

I have thought about this experience during my research on youth and school violence. At the time of the meeting with the director, I attributed the students' fears to an unfortunate stereotype of people from the United States. More recently, I have come to believe that they may have been right to assume the worst. After all, I was coming from a country that even U.S.-generated statistics proved to be among the most violent in the developed world.[1] In Colombia, specifically, the United States has virtually paid the bill for a devastating war between drug barons, guerrillas, and the government, which has proved once again U.S. propensities to solve problems, and to help other countries to solve problems, through military might.

Whether people in the United States are willing to accept it or not, violence is a defining characteristic of U.S. culture. This is not just the unfortunate outcome of high rates of gun possession, poverty, increased militarism, prejudice, and other factors that figure in highly as causes of lethal violence—it is also because the U.S. has benefitted from violence. Through violence, the country has sustained economic and political might abroad, has bolstered domestic and international expansions, and has served international interventions. Within its borders, violence has supported enslavement, patriarchy, class stratification, segregation, imprisonment, and has brought the country wealth through the distribution and sale of weapons on world and local markets. Those working on violence prevention must keep this reality in mind. Violence is not the explicit reserve of schools, or of youths, or of cities—it is characteristic of a U.S. culture that is indebted to and in some cases addicted to physical assertions of power.

The connection between different forms of violence is a crucial one, and it is at the heart of this book. School violence, youth violence, violence against women, urban violence, militarism, media violence, and so on, are part of a continuum. They are not singular and inexplicable occurrences in an otherwise peaceful society. What do we make of a boot camp chant discussed by a marine who entered the army through his high school's Junior ROTC program? Running obstacles, he sang in unison with other cadets: "Rape the town and kill the people, that's the thing we love to do! Rape the town and kill the people, that's the only thing to do! Watch the kiddies scream and shout, rape the town and kill the people, that's the thing we love to do!"[2] Are we to dissociate the school from the military and say that one has nothing to do with the other—in spite of increased numbers of Junior ROTC programs in U.S. high schools?

What are we to think when middle-school kids dress up in military camouflage from head to toe and open fire on their school, killing four children (all girls) and a female teacher, as occurred in Jonesboro, Arkansas, in 1998. How could these kids even know how to shoot—and to shoot so well? One, who was 11 years old, learned from his father at their local Jonesboro Practical Pistol Shooters Club. These are just two examples of the way school violence is integrally linked up with broader cultural and structural issues in the United States. To prevent any type of school violence, we must consider the problem within this more expansive national context—not root it out and pinpoint it as an isolated entity that we solve with a new packaged program.

The ways in which the United States has made use of violence to sustain might and leverage in world markets, political circles, as well as in actual battlefields, are not the concern of most people in the country; therefore violence prevention and crime policy has never focused attention on violence committed systematically in political arenas. Rather, the push has been to counter rising lethal violence in schools and among youths. Since "race riot" and "urban uprising" entered the American lexicon in the 1960s, and through the implementation of drug laws by Governor Rockefeller in the 1970s, the two hands of violence prevention in the United States have been the stiffening of sentences for criminal offenses and the mass building of prisons to house growing populations of mostly young black men.

In the 1990s, zero tolerance became a part of the language about crime, youth, and schooling, and sealed support for "get tough" policies. What zero tolerance has meant for the prison industrial complex has been quite vast. Prison populations have sky-rocketed, and with hardly a peep, by 1995 forty-eight states passed laws to facilitate the prosecution of juveniles as adults—and to therefore place children in adult prisons where they are at a higher risk of not only attack and rape, but of suicide. Moreover, in spite of continued abuses of inmates at prisons, the Prison Litigation Reform Act of 1996 made it easier for local governments to end federal court oversight of prisons. The federal court oversight was seen as necessary after decades of abuses of inmates by prison employees, that in some cases have led to deaths and reports of torture.

In spite of its ineffectiveness and meanness, zero tolerance gained political leverage in federal law, in national crime policy, and finally in schools. It did so for several reasons: first, it was the embodiment of the "get tough on crime" movement that carried Republicans to Congress in 1994. "Zero tolerance" is also a trendy phrase that easily rolls off the tongues of politicians eager to show that they are not soft on crime. It provides cover for defensive school administrators—it communicates that court houses, schools, and other institutions are getting tough on crime. It proves that lawmakers, administrators, and judges are doing everything possible to stamp out violence even if it means that they turn schools into prisons and prisons into modern-day dungeons.

Zero tolerance refers to those policies that show a hard-handed and extremely punitive way of dealing with kids and criminals—it proves little more than the ability of the U.S. judicial system to beat down people who are already beat. Behind zero tolerance are federal policies—such as the Gun-Free Schools Act of 1994—and general negative feelings about youths that have guided responses to young people's problems. Zero tolerance is represented in the response of one school that suspended an elementary school student for bringing a water pistol to class, and of another school that suspended a student for giving Advil® to a friend who had a headache. A report by the Advancement Project and The Civil Rights Project at Harvard University, made note of just a few other cases in schools involving zero tolerance.[3] Some of these included:

- A six-year-old African-American child was suspended for ten days for bringing a toenail clipper to school. A school board member said, "This is not about a toenail clipper! This is about the attachments on the toenail clipper!"
- A kindergarten boy in Pennsylvania was suspended for bringing a toy ax to school as part of his Halloween costume.
- A 14-year-old boy mistakenly left a pocketknife in his book bag after a Boy Scout camping trip. At his hearing, the boy's Scout Master testified on the boy's behalf. The student was expelled under the district's Zero Tolerance Policy, which requires expulsion for possession of knives. As a result of an appeal by the Legal Aid Society of Greater Cincinnati, the student was readmitted to school, but had already missed 80 days of school.
- An African-American 9th grader was expelled for one year from a predominantly white school district and sent to an alternative school because she had sparklers in her book bag. She had used them over the weekend and forgot they were in her bag.
- An African-American male 7th grader bet a schoolmate on the outcome of a school basketball game. The schoolmate, who lost the bet, accused the boy of threatening him for payment. The school district conducted no investigation but instead notified law enforcement officials. The 7th grader was charged with felony extortion and expelled.

There seem to be endless real-life stories that prove the unfairness and outright stupidity of zero tolerance policy and of the people who mindlessly enforce it. At the beginning of the school year in one Mississippi school, black students on a bus were playfully throwing peanuts and one accidently hit the white female bus driver, who pulled over to call the police. The police arrived and diverted the bus to the courthouse, where students were questioned. Five African American boys in high school were then arrested for felony assault, which carries a maximum penalty of five years in prison. The Sheriff commented to one newspaper, "This time it was peanuts, but if we don't get a handle on it, the next time it could be bodies."

Just imagine it: A life of crime—including murder—that all started with peanut-throwing on the school bus! As a result of this "assault with a peanut" incident, all five boys lost their right to ride the district's buses. School was thirty miles away, and the boys' families lacked transportation in this poor rural area of the Mississippi Delta, and as a result the students dropped out of school. One boy remarked, "I didn't have a choice—I didn't have a ride." His favorite subject was math (with 'A' grades), and he had grand ambitions. He stated, "I [would have] gone to college. Maybe I could have been a lawyer." Felony charges for peanut throwing, and in other incidents, expulsions for misbehavior and suspension for Halloween costumes—all this and more are the linchpins for feeding the prison industry newer bodies of mostly poor and minority students. As the Harvard report stated: "What was once considered a schoolyard scuffle, can now land a student in juvenile court or even worse, in prison." Furthermore, if the student is poor and non-white, the likelihood of this happening is greater.

Zero tolerance is the link between schools and prisons. Not only is it a policy that steers students from classrooms, through the labyrinths of the justice system, and into prison cells, but it is a philosophy that is shared by both schools and prisons in equal measure. Zero tolerance is the driving force behind one of the fastest growing ventures in the United States: the private prison industry. It is symbolized as well in draconian prison policy and the subsequent inhumanity that defines much of the criminal justice system. Not only does the United States imprison juveniles, but the country is unique in the world for being the only country in 1998 and 1999 to put to death people who were minors when they committed their crimes. As Wisconsin U.S. Senator Russ Feingold made plain, "I don't think we should be proud of the fact that the United States is the world leader in the execution of child offenders."[4]

Everybody who has ever filled out a job application, sought some form of social services, or applied for a driver's license knows that there is nothing that hurts young people more—that prevents them from obtaining a job and getting their lives together—than a criminal record. Even so, this is what we give young people whose criminal behaviors have been for the most part nonviolent and in many cases non-threatening to people around them.

There is agreement as well among many sociologists, some judges, and even a few politicians: If you want to ensure continued criminal behavior, take a kid who has bought some marijuana from a friend and sold a bit to an acquaintance, lock him up, in the best environment possible have him learn from others how to be a true criminal, and release him into the same kind of life he had before but with the added albatross of a criminal record. The recipe is ripe for the making of criminals. In fact, this is exactly what we do. When people ask why, rolling off the tongues of school administrators, prison wardens, judges, and politicians, are the same two words: "zero tolerance."

In schools, zero tolerance has been the rationale for the deployment of school police officers, the suspension and expulsion of students for misbehaving in class, and the buildup of security devises in schools. My first experience with a metal detector in school was during a middle-school science lab when we used a small handheld metal detector for an experiment—now, more often, students find themselves on the receiving end of one passing into a school. It is not just urban schools that have increased security in this way. A newly built middle school in a wealthy suburb not far from one of the schools discussed in this book opened in September 2000 with the following features: electronically latched doors, close-circuit television, specialized alarms, and sites at exterior and some interior doors where swipe cards would be needed to enter. The close-circuit televisions, with tapes that ran 24 hours a day, were hooked up to cameras at the school's five entrances and areas such as the cafeteria and gym. Such security devises often cost school districts hundreds of thousands of dollars to install and for upkeep. The security features in this school were seen as necessary after another school in the district had to spend $21,000 to make repairs caused by vandalism.

While an array of individuals—including the wealthy, the poor, the urban, the rural—have been touched by zero tolerance, it is generally the poor and nonwhite who suffer the most from it. The reason why is simple: People outside of mainstream society have always been the ones to be most penalized by crime policy. For a variety of reasons, prisons are overcrowded with black men, minorities make up the rolls of school suspension and expulsion reports, and young people caught in the labyrinth of out-placements, social service agencies, boot-camps, detention facilities, and locked school facilities, are mostly poor and/or nonwhite. These are people without the political power, gumption, and knowhow to pull themselves out of a vast criminal justice system that extends from the school to the prison. Part of the reason that zero tolerance has had such a stranglehold on justice policy, in spite of its ineffectiveness and in some cases inhumanity, is because politicians have convinced themselves and others that delinquents have been given every chance possible to straighten out. Pundits will point to the 1960s and the failure of liberal reforms and "rehabilitation" to stem violence. This suggests that only a backlash against young people will work to rein them in. They will refer to Wall Street as well and note that the economy is booming: There is no reason for violence with jobs so plentiful.

These arguments neglect to account for the fact that in spite of so-called liberal reforms, the United States has never known a sustained time of true national violence prevention. Instead, we have been seduced by punishment. The rise of the professions and psychology that shaped crime policy through the 20th century has not helped to set up a system of violence prevention, but one of institutionalization, confinement, and neglect. With the backing of professionals, prevention has been drowned out by incarceration, the mass suspension and expulsion of students from school, and the labeling and drugging of children. In reference to the economic argument—where jobs are seen as so plentiful: In spite of the fact that rich people have gotten richer in the United States during the latter part of the 20th century, the booming economy for some was little more than something they heard about in the media. In spite of glowing news, poverty in the United States continues to grow, especially in Connecticut and New York, two states that are focused on in this book. The number of high-poverty neighborhoods (defined as census tracks with 40% poverty or higher) have increased since the 1970s, and most jobs that have been created are low pay, temporary, and lack adequate benefits. For the middle classes, especially the black middle class, the picture is also grim. Prosperity and federal policies following World War II that helped to propel people to a relatively strong middle-class status are slipping away, and in the coming years we are expected to see a downward economic slide for all except those of secure and vast wealth.[5]

It has been said that we teach kids to be violent then punish them when they act as expected: Some are raised in squalor, surrounded by violence, and we imprison them when they act like everybody else around them. We fill them with military training and expect them to be "peace keepers." Advertisers and manufacturers flood them with violent media, and we expel kids from school when they act like the new media musclemen. Corporations pump out more deadly weapons at breakneck speed, and we say, "blame the person, not the gun"—and especially not the gun manufacturer. It is also said that we have given children every opportunity to lead peaceful and productive lives, and instead, they have turned against civil society. They run amuck in the streets, have no respect, and have lost all moral reasoning. Seeing past such extremes in debates about violence is the intention of this book. In conversations with students and inmates I have met some who have been truly out of control. They will be the first to admit it. I have also seen that a person's behavior can not be cut off from circumstances and the places where that behavior has been cultivated.

The Research Story

At Zero Tolerance examines youth and school violence and proposes several prevention strategies by drawing on qualitative research conducted in two high schools, a prison, and on my own experiences working in schools on violence prevention. In the two urban schools, ethnographic research on violence and violence prevention was conducted in 1997–1998 in one school in New York and through 1999–2000 in another school in Connecticut. In other writing I have referred to the New York school as Brandon High, the city where it is located as Brandon city, and will continue to do so in this book. I will refer to the Connecticut school as Rosemont High and the city as Rosemont. In the prison, in 1998, I participated in and conducted research on two violence prevention programs that attempted to teach violent inmates conflict resolution skills. I also interviewed inmates about their school experiences and their ideas about violence and violence prevention. It was a medium security prison which I refer to as Godwin Prison. From 1998–1999 I worked in an elementary school with staff to develop a peer mediation program and conducted participatory action research on the process.[6] All these experiences, along with studies of urban policy and school reform, enter into my discussions in this book.

Throughout the writing I have held strong to two beliefs: First, that violence is best understood when the life experiences of those caught up in violence are the starting points for reform; and second, that violence prevention is more effective when it intends to advocate on the behalf of youths whose lives are infiltrated with poverty, abuse, negative peer pressure, stress, boredom, depression, and perpetual conflicts with others. The basis of this approach, as Bruce Jacobs noted in his qualitative study of crack dealers, "is the notion that complex and intricate relationships among parts of an organism cannot be explored out of the context of their whole."[7] Any study or discussion of violence must examine the behaviors of young people but not stop there as is often the case at a time when each and every move by youths is put under a kind of moral microscope. Individuals must also examine the behaviors of adults who interact with youths through various kinds of systems, including school systems, juvenile justice systems, and social service systems. While qualitative research may take as its starting point the "voices" of youths, youths' experiences and actions must always be viewed in connection with more far-flung realities regarding, on the one hand, the personal institutions that are continually a part of discussions about violent kids, including families, gangs, peers, and neighborhoods; and public institutions, including all kinds of schools (alternative, private, special education, general education, and vocational and technology schools), detention homes, prisons, and social service agencies, that sometimes house and steer the most troubled students to adulthood.

For several years, I have taken most opportunities available to me to sit in on and observe violence prevention programs, to interview students and inmates about violence, to follow policy regarding violence and violence prevention, to attend meetings where concerns about violence were at the forefront of conversations—in short, to research as a participant issues regarding the connection between youths, schooling, and violence in society. At times, my entry into the research site has been quite easy, as when, as a research associate I studied violence at Brandon High. As part of a university-based research team, assurances from the school district that I could conduct the research had already been arranged by the director of the project.

At other times, my entry into the research site has been more difficult. As a participant in the violence prevention programs at Godwin Prison, I had the opportunity to seek permission to interview young violent offenders; it took several months to obtain permission from the State Department of Corrections, and even after obtaining this permission, I met obstacles.

The circumstances involved in my attempts to interview inmates are telling. After obtaining permission from the State Department of Corrections to begin my interviews, I received a phone call from the Deputy Warden of the prison to tell me that I could not tape-record the interviews. I felt it important to record the interviews, and since the approval of my research by the State Commissioner of Corrections had included my request to use a tape recorder, I persisted to state my case. From the Deputy Warden, I was forwarded to the Warden, who was not in at the moment. After about a week, the Warden finally answered my telephone calls. He was kind, but told me that I needed to fax him the questionnaire that I intended to administer. I told him that I did not want to administer a questionnaire, but wanted to conduct interviews. He told me he would call me back, saying he had to check with "the State."

I waited another week or so, then called him. He told me again that I only needed to fax him the questionnaire. I reminded him that I did not have a questionnaire, but wanted to interview inmates. He asked me, "But don't you have a questionnaire for the interview?" I told him that I could send him a list of questions I intended to ask the inmates, and he told me that this would suffice. I wrote a list of questions that day and faxed them to the Warden. After waiting for about two weeks for a response, I contacted the Substance Abuse Office at the prison. From a program I had participated in, I knew a worker there. I asked him if he heard of my request and he said that he had. He transferred me to a counselor in the office, who told me that the Warden had turned over my paperwork to the Deputy Warden: Since I would conduct the interviews in the Substance Abuse Office, the counselor had received a copy of the letter to the Deputy Warden. I called the Deputy Warden, and after faxing him the same set of questions that I had faxed the Warden, he gave me permission to tape-record the interviews.

Such delays are a natural part of doing research, are indicative of institutional bureaucracies, and reflect current concerns to protect people who agree to participate in research. However, such delays also demonstrate institutions' reluctance to have outsiders see what is not usually visible to the public eye. Institutions such as prisons and schools operate mostly outside the public purview.[8] Research that requires one to enter into a place and to have the relative freedom to speak to people and observe the institutions' functions are threatening to those places that wish to avoid public scrutiny. I have never fooled myself into thinking that people who run prisons and schools appreciate what I do; for most of them, I have been a genial and nosey outsider with credentials. While I have been given much freedom by many school and prison staff, I have also been shunned and looked at suspiciously. In one high school, the director of school security, after two weeks of showing me crime reports from the school, refused to release the reports to me because he felt that my knowledge of the material would jeopardize the school's reputation; this, in spite of my repeated assurances about my ethical and professional obligations to confidentiality in research. In another case, a school social worker who had agreed to work with me refused after I had wondered out loud about students in self-contained classes not being urged to make use of the school's peer mediation program.

Research that requires immediacy with people's lives and interactions of a personal nature is qualitative, and has been compared to documentary filmmaking, investigative journalism, and *flaneurism*, and I too have felt these roots. Like documentary filmmaking, I have attempted to present life circumstances as a chronicle of daily events and to focus on those who can not represent themselves for lack of power and access to the media and other public outlets.[9] In the tradition of investigative journalism, I have insisted on my right to know. Public institutions need to be run by the public, but to do so, the public needs to know what is going on inside them. Finally, as I meander school hallways and prisons, and sit in on classes, workshops, and community meetings, I have felt like some kind of *flaneur*.[10] Detached and critical, I observed and took in the sights and sounds around me with the mind and methods of a researcher but also with feelings of connectedness with the places and people I have gotten to know. Unlike a camera affixed to a wall that takes in all sights in equal measure, I sort out opportunities to understand what was violent about schools and how best to address the problem. My judgments have been informed by reams of field notes and interview transcripts, by my understandings of policy, and by my analysis of research done by myself and others.

Because my arguments tend to support and lend credence to the experiences of young people who challenge more reactionary perspectives that have demonized children, I have also felt a sense of advocacy in my work. I have felt it important to present an accurate portrait of school violence that does not continually blame students but tries to understand what students mean when they say that they are not at fault when an incident of violence occurs—or, in the words of one student I had gotten to know, that "some school people not only don't *understand* the problems we have, they can't *stand* us."

Experiences and research has shed light on everyday events that seem to represent the problems of a nation. For example, one day when I was leaving an elementary school a woman was in front of me pulling her shouting daughter by the hand. She seemed angry and embarrassed with the scene that her daughter was making, and I could not say that I could blame her for her uneasiness. The girl was yelling, half-crying it seemed, "I don't like school. And I don't like that Margarita." The woman kept telling the girl, "I do not know what is wrong with you today!" The girl repeated herself, stating her dislike for something in school and a person I assumed to be a fellow student. It struck me that the girl was telling her mother what was wrong. Whether or not the girl would get punished if she continued to shout, I do not know. But I do know that there was something wrong that was causing the girl to have an emotional blowout—and that it was likely that she would get punished for her behavior. I also know that the girl was telling the woman what was wrong, but the adult was not hearing it.

Chapter 1

The Kid Crackdown

Since the 1977 Safe Schools Study was conducted by the National Institute of Education, several large-scale studies of school violence have taken place in the United States. These have included the 1989 National Crime Survey, which included the School Crime: A National Crime Victimization Survey Report; the Metropolitan Life surveys and their subsequent reports issued in 1993, 1994, and 1999; reports distributed by the U.S. Department of Education's National Center for Education Statistics in 1995 and 1998, and others.[1] While these large-scale studies vary in their findings, and challenges and reinterpretations of their results have been undertaken by several researchers, they all conclude that, whether or not rates of violence have really decreased, the United States remains a country suffering terribly from the physical, social, and economic costs of violent crime. The lives lost, the suffering of survivors, and the money spent on policing, prevention, and incarceration, are overwhelming. No blip or dip on a statistical scale can undo the fact that violence is a prevalent and devastating part of many people's lives.

While studies continue to be done, federal legislation has made available large sums of money for a variety of efforts to counteract violence, especially in schools. Taken together, these studies, and the legislation that they have sometimes influenced, signal a unique, though not entirely new, kind of reaction towards violence—a reaction that can be characterized by the swift development of violence prevention and conflict resolution programs in schools, a renewed call for strict disciplinary and judicial procedures, and new attempts at gun control laws. These three strategies are represented in legislation throughout most of the 1990s, including the Safe and Drug-Free Schools and Communities Act of 1994, which reads, in part, that "drug and violence prevention programs are essential components of a comprehensive strategy to promote school safety and to reduce the demand for and use of drugs throughout the Nation."[2]

In 1994, the Goals 2000: Educate America Act was passed. This included Title VII (the Safe Schools Act), which allocated up to $3 million to school districts to develop violence prevention programs. Also included was Title VIII (the Gun-Free Schools Act), which added to the national scene the rhetoric and reality of zero tolerance policy by mandating the expulsion of students who brought firearms to schools.[3] When the Crime Control Act of 1990 was passed by the U.S. Congress, it included the Gun-Free School Zones Act, which made it unlawful to possess a gun within 1,000 feet of school property or municipal playground.[4] Four years earlier, the Drug-Free Schools and Communities Act of 1986 included treatment and counseling for students deemed violent, in-service training for teachers to learn violence prevention and conflict resolution strategies, and money for community, police, and school liaisons for the prevention of school and community violence.[5]

Missing from most of these national attempts at school violence prevention is any indication that the developers of violence prevention and crime control initiatives understand the circumstances in schools, in students' lives, and in communities, that lead to violence. One must ask oneself what kind of legislation or prevention program is going to solve the problems of one tenth grader I interviewed in a Connecticut school whose circumstances are dramatic but by no means uncommon for many students in the United States. Olivia grew up in North Philadelphia, one of the most dangerous areas of a city that is considered among the most dangerous in the United States. As a young girl, waiting in a car for her brother to come out of a store where he was buying pet food, Olivia watched as rival gang members shot him dead just several feet from where she was sitting. Several years later, she was in an apartment sleeping when drug dealers broke in in the middle of the night and tied up and tortured her father with a cigarette lighter for not paying for drugs he had purchased.

In junior high school, after surviving an attempted rape from a family member, Olivia was moved from Philadelphia to a city in Connecticut, where she had relatives. She did not get along with the relatives and fought with them constantly. In high school she was placed in a self-contained special education classroom due to behavioral problems and because she had told a school psychologist that she had thought about killing herself. After I interviewed her, she was arrested for assaulting the father of her son with a beer bottle because he refused to pay child support. Later, while awaiting trial, she was suspended from school for continual confrontations with other students. She had not returned to school after her suspension, and, after weeks of not being able to find out from school personnel what had happened to her, I assumed that she had dropped out, had been imprisoned, or had fought again and had, this time, been killed.

Like other students whose lives are wracked by violence, Olivia was as much victimized by violence as a perpetrator of it. If there is one thing that I have learned from my research, it is this: The main cause of violence *is* violence. Public policy and school responses to violence too often view students as either perpetrators of violence or victims of it, but rarely as people stuck in the middle of the two. In general, students' frustrations, fears, violent actions, and emotional traumas are not addressed by policy or violence prevention programs that aim to alter behaviors without changing the circumstances in their lives that put them in positions of always attacking and defending themselves. While violence prevention policies and prevention in schools are commendable, they often neglect to account for long histories of victimization and the nature of the complex and violence-infested worlds in which many young people live. In this way, they too often join national discourses that view youths as out of control, immoral, and delinquent, and not as people in need of long-term attention and care.

Getting Tough

There is nothing worse than behaviors and policies that see it as advantageous to get tough on kids who already have it tough. Like the adult who lashes out at the young person because of pent-up frustration, zero tolerance policy is not a means of violence prevention and "pro-active discipline" (as it is sometimes dubbed); it is an almost uncontrollable response by adults to cast blame and to take out their own frustrations and fears on young people. As is often the case, frustrations are taken out on people who do not ordinarily deserve it and are often more powerless and defenseless than the one doing the lashing. In some cases, federal policy that has ushered in zero tolerance has led to inappropriate and harsh sentencing of students. In one well-known case, students from a school in Detroit were given two-year expulsions for getting into a brawl at a football game. Without excusing the behavior, one may be critical of the justification of the punishment; will removing students for half their high school careers provide them with what it takes to act nonviolently and not brawl again?

The origin of zero tolerance policy dates back to the 1994 Republican takeover of Congress and the party's promises to Americans to get tough on crime. That same year, the Gun-Free Schools Act was passed by Congress along with the Safe Schools Act. Largely a result of

President Clinton's Goals 2000: Educate America Act, the Gun-Free Schools Act stated that

> No assistance may be provided to any local educational agency under this Act unless such agency has in effect a policy requiring the expulsion from school for a period of not less than one year of any student who is determined to have brought a weapon to a school under the jurisdiction of the agency except such policy may allow the chief administering officer of the agency to modify such expulsion requirements for a student on a case-by-case basis.[6]

While the law made room for expulsion policies to be modified on a case-by-case basis, it has also had the effect of enforcing a rigid and sometimes unjust form of discipline in schools, since the reality of the Gun-Free Schools Act and other zero tolerance policies go beyond weapons. For example, in 1997, Senator Jesse Helms introduced an amendment to the Gun-Free Schools Act that would require local educational agencies to expel not only students who brought weapons to school, but students in possession of an illegal drug or drug paraphernalia. As the act has been instated, individual schools have added to the original policy, calling for zero tolerance for everything from disruption of classes to "public displays of affection" (PDA). As an integral part of the crackdown on kids, like other "get tough on crime" measures, zero tolerance strategies are often forces in schools that give impetus to rules, policies, and new abilities to justify the expulsion, exclusion, shaming, labeling, and alternative placements of students who are sometimes deeply troubled.

While the suspension and expulsion of students has long been considered by many to be an injustice toward children who need more schooling, not less, zero tolerance has made it easier to remove students from schools and put them in greater contact with the individuals in their lives who may be central to their problems in the first place. In Brandon High, for example, reports of fighting had remained steady for several years, but suspension rates had gone way up. During the first four months of the 1997–1998 school year, more than five hundred students were suspended; over two hundred were in-school suspensions. Teachers and administrators consider the first few weeks of school, in the words of one teacher, "a kind a clearinghouse time," a time of clearing out from classrooms troublesome students who could be labeled socially or emotionally disturbed (SED).

During the 1999–2000 school year, the Rosemont school board broadened the powers of schools in the district to expel not only students who brought weapons or drug paraphernalia to school but students who "continually disrupt the educational process." No longer was the disruptive student sent to the office, since common wisdom in schools says that principals no longer want to deal with disruptive students as they once did. Instead, security officers take charge and follow standard procedures that require the expulsion of students who may be nothing more than goof-offs.

The push to get tough on children has not been the sole preoccupation of schools but of a nation that has made a mad rush to prosecute juveniles as adults and fill prisons beyond their legal capacities. As I noted earlier, between 1992 and 1998, forty-nine of the fifty-one state legislatures (including the District of Columbia) made changes in their laws to make it easier to prosecute juveniles as adults and incarcerate them in adult facilities.[7] In contrast to juvenile facilities, adolescents in adult prisons are five times more likely to be sexually assaulted, twice as likely to be beaten by staff, 50 percent more likely to be attacked with a weapon, and eight times more likely to commit suicide.[8] This is a lot of abuse, assault, and suicide, given the fact that the United States imprisons more people than any other Western democracy.

In England, where the rate is the highest among Western European democracies, one resident per 800 is imprisoned. By contrast, in the United States, one resident per 150 is imprisoned. In general, the United States has a prison rate that is six to twelve times higher than other Western countries.[9] However, the United States was not always a leader in draconian judicial policy; in the 1930s, its incarceration rates were comparable to or lower than European countries. Recent years, though, have been marked by iron-fisted policies, the swelling of prison populations from 330,000 in 1980 to nearly two million in 1998, reduction of constitutional rights of inmates, expanded use of the death penalty, adoption of "three-strikes" and minimum-sentencing laws, life-without-parole sentences, and the development of a new civil service job—the prison gerontologist.[10]

As with most get-tough measures, the results of zero tolerance policy have not affected all people in equal measure but have come down hardest on mostly the poor and nonwhite and have not just affected individuals but entire communities. The high prison rate for black men, which soared during the mid-1980s as the blue-collar job market collapsed and wages for less skilled laborers declined, has not only derailed lives but has contributed to out-of-wedlock births, an increase in female-headed families, greater competition among black women for eligible husbands, and social dysfunction in neighborhoods.[11]

During my days in Godwin prison, first participating in a violence prevention program and then interviewing inmates, I was struck by the number of black and Latino men in the facility; at times, it seemed that the only white people in sight were those running the place. During the first workshop with inmates, only three of the twenty-two participants were white. According to criminologist Michael Tonry, a number of studies during the early 1990s determined that between 23 percent and 56 percent of young African-American males were under justice system control and over half of the prison inmates were nonviolent offenders.[12] In recent years, prison populations have skyrocketed, leading to dangerous overcrowding and the development of a huge private prison industry. As the War on Drugs marched through cities in the 1990s, prisons became clogged, not with serious offenders but with problem kids trying to make a buck selling drugs on street corners.[13] While it is important not to excuse drug dealing, one must wonder if imprisonment is the best way to deal with sellers and users of drugs.

Does this crackdown rehabilitate problem kids and solve our society's problems?

A similar question could be asked of schools. Does the suspension and expulsion of students for fighting and other forms of violence solve problems, or do students return to school the same, or worse, as when they left? A common complaint among school personnel was that students often came back to school from suspensions with the same kinds of grudges and anger that sent them out in the first place. In addition, these students now harbored a hatred for the school staff who suspended them.

Too often, zero tolerance treats matters that are best dealt with at the school and family level as criminal offenses to be dealt with at judicial levels.[14] These are not sensible reform strategies; they are symbols of U.S. frustrations with crime, and they represent U.S. toughness and desire to teach a lesson. While such policies have succeeded in emptying schools temporarily of troubled kids and filling prisons, they have failed to create a society that is more humane and safe. For anyone who argues that zero tolerance has led to decreased rates of violence, one must consider that the harshest crime control policies date from the mid-1990s, several years after crime rates began their decline.[15]

School Violence Prevention

Violence prevention in schools has taken on many forms, some of which reflect national trends to punish and to rely on security and policing measures to control public places. There is little happening in schools that can not be connected, somehow, to national movements; in this case, zero tolerance has taken place within the context of increased national use of law enforcement and incarceration.

But violence prevention in schools does not end with zero tolerance. It has a more kindly face as well, one based not so much on processes that are judicial but rather educational.[16] For example, conflict resolution programs often aim to change students' behaviors through instruction and modification techniques that are pedagogical and based in social learning theory.[17] In a similar way, peer mediation is often considered an educational experience; students not only have problems resolved but learn to deal with future problems.[18] A school psychologist at Brandon High referred to this as the "secondary learning" that students do as mediators. However, these two processes—the judicial and educational—are rarely mutually exclusive. As an alternative to suspension, peer mediation programs are supported and even attended by students because of the threat of judicial processes ("It's either suspension or mediation," administrators tell students). The Drug Abuse Resistance Education (DARE) program is another example of this: as a kind of educational program that aims to teach students the dangers of drugs, alcohol, and violence, it is also intimately tied to judicial processes. In this case, the program is directly linked to the police department, since DARE teachers are law enforcement officers and may be called upon to arrest a student if necessary—and students know this.

Within judicial processes are issues that surpass the strictly punitive and include, as well, new technology and surveillance measures that aim to prevent violence. Security technology is a way of doing more with less people; video cameras in schools enable school personnel to monitor multiple hallways with only one person behind the console. The techno-security built up in city schools has been described by several authors, including John Devine, who has explained in vivid detail what it is like to spend time in New York City schools that seem to have been overtaken by a siege mentality: "Funds are appropriated for more and better trained guards, metal detectors, X-ray scanning machines, electromagnetic door locks, alarm systems, emergency telephones, and other security equipment," not to mention school police officers (who are officially called "school resource officers").[19] Rosemont High, for example, had three types of security personnel: a police officer who answered to the Rosemont Police Department, five security officers who answered to the Rosemont board of education, and three guards, derogatorily called "Murphy guards" or "rent-a-cops," in reference to the private company that "rents them out."

While increased security is a trend at many city schools, as noted before suburban and rural towns are buying into the process as well, sometimes at great cost to budgets and to school climates. In another town not far from Rosemont, the town council, in 1999, approved $47,000 for school security in its middle and high schools, in addition to their already employed security teams. Money was appropriated for the purchase of "proximity readers" (a card system that enabled access to buildings), TV monitors for front entrances of schools, electric door latches, re-key entrance doors, and motion trips (which indicate to the main office if somebody is near the front entrances).[20] In some counties, school districts spend $100,000 to $150,000 for security systems, with a cost of $400,000 for annual upkeep, repair, and replacement of systems.[21]

As one form of violence prevention, this security-based response to school violence reflects not only fixations on surveillance tactics but an era that can be defined by increased technology in all facets of life. Policing and violence prevention in schools has been infiltrated by the technology revolution, and the result has been a shift to high-tech policing. In other words, the security buildup is not just the result of zero tolerance, it is also an outcome of private security companies that have seen schools, like businesses and homes before them, as a new niche in which to sell their wares.

In the educational realm as well, violence prevention has meant an economic boom for curriculum developers, trainers, consultants, and even university teachers such as myself, who prosper when schools call on professionals to attend to problems associated with crime and violence. The development of new violence prevention programs and curricula, including peer mediation, character education, and DARE programs, and their accompanying videos and CD-ROMS, have opened a new niche for marketers as well as educational researchers and criminologists. It has altered the role of school social workers and counselors, and even health and gym teachers, who are called upon not only to teach their content areas but to incorporate or teach conflict resolution.

For schools, violence prevention programs meet several unique needs. They attempt to prevent violence. They give mostly high-achieving students the opportunity to join a team or club (such as a peer mediation team or a student support team) that looks good on college applications. Finally, they enable schools to say that they are doing something about violence as these efforts are touted in meetings and in the press as evidence that a particular school or school district is responding to a current problem. Having a program seems to signal to the larger community that the school is addressing parents' worries; it attempts to put people's minds to rest.

New violence prevention programs in schools have increased dramatically in recent years, and, while programs in different schools differ in dramatic ways, most are truly well-intentioned attempts to deal with what is seen as a crisis situation. Even so, the proliferation of programs can be misleading. I have become aware of many violence prevention strategies, and, while their names and acronyms differ—peer mediation, conflict resolution, character education, DARE, PAL, Second Step, student support team, student outreach program, pupil assistance service, to name a few—their strategies of violence prevention are not nearly as far-reaching as their names suggest. Most strategies are fundamentally similar and are either based in judicial processes or educational processes, or a mixture of the two. In essence, most are, in the case of judicial responses, spinoffs of national "get tough" policies, or, in the case of the educational programs, variations on the theme of behavior modification. This is, in part, due to the history of schooling. Schools in the United States have always had both an educational and custodial function, and the hookup between the judicial and educational dates back to 19th-century truant officers and "child-savers."[22] However, the technology revolution is a new component to the story and has created, in some cases, a police-state-like atmosphere in schools where cameras keep close watch, the crackling of walkie-talkies becomes part of the auditory fabric of hallways, and even parking spaces are designated for police cars.

"Gun Control Means Using Both Your Hands"

On my way to Rosemont High, a car passed with a bumper sticker that read: "Gun Control Means Using Both Your Hands." That morning I read in the Rosemont newspaper about a new controversial Connecticut law that would enable police officers to confiscate the guns of individuals whom they deemed unstable. This was a first-in-the-nation gun law that was drawing a lot of fire from critics concerned about illegal search and seizure and increased power in the hands of police officers. The police had been, in recent weeks, on the front pages of newspapers for accusations of abuse, and, in one case, the shooting death of an unarmed twelve-year-old African American boy. Proponents felt the new law was another move toward sensible gun control that would keep guns out of the hands of people who were obviously unstable but legally entitled to own a firearm.

The bumper sticker and the new law represented to me the mixed signals of gun ownership in the United States. While it may seem that federal policy has seriously attempted to place restrictions on gun ownership, most attempts at gun control in the United States have been minimal and have met serious resistance. Though there has been long and sustained opposition against gun control by members of the National Rifle Association, since the 1930s gun control legislation has squeaked through Congress. In 1938, the first federal law to single out youths under the age of eighteen was passed when it was determined that adolescents under that age were not permitted to acquire guns. The federal Gun Control Act of 1968 raised the minimum age for handgun ownership to twenty-one. In more recent years, the Gun-Free School Zones Act of 1990 made it unlawful to possess a firearm within 1,000 feet of a school or municipal playground, and then in 1994, as noted earlier, the Gun-Free Schools Act required that a student who brought a gun to school be expelled for a one-year period. Amid these forms of legislation have been other, more controversial, attempts at gun control, including the Brady Bill, which finally passed Congress in 1993 after many years of rejection and required a seven-day waiting period for those wishing to buy a gun.

In spite of this flurry of legislation, the United States remains heavily armed.[23] It was estimated by the U.S. Bureau of Alcohol, Tobacco, and Firearms that in 1990 there were at least 200 million guns in circulation in the United States and that between 40–50 percent of households store guns. The outcome of such a domestic arms buildup has been severe, especially for young people. In 1992, for example, 5,262 young people (ages between five and nineteen years) died from gunshot wounds; 62 percent by homicide, 27 percent by suicide, 9 percent by unintentional injuries, and 2 percent by undetermined circumstances. This made firearm incidents the fifth leading cause of death for five-to-nine-year-old children and the second leading cause of death for children ages ten to nineteen. In addition to these deaths, an estimated 23,167 school-age children suffered nonfatal firearm injuries that were treated in hospital emergency rooms from June 1992 through May 1993.[24] In 1999, Louis Harris and Associates reported that about half of public school teachers (53 percent), students (47 percent), and law enforcement officials (51 percent) said that it was easy for students at their schools to obtain a gun.[25]

Such statistics may cause us to believe that weapon possession by U.S. citizens is not only rampant but unstoppable. However, there is other evidence that suggests that most U.S. citizens (about 70 percent) are proponents of stricter gun control legislation. In 1993, for example, the year the Brady Bill passed Congress, 88 percent of U.S. citizens polled in a national survey supported the seven-day waiting period. In addition, fourteen different National Opinion Research Center surveys from 1973 to 1991 showed that from 69–81 percent of U.S. citizens favored conditioning gun ownership on prior possession of a police gun permit. In addition, while the National Rifle Association (NRA) attempts to convince people otherwise, nearly half the U.S. population is in favor of complete prohibition of handguns.[26]

When we consider the combined figures of gun ownership and gun control, we can draw several conclusions: First, gun ownership in the United States is not only rampant, but a national health crisis, especially for young people; second, stricter gun control legislation is made controversial, if not nearly impossible, not because Americans are overwhelmingly against it but because politicians are fearful of the NRA and are unduly wedded to their campaign contributions.

To attend to the problem of guns, cities have attempted gun buy-back programs, and in some cases, have turned to litigation. New Orleans, Miami, Chicago, and Bridgeport were some of the first cities to sue gun manufacturers for their production of handguns and in particular for oversupplying states where gun laws are lax (notably in the South). They have accused gun manufacturers of cutting costs by not including the most advanced forms of safety devices and of increasing production of more deadly, higher caliber weapons to compensate for lagging sales of lower caliber guns.[27] Such lawsuits are desperate tactics that take their lead from the largely successful tobacco suits of the late 1990s. They are tactics born of frustration, as are most responses to violence—frustration with the devastation that gun ownership has caused and frustration with political figureheads who seem unwilling to do anything about the problem. However, unlike zero tolerance, which takes out frustration on youths, this frustration is aimed at the business people who supply youth with "better," meaning more deadly, products.

The Violence of "School Violence"

School violence is defined in a number of ways and incorporates a range of behaviors. Certainly, lethal forms of violence enacted with weapons are one form of school violence, and the attention this has received beginning in the late 1990s has been a feature of the news as well as large-scale studies by researchers. What most of the research on gun possession in schools holds in common is the conclusion that, as one study noted, "youth who are caught up in extreme violence anywhere in the community, whether as victim or aggressor (and often both to a degree), are likely to carry weapons to school."[28] Simply put, kids who bring guns to school are those whose lives are embroiled in violence, often as victims. A 1998 National Institute of Justice study noted that family and friends were the primary sources of guns for youths.[29] This was consistent with a study in Boston that also noted that most guns used in firearm homicides are obtained through an underground market of buying, lending, giving, and trading guns, which the legal market initially supplies.[30] Gun violence by kids who are victims as well as perpetrators of violence, who are "caught up in extreme violence," and have the family and peer connections to obtain a gun, represent the most frightful form of school violence.

Other forms of school violence are not as lethal as gun violence but are more persistent and nearly as damaging; these include sexual harassment, jumpings, fights, bullying, threats, and forms of prejudice. In the schools I have studied, these have been the kinds of behavior that were of greatest concern to most school staff. Even the National Institute of Justice study on gun use by high school students noted that only two percent of school administrators considered guns a serious problem in their buildings. In the words of one school administrator I interviewed, "the problem here is ongoing fighting, taunts, and disrespect of students against students and sometimes teachers." Students can have similar reactions. One boy in Brandon High captured the sentiment of other students when he explained: "I don't think we should be worrying so much about what might happen and should deal with what is happening. Like, there is a fight almost every week and kids are just getting down on each other everyday."

Those who are not convinced that there exists a connection between these low-level types of violence and more lethal forms need to listen to students explain how angry words, and even unwanted stares, lead to fighting and, in some cases, weapon violence. One student I interviewed in Rosemont High, a senior, had once been a member of a well-known gang in the city but was very determined to graduate from high school. He had been in a detention center after being caught robbing a store, had returned to school, and was placed in a self-contained class. When I interviewed him, he was living with his girlfriend, who had just quit school. In spite of these setbacks, Raul was a clear thinker with a determined mind. He knew what the story was when it came to violence in his city:

> If someone is going to fight, it's usually because of what was done to them. That's how it is for me and almost everybody I know. Nobody fights for nothing. You either been disrespected, challenged, people haven't been straight with you. You got knuckleheads who call you 'faggot,' and then you fight, and after the fight, if you don't like the way it turned out or the problem presents itself again, you take it to the next level. It's like everything in life. . . one thing leads to another.

The research on bullying and harassment not only reports on findings but, unlike studies of gun violence, must work to convince individuals that such behaviors are indeed violent.[31] This is because people too often write off forms of harassment and bullying as "boys being boys," or a "natural part of growing up"—expressions I have heard from school staff. Also, school staff do not always know what to do in the case of such behavior. As one counselor told me, "You see kids and it's hard to tell what's going on, then you do intercede, and even in private, students won't say a word or have such conflicting stories, so you begin to say to yourself, is this really worth it?" One teacher called situations of bullying and harassment a "mosh pit of unknowables. . . you just hope it will go away." Of course, such incidents do not just go away; they, in fact, get worse.

Though schools will never be able to abolish such behavior, they are capable of reducing incidents. This is accomplished by doing the difficult: interceding when there is a problem between students and having a clear school policy on the problem. As one group of researchers noted: "By far, the most effective violence intervention described by the children, teachers, and administrators was the physical presence of a teacher who knew the students and was willing to intervene, coupled with a clear, consistent administrative policy on violence."[32] However, such responses to violence are not ordinarily undertaken by schools that are reluctant and unsure of how to intercede, and, in some cases, do not even consider kinds of aggressive behavior to be violent. Furthermore, in this time of zero tolerance, when people are called on to intervene, too often they are the guards and police officers in the schools, not the administrators and teachers who should be interacting with the students the most.

There exists a continuum of school violence with mild forms of teasing at one end of the spectrum and school massacres at the other. When attempting to address school violence in a particular school as a community, or in all schools as a nation, each form must be considered simultaneously. This is not only because each form is violent and therefore in need of some attention, but because there are important connections between different types of violence, even between the extremes. Teasing, in conjunction with other factors, can lead to gun violence or suicide.[33] Even in young children, bullying can be a precedent for other violent behaviors later in life, including sexual harassment and fighting.[34] Both the teachers and students I interviewed were generally in agreement that most physical confrontations were the result of previous verbal exchanges or harassments. For many students, being disrespected was considered the crucial ingredient that led to serious violence, including weapon violence in schools. To deal with weapon violence or fights without dealing with issues of respect sets the stage for, at best, a quick fix with a short life span.

The blurring line between perpetrator and victim disappears almost entirely when we consider that many acts of violence are "started" by individuals who have been victimized in the past, including those who are victims of domestic and sexual abuse.[35] When a student is suspended or expelled from school for fighting, the fight itself, while often seen as an isolated incident by most school personnel, is often one confrontation in a long stream of violent interactions that may have consisted of threats, bullying, jumpings, and violence in the home and community.

When a school does not intervene in such cases, it takes part in another form of violence that is not often a concern for staff but is discussed in academic literature and apparent in some schools. Forms of symbolic or systemic violence are enacted on students by school systems. Juveniles have no choice but to go to school, so when schools become places where students' chances of success are smothered due to either personal, cultural, or economic factors, there occur grave injustices.

Various authors have confronted the fact that schools can become hellish places for students because of cultural and financial inequities, prejudice, and mistreatment.[36] Sometimes these injustices can be, or can rightly be interpreted to be, violent in nature, especially when school system actions stigmatize or humiliate students. Some young people have the resources and gall to physically confront others in schools; school systems are in a different position and use symbolic forms of violence to lash out. Threats, bullying, and harassment are not only the actions of students; some school staff also bully, threaten, and harass, but often in more subtle and even institutionally accepted ways. When these behaviors and others, including segregation, overmedication, and unjust placements, become institutionalized, the violence becomes systemic in nature. It remains deeply interpersonal, but it has added behind it the weight of the public sector; it becomes a kind of state-sanctioned imposition of dominance. Not only is this a form of violence, like teasing and bullying, it leads to other kinds of violence. Students not only lash out at each other; they also lash out at schools and staff, often because of what one student called "the beating down" that they get from school staff when they are unjustly accused, singled out for the most severe disciplinary measures, or segregated in self-contained classrooms.

Just as we cannot examine violence by ignoring the associated issues of systemic and interpersonal abuses in communities and institutions, we cannot prevent violence by focusing solely on one form of violence and not another. There exists not violence in schools, but *violences*, a range of behaviors that extends from the most mundane to the fatal. In addition, there exist forms of systemic and symbolic violence, including some aspects of zero tolerance. Reduction in systemic violence is important to include in violence prevention strategies because it takes as its starting point reduction of violence by youths and schools, not just youths. It also keeps focus on the fact that many forms of violence are interconnected, one indirectly influencing and sometimes even causing the other. Ask girls in school about conflicts that have caused them pain, and many will talk about their fears of not only the delinquents but popular and high-achieving students (both boys and girls) who carry with them not guns and box cutters but an arrogance and bravado that can penetrate them like a knife. When schools are incapable of dealing with the harassments, tensions, and even rapes that accompany such behaviors, these girls are doubly victimized: by the aggressors and by the school.

Working Toward Solutions

In order to prevent violence, we must first understand the nature, causes, complexities, and contradictions of violent situations. We must look beyond students to examine the problem in a manner that would take into account the historical, economic, and cultural foundations of school violence in all of its forms, including weapon violence, harassment, fights, bullying, "jumpings," threats, systemic violence, and forms of aggression caused by cultural prejudices. We need to link structural issues of policy, discipline, community politics, and inequality to concerns involving behavior, race, power, gender, gangs, sexuality, and social class. In addition, we need to view violence in what Jeffrey Fagan and Deanna Wilkinson called an "event-based approach," which views violence within a mix of interactive parts "as complex interactions among people, personal motivations, weapons, the social control attributes of the immediate setting, and the ascribed meaning and status attached to the violent act."[37]

To account for the "situatedness" of violence, and not just its sweeping "causes," does not deny the importance of individual character traits that lead people to act violently, but it does recognize that there exists no direct link between personality and violent behavior. All decisions that people make, including those involving violence or potential violence, are made within a context, and violence prevention must deal with that context. The nature of the event, the history of the situation, the availability of weapons, what people have to lose when violent, the relationship between those involved, and the meaning that individuals make of hostile situations, all factor into decisions about one's behavior. Understanding and shaping prevention strategies that recognize these interactions and multiple forms of violence will require that we move beyond single violence prevention programs that hone in on students' behavior, and, instead, make a concerted attempt to confront the darker sides of American life which contribute to violence: community losses, family problems, lack of meaningful and secure employment, cultural tensions, distrust, peer pressure, youths' feelings of isolation, frustration, and hopelessness, male bravado and sexism, access to weapons, and a U.S. culture entrenched in militaristic and punitive ways of acting.

Zero tolerance mimics violence. While one may lash out with fists or weapons, societies choose to lash out with persecution, segregation, and incarceration. After declaring war on street crime and drugs, the United States has gotten around to declaring war on school violence. In the case of zero tolerance, though, the war is being waged not on behalf of students but against them.

Although the United States is quite adept at using one form of violence to deal with another, in international as well as domestic circles, violence prevention will be only minimally successful if harsh punishment is what dominates strategies. Punishment can never deal with the context of the problem, can never approach doing something about the prior victimization, the easy access to weapons, and the family breakdown that engulf the lives of many violent offenders.

In addition, judicial means of punishment often increases the likelihood that the punished one will act violently in the future. According to criminologists Robert Sampson and John Laub, arrest, conviction, and imprisonment stigmatize individuals and create impediments that prevent them from establishing social ties with conventional adults and activities. This, in turn, often leads to joblessness and other problems that increase commitment to deviant behavior.[38] When violence prevention does not take into account the context of the problem, it is assumed that because youthful hands hold the guns or strike out at others, they alone are the culprits, as if all people acted in social vacuums where nothing else went on in behavior except messages between kids' brains and their fists.

While zero tolerance focuses on kids for punitive consequences, violence prevention programs usually zero in on kids for behavior modification. Students' efforts to restrain themselves from violence and to learn peaceful ways of acting are important aspects of violence prevention. All programs that can accomplish such tasks are commendable. Peer mediation, student support services, intervention and prevention programs, and character education are hallmarks of violence prevention in schools. This is good. However, what also needs to occur is a far-reaching violence prevention strategy that takes as its starting point not students but the circumstances that lead to their problems.

If there is one thing that institutions such as schools do well, it is to reproduce in the institution what is already instituted in the larger society, and this is as true with violence as it is with racial and social class inequities. If students are to be responsible for the way they act, institutions and communities must be responsible for their behaviors and offerings to young people. What society offers to some students in the form of decrepit schools, lack of attention and care, and squalid neighborhoods is a crime in itself, a form of systemic violence. The United States has yet to view violence as an outcome of a national history that has been violent, of an economic system that creates the social isolation and hopelessness that causes some violence, and a culture that has come to accept and even prosper from everyday forms of aggression against the less powerful in the world. Unfortunately, this context of violence is not even recognized until it is the white and middle-class kids who become embroiled in the mayhem. As a result, surrounded by violence and with no other places to retreat, U.S. society has lashed out with a frenzied attempt to tolerate no more.

Chapter 2

From Child-Saving to Zero Tolerance

Where we are today as a society confronting violence is a result of many factors. These factors include the influence of history on present situations, especially in regard to the long legacy of violence and punishment in the United States; the creation of social science theories of violence that partly steer national responses to the problem; and the shape and forces of our institutions as they interact with youths of different ages, races, genders, abilities, and social classes. To understand this history is to know how we have arrived to our current state of thinking about the problem and the subsequent incorporation of zero tolerance to deal with it.

Zero tolerance as a prevention strategy is based on certain theories of delinquency and is the result of a U.S. history that has endorsed harsh punishment of juveniles as an effective means of curbing violent crime. There are assumptions about the effectiveness of punishment and the state of the violent mind and body that give purpose and support to the policy. In order to unravel zero tolerance and replace it with more caring means of violence prevention, we must unravel the assumptions that give zero tolerance life; to do this, we need to confront the history that gives zero tolerance its institutional bases.

There are as many theories of violence as there are forms of violence, and these theories have been discussed in exhaustive detail in a number of books and articles.[1] Rather than rehash them here, briefly speaking, theories of violence fall into several categories. There are social learning theories which interpret violence as "learned behavior," an outcome of students appropriating from their environments and popular culture aggressive behavior and then considering violence a norm they replicate in their own interactions with others.[2] There are rational choice theories that identify poor reasoning skills as the cause of violence. Here, individuals weigh the consequences of a violent crime against the possible benefits and make the *rational choice* to be violent—in a sense, individuals determine that "crime pays."[3] There are structural theories of violence that focus on social and environmental conditions such as poverty; here, violence is viewed as a systemic problem having to do with inequities in the world and a general breakdown of relations between people, which leads to social isolation, frustration, and aggression.[4] Biological theories focus on medical conditions and biological traits of violent offenders and have roots in eugenic explanations of criminal behavior, where criminal tendencies are identified in people's physical and psychological "stigmata"—essentially, in a person's natural makeup.[5] Finally, interactionist theories incorporate some combination of social learning and structural theories and view violence in connection to how people make sense and interpret their experiences and circumstances.[6]

In a sense, these theories have become commonsense ways of thinking and talking about what is deemed a crisis among youths. They reiterate in more clinical and academic terms conversations that are informal and ongoing, where remarks are made in school hallways and in the popular press about disintegrating families, or the influence of peers, or about kids not knowing the consequences of their actions. In

Brandon High, for example, a school counselor insisted that the problem with violent behavior stemmed from what kids learned from influential people in their lives, including gang members, families, and peers.

> You want to solve violence, you have to have kids unlearn what they have learned since the day they were born. It is like training, I hate to say it, like training an animal—after all we are all animals. If you have a vicious animal, then you have to teach it not to be vicious. It's retraining, but isn't that what education is about. Training people, educating them. In this case, educating them to be relaxed and quit setting themselves up for jail, which a lot of these kids are doing.

One can hardly spend a day in a school talking to administrators, teachers, and students and not hear this notion of violence being expressed: that students' "locus of control is external," that they are in need of behavior modification, that they need to be "reeducated" or "retrained"—these are the comments that reflect a theory of violence as learned behavior.

Others in schools have different views. While a school social worker in Rosemont High would not disagree with the fact that some kids learned how to be violent from people they knew, he felt it important to focus on the environment kids came from. During the year that I spent with him, he noted in matter-of-fact ways that one could not deny the hard reality of facts: Of the 158 students with behavioral problems who were assigned to him for counseling, only a few that he knew of were middle to upper class and had an intact family:

> You see who I am meeting with every day. It is very rare that I am talking to somebody with two parents in the family, a structured home, somebody in a middle class neighborhood, and somebody with a family that makes a decent and steady salary. It's the family, the neighborhoods, it's not having money to buy things, or if you do have the money, then spending it on Pokemon cards, Nikes, and clothes twice as expensive as mine. Goals and priorities are completely out of whack. Through no fault of their own, many kids are at a

crisis situation. There is no family, they live in the projects, they are surrounded by shit—and I mean that literally. They feel that they got nothing to lose—and you know, they're pretty much right.

Such explanations are ways for people to make sense of what is seen as a crisis situation. However, they are also ways of speaking within certain parameters that are learned. The social worker in Rosemont High drew on his own training in sociology to view violence within the context of kids' neighborhoods and within structural theories that pinpoint poverty and community dysfunction as the root of the problem. The school counselor defined violence through his own training in learning theory and therefore associated the problem with cognitive processes.

Those involved in violence prevention must start with the messy business of understanding how U.S. society interprets the realities of violence through such professionalized accounts because these accounts shape prevention strategies. When schools hire more security officers and buy into technology to solve problems, the underlying belief is that violence will be minimized if students are watched closely and there exist deterrents. This is a belief based in rational choice theory—the assumption that individuals make rational choices to be violent. Therefore a threatening judicial system is set up to convince youths that crime does not pay. When schools invest in behavior modification and conflict resolution programs, the assumption is that violence is learned behavior. Here, we are back to kids' cognitive processes that are in need of fixing. These are, in fact, the two primary ways how violence prevention is conducted in schools: through processes that are judicial and processes that are educative or cognitive.

Judicial processes of school violence prevention, rooted in rational choice theory, assume that students weigh the consequences of a violent act against the apparent gains and decide, in a rational sort of way, to go ahead with the fight, assault, or worse. Such a theory can be heard in the writing of the researchers Jeffrey Fagan and Deanna Wilkinson, who explain that "a violent event involves a sequence of decisions by the perpetrator, and the individual evaluates alternatives before carrying out a violent action."[7]

With this theory in mind, one comes to believe that students can be controlled if they are convinced of the nearly omniscient power of the school to watch, to apprehend, and to quickly and severely punish—hence, the rush to hire security officers to monitor school hallways. On the other hand, violence prevention that takes as its starting point educational processes are rooted in social learning theory: in contrast to judicial processes, this is a kinder and gentler route to violence prevention. When the educators Vicky Dill and Martin Haberman claim that "our schools must take the lead in introducing students to an alternative culture of nonviolent options through gentle teaching and moral vision" they are working within this theoretical framework.[8] Rooted in social learning theory, violence is seen as something that is caused by outside influences ("environmental determinants") interacting with cognitive processes that affect people's behavior in a way that causes them to be violent.[9] While some may conclude that the natural solution then is to change "environmental determinants"—or the circumstances of people's lives—this is often considered too utopian or beyond the scope of schooling; therefore, the problem is addressed pedagogically through the realignment of students' cognitive facilities.

While judicial and educative processes are in some ways two disparate methods of preventing violence, when taken together they lay the foundation for zero tolerance in schools. While cognitive theories are a "gentler" way of violence prevention, they share with zero tolerance the belief that individual students are the locus of the problem. Neither zero tolerance nor cognitive theories of violence could exist in schools if it were not for the fact that the overwhelming belief in the United States is that prevention should focus on young people, not, for example, on society or social policy. In the second case, rational choice theory shares with zero tolerance the belief that kids need to be watched and threatened, and that punishment is an effective way to get children to toe the line.

The popularity of zero tolerance is, in part, a result of a confluence of ideas developed amid the furor to instill judicial and educative processes of violence prevention in schools. Zero tolerance did not just spring up out of nowhere, and it is not only an outcome of broader "get tough" policies seen in policing and incarceration strategies. It is also an extension of violence prevention theories that have pinpointed individuals as the root of the problem and determined that judicial responses to violence are the most effective means of dealing with the problem.

How we have arrived at this state of thinking and social reform in the United States is a long story that has many characters, contradictory scenarios, and episodes. The story is historical in nature and includes circumstances involving the development of the helping professions, the creation of their institutions (asylums, schools, prisons) and their theories of delinquency, issues regarding industrialization and urbanization, matters concerning the rise of science and especially the eugenics movement, and the development of the juvenile justice system and its means of creating links between schools, courts, and police departments.

Foundations of Zero Tolerance

What follows is an account of the changes and developments since the 19th century that have helped to mold current zero tolerance ways of thinking and conducting business in school. While the account lacks details that would appear in a more extended history, the overview is a way of understanding zero tolerance in relation to science, demographic changes, social progress, and childhood. To unroot zero tolerance from schools, one must know from where its roots spring.

Nineteenth-Century Roots

The rise of professional experts on deviance, the building of institutions for delinquents, and the development of theories of violence, have all played a part in our current zero tolerance responses to youth and school violence. During the 19th century, the professionalization of social work occurred at the same time that science was steeped in positivism and evolutionism—an era when immigrants began filling cities and progressives focused on social reform through the development of institutions such as schools and reformatories. Many contradictory outcomes were the result. Although none directly led to zero tolerance policy, they did set the stage for the professionalized and institutional responses to delinquency that support zero tolerance in schools today.

As Joseph Kett noted of the times, "Those who sought to reform juvenile delinquents in mid-19th-century America spoke the lofty language of nurture and environmentalism."[10] While the focus was on environments, specifically the urban centers and their associated slums, factories, and tenements, the progressive reforms were largely aimed at children's removal from the environments, not so much the betterment of the places. This was done through various institutions to deal with greater numbers of immigrant and delinquent youths—the most lofty institution of the time being the common school. What also sprang up were poor houses, asylums, and detention homes. The effect on society of institutionalization has been widespread. It corresponded with the professionalization of childhood as normal schools for teachers and graduate programs in psychology began to emerge. The movement did not start with the intention to get tough on children—it, in fact, had quite the opposite intention—but it did end that way.

The professionalization and institutionalization of youths, and especially delinquent youths, made way for what Michel Foucault called the "present scientificio-legal complex from which the power to punish derives its bases."[11] The monitorial Lancasterian schools were an example of this, for they represented the fixation on castigation as a means of "molding" students into complacency, and held dear the belief that schooling should be accompanied by an iron-gripped control of students' behaviors and bodies. The Lancasterian schools were popular in Europe as well as in the United States, and were developed by Joseph Lancaster, who advocated structure and harsh punishments for students—including the use of wooden shackles, hanging baskets (in which to suspend students), and paddles and whips. A discipline-driven and highly structured environment was common in many of the first public schools, especially in the cities. An anonymous critic of a New York City public school described a classroom in 1868 in the following way:

> They sat, the girls on the one side and the boys on the other, each eye fixed upon the wall directly in front. There was no motion....The rows of children, right and diagonal, were as regular as rows of machine-planted corn. A signal was given at which every face turned instantly, as though on a pivot, toward the face of the directress. She bade them good morning, and, in one breath, the whole school responded. At another signal every face swung back on its pivot to the original position.[12]

In addition to this way of automating children, students were whipped, humiliated, shackled, and beaten with paddles. To control, monitor, and to punish even physically was and to some extent remains a defining aspect of many schools. The beliefs that uphold such practices lay the groundwork for the scientific and legal legitimacy of zero tolerance punishment.

However, there were different and sometimes competing views of youths in the 19th century. In a sense, Puritan hardliners butted heads in art, philosophy, and social action with liberal reformers. The methods of Joseph Lancaster met with ideas laced with Romanticism, middle-class sensibilities, and the belief that children needed care and nurturing, not torment and flagellation. Historian Sterling Fishman explained that in the 19th century, "education was depicted as a gentle and affectionate activity rather than a violent or potentially violent one," and though Lancasterian schools still existed, they were sometimes caricatured and criticized for their abusive treatment of children.[13]

Middle-class professionals, progressives, and a host of "child-savers" viewed children as innocent, precious, and in need of guidance and protective care. British Romantic poets made the case for their innocence at the same time that they reflected children's idealized images. Consider the writing of William Wordsworth, one of the more prominent Romantic poets:

> Oh! mystery of man, from what a depth
> Proceed thy honours. I am lost, but see
> In simple childhood sometime of the base
> On which their greatness stands....[14]

Woven into these notions of childhood was a distancing of the youth from adult society. What emerged as the child-study movement redefined the child "as a person with distinctive attributes— impressionability, vulnerability, innocence—which required a warm, protected, and prolonged period of nurture...[and] educators and moralists began to stress the child's need for play, for love and understanding, and the gradual, gentle unfolding of the child's nature."[15] Such progressive notions not only gave rise to child-centered philosophies in education, but to lasting reforms in law, education, and social services, including compulsory education, child labor laws, kindergarten and playground supervision, the juvenile court, child welfare, and reform schools. These reforms were all seen as a means of dealing with the specific needs of children and helping them in protective and caring ways—and, in some cases, they were.

But while the "gentleness" of these beliefs stand in stark contrast to zero tolerance policy, the rhetoric did not always reflect the reality. The child-saving movement also corresponded with the rise of the professions, an increase in clinical studies of youths, strong scientific beliefs in an objective reality, and the conclusion that the state can

monitor and control society and intervene in the lives of youths as
parens patriae, or surrogate parents. As mentioned, in time these beliefs
led to the building of a variety of institutions meant to isolate, insulate,
and control deviants—prisons and penitentiaries for criminals, mental
asylums for dependent youths, and poorhouses for paupers or the able-
bodied impoverished."[16] While the benefits of such institutions were
upheld by the scientific-legal community of the times, as Erving
Goffman pointed out in his study, *Asylums*, such institutions have the
effect of eventually stripping individuals of the very capabilities that
prove that they are, in fact, responsible: self-determination, autonomy,
and freedom of action.[17] The expertise that professionals of the time
provided, their so-called objective studies of children, and their training
and similar educations in the professions provided the authority and
scientific rationality to convince others that violent behavior must be
addressed through reforms provided by state interventions and
institutions. As criminologist Barry Feld noted, "Progressive reformers
embraced many child-saving programs to respond to the myriad threats
to child development: inadequate and broken families, dependency and
neglect, poverty and welfare, education and work, crime and
delinquency, recreation and play."[18]

Inherent to the child-saving and Progressive movement was the
belief that violence and delinquency was caused by urbanization,
poverty, and social disorder, especially in cities. For this reason, many
of the first reform schools were located in rural and pastoral settings,
away from the evil influences of city life. These reform schools reflected
the same rationale that propelled European "rustification" experiments,
the "cottage plan" which attempted to replicate a family environment
in reform schools, and Charles Loring Brace's Children's Aid Society,
which placed orphaned and abandoned children with rural families,
usually shipping them from New York City to the Midwest.
Developments in alternative education, such as Summerhill, also
represented the belief in the purity and reformative qualitites of rustic

settings.

Even today, detention facilities for delinquent children have on their "campuses" what continue to be called "cottages"—as was the case in the Rosemont school district. While the basic philosophies of the child-saving movement went against current notions of zero tolerance, the movement did lead to greater connections between children, the professions, institutions, and the criminal justice system. Today, these connections support zero tolerance, since the policy could not exist if it were not for the professionalized accounts that support the isolation and institutionalization of individuals deemed violent—a reality that began with attempts to identify and rehabilitate delinquent youths in sometimes well-intentioned ways.

In addition to the belief that criminality was a result of the environment, there existed in the 19th century the conviction that violence was the outcome of the stunted development of individuals. Youth itself was deemed a time when individuals teetered precariously between primitiveness and civility. As the educational researcher Nancy Lesko noted, "Adolescence [in the 19th century] was deemed the dividing line between rational, autonomous, moral white bourgeois men and emotional, conforming, sentimental, or mythical Others, namely primitives, animals, and children."[19] Youths who did not pass into a stage defined as "rational" and "civilized" not only remained infantile, but were prone to violence, and as such, were quite different from those who "naturally" passed into this stage. Some professionally trained criminologists and psychologists, influenced by social Darwinism, concluded that criminals were biologically different from other human beings—that they were, in a sense, more primitive than those who did not display violent behavior.

As a kind of anachronistic throwback to more primitive and undeveloped times, criminals were, in some ways, a unique form of character, whose distinctiveness could be measured and empirically viewed by professionals who measured the size of their skulls, compared the slope of their foreheads, and the absences of their earlobes. Cesare Lombroso, the 19th-century Italian physician and psychiatrist, was at the forefront of this movement to explain criminal behavior through eugenic theories of human development and advancement. In the United States, the movement was not only driven by a belief in "scientific rationality" that bolsters even today rational choice theory, but it confirmed racial prejudices against 19th-century immigrants, because the physical features that defined criminals corresponded with the physiognomy of the southern and eastern Europeans that were entering the U.S. at the time.

As mentioned earlier, zero tolerance is based, in part, on the belief that individuals make the rational choice to be violent. In this way, the choice to be violent is determined, an almost natural part of criminals' thought processes. Today, the connection between rational choice and biological factors are reiterated by a host of researchers, including Nathaniel Pallone and James Hennessy who, when describing violent individuals, focus on the "impulsivity" of "actors with a high taste for risk, which may be construed as the product of neurologic or neuropsychological dysfunction." They claim that criminality is often a matter of offenders who "self-select those psychosocial environments that are peopled with like-minded (and likely also neurogenically impulsive) others." They conclude that "such self-selection in essence constitutes 'rational choice' on the part of such actors that functions so as to create the proximate opportunity for criminal violence."[20] Here, biology and choice are never really separated: Individuals choose to be with people like themselves, and as a group they are people with the same kinds of biological dysfunctions that contribute to their violent tendencies and their wants to be together.

A confluence of circumstances and developments—including the eugenics movement, immigration, social Darwinism, enlightenment principles of science—provided the milieu for the development of biological and rational choice theories of violence. Today, the view could be classified as the "youth as wild animal" theory. It is a way of conceptualizing kids as "violent offenders," "outcasts," or "delinquents" who need to be watched carefully, locked up, and even destroyed, if necessary. Even popular choices of words, such as the aggressive youth as "predator," reflect this classification; consider as well the school counselor's explanation of violent students as "vicious animals." These notions of violence pave the way for reform strategies that have more to do with zoo keeping than rehabilitation.

Such ideas are also the backbone of medical models that have sought greater use of prescription drugs, such as Ritalin, on students. The American Medical Association determined that the use of methylphenidate (the generic form of Ritalin) had increased twofold to threefold for children two to four years old, for whom the drug is not recommended by the Federal Drug Administration. In Rosemont High, it was estimated by one school social worker that as many as 80% of the students labeled as having behavioral problems were taking prescription drugs for their conditions—quite a bit of drug-taking considering that about 400 students in the one high school were labeled with behavioral problems.

Twentieth-Century Roots
In the early 20th century, psychology and Freudian psychiatry gained credence and further professionalized concepts of criminal behavior. As Sol Cohen has remarked in his study of psychoanalytic pedagogy, the topics of education and childhood were staples of discussions at meetings of the Vienna Psychoanalytical Society.[21] The rise of psychoanalysis and psychology had the effect of considering cognitive as well as environmental processes in the development of the violent psyche. One of the first developments in this regard was the establishment of Dr. William A. Healy's Juvenile Psychopathic Institute, which had close links to Chicago's new juvenile justice system. The Institute attempted to better understand the "inner worlds" of troubled youths and to foster the spread of the Child Guidance

movement—a movement that used testing, evaluation, and therapy as a means of administering intensive psychological treatments to solve problems of deviance.

Amid these developments, there began a shift in focus on criminality: in some ways what emerged as psychology combined rational choice and environmental theories into a social learning theory of violence. At the forefront of this shift was the nature *vs.* nurture debate: what were the effects of environments on the decisions that human beings made that led to their violent actions? While this debate has taken on many forms in several disciplines, including criminology, medicine, law, and sociology, the work of psychologists of the time, who were given greater respect on account of Freud's popularity, fed the emerging field of child development, and provided the background for the writings of prominent educational theorists, including G. Stanley Hall, Jean Piaget, and, to some extent, John Dewey. A defining characteristic of the field of psychology was the question of whether individuals had the ability to determine their behaviors in the face of overbearing environmental factors, and if so, to what extent.

In the early and mid-20th century, B.F. Skinner became renown for developing a science of behavior that linked environmental, rational choice, and biological accounts of violence. Essentially, Skinner wanted to show that behavior could be controlled and even predicted. In an early book, *The Behavior of Organisms*, he attempted to answer two questions: "What is the structure of a science of behavior" and "how valid can its laws be?"[22] Skinner was most interested in determining what he called the "predictable uniformity in behavior." While in the same book he argued that there exists "a large body of behavior" that does not seem to be elicited, "in the sense in which a cinder in the eye elicits closure of the lid," he continued to search for examples that proved that people are, in a sense, mostly passive recipients of outside stimuli that control their behaviors.[23] When Skinner made the assertion, even in 1971, that "a person does not act upon the world, the world acts upon him," he described a relatively bleak picture of individual freedom, and reiterated the automaton-like behavior that occupied the stage for his best-selling novel, *Walden Two*.

Skinner's life-long focus on a science of behavior (sometimes called a "system of behavior") has framed people as individuals who react almost instinctively to outside influence, with little ability to determine for oneself how one will respond. His views departed from those of the child-savers in the means of correcting violent behavior. While the child-savers' strategies were housed in discourses of rehabilitation, Skinner's were housed in behaviorism. According to Skinner, in order to change a behavior, including violent behavior, other kinds of influences must interact with the individual—influences that would counteract those that provoke violent behavior. These influences can include positive reinforcement in the case that a youth acts non-violently, but also punishments and deterrents such as prison—or more specifically to schools today, suspension, expulsion, outside placements, arrest, and other zero tolerance strategies—in the case that someone acts violently.

Behaviorism is widespread in schools, and is seen as something that joins the moral and the scientific: Punishment develops upright citizens ("spare the rod, spoil the child") and is supported by clinical tests (albeit, in Skinner's case, clinical tests on white rats).[24] In the behaviorist mind, it seems only natural that a student who acts appropriately will continue to do so if he or she is rewarded for such actions; likewise, the student who does not act appropriately will, in time, do so if he or she is punished for such behavior. This manipulation of behavior, like a watered-down form of social engineering, fuels zero tolerance in schools. Not only are we led to believe that punishment leads to appropriate behaviors—by extension, harsher punishment will get us there faster.

In the years that have passed since Skinner developed his behaviorist notions of violence, attempts to make sense of the interaction between environments and individuals in the development of behavior have moved away from his more deterministic models, but Skinner's ideas are by no means dead. They have been transformed and built upon by a range of scholars—they have entered into discussions about poverty, genes, cultural deficits, social policy, and intelligence. On a positive note, he is sometimes commended for making the point that environment does affect behavior, that it is not just biological, medical, or a matter of rational choice. While Skinner's notions of behavior lack understanding for the way people have the power to guide their own destinies or filter through interpretations of experiences, his theories challenge even more damaging eugenic explanations of violence. While the "eugenics movement" may be over, eugenic notions of intelligence and behavior continue to resound. With its blather about I.Q. scores and its science-sounding veneer, such ideas were popularized, for example, in the 1994 publication of the *The Bell Curve*, a book that, in the words of Jacqueline Jones, "is simply the most recent in a long line of efforts to prove the congenital inferiority of poor people in general, and black people in particular.[25] Aside from this, though, Skinner has been responsible for a particular view of humanity that is guided more by science than by understandings regarding the complexities of interactions between behavior, identity, and social contexts.

Following up on Skinner's work in the 1960s, and in some ways improving upon it, social psychologists described a new kind of behaviorism; one that put more emphasis on how individuals imitated as well as interpreted and *interacted with* the mixed messages of society. New developments during the 1960s, including greater focus on social learning, labeling, and interactionist theories, as well as radical and liberal ideologies that challenged the institutionalization of those considered deviant, began to undo some of the child-saving, eugenic, and behaviorist notions of delinquency. In a sense, understandings of violence turned to cognitive theories, including social learning, and there developed a concern for how individuals interpreted their surroundings, not just responded to them.

The development of social learning theory signaled a departure from behaviorism, and while it continued to focus on individuals as the root cause of violence—in that it was their learning that caused the problems—it did challenge more deterministic views of individuals as naturally, biologically, and instinctively violent. Albert Bandura, who is often considered the forefather of social learning theory, explained that "people are not simply reactors to external influences. They select, organize, and transform the stimuli that impinge upon them."[26] Why is it, one may ask, when two people are faced with the same stimuli—perhaps a threatening person—one reacts with fists and another with flight? As mentioned earlier, social learning theory is a phenomenon that supports some aspects of zero tolerance in that the individual students' cognitive processes are deemed in need of adjustment, which, today, is done within zero tolerance strategies of "teaching a lesson" through punitive measures. However, it also leads to a softer kind of zero tolerance that is wrapped up with ideas about pedagogy, not just punishment: it is the "gentler" form of violence prevention that links deviants with strategies meant to *teach* them appropriate behavior.

The way that people learn, according to social learning theory, is through modeling and imitation. Bandura explained that "most human behavior is learned observationally through modeling: from observing others one forms an idea of how new behaviors are performed, and on later occasions this coded information serves as a guide for action."[27] In tests that became well-known in academic circles, Bandura used a Bobo doll (an inflatable clown) to show that children, after watching an actor be rewarded for beating the doll, imitated the actions in laboratory tests. Since these mid-1960s tests, social learning theory has been at the forefront of explaining how influences such as media affect young children. In his book, *Social Learning and Personality Development*, Bandura and his colleague, Richard Walters, concluded that "imitation plays an important role in the acquisition of deviant, as well as of conforming, behavior," and reiterated in their own work the basic explanation put forth several decades earlier by the anthropologist Gladys Reichard, who stated that "children do not do what adults *tell* them to do, but rather what they *see* other adults do."[28]

While Bandura and other researchers who adopted social learning theory pointed out how children in the U.S. were influenced by what they saw—especially in terms of their families—anthropologists such as Margaret Mead and Douglas Fry showed that other cultures, too, were prone to imitate the actions of those in their communities and families. In one study, Douglas Fry examined two neighboring Zapotec communities in Oaxaca, Mexico. One community was more aggressive than the other in terms of wife beating, assaults, homicides, and fighting. Through long-term observation he showed that the parents in this community disciplined their children corporally more often than in the community that was peaceful. He found that children in the less violent community were disciplined verbally, not corporally, and that the children were not only less violent, but more obedient to their parents.

Fry explained, "in place of heavy reliance on corporal punishment, La Paz parents raised non-aggressive children through a combination of conveying expectations of non-aggressive [behavior], respectfulness, and obedience, modeling and rewarding such behaviors, and preventing and correcting transgressions verbally."[29] This focus on aggressive child-rearing practices confirms the work of Bandura and Walters who, in their study of adolescent boys, explained that "punitive methods of discipline not only further alienated the boys but also fostered the hostility and aggression with which the boys had responded to emotional deprivations."[30]

Interestingly, Bandura and Walters noted in their book, *Adolescent Aggression*, that "the majority of boys who display repetitive antisocial behavior come from broken homes, or live in high delinquency or deteriorated areas [but] such boys were excluded from the present study."[31] For a variety of reasons, Bandura and Walters wanted to study children who were not deprived in the traditional sense. While the work of Bandura, Walters, and other social learning theorists have been helpful in documenting what Fry called the "intergenerational transmission of conflict," the work does not focus on social environments as much as family practices. While their work will support assertions that parents need to model good behavior if they expect their children to be good, the work does not address the broader socioeconomic factors involved in why the parents may be bad influences in the first place. For these kinds of considerations, we must leave the world of psychology and pay heed to the people who know of these problems the best—the violent offenders themselves.

From Zero Tolerance to Understanding

Zero tolerance policy joins equally with notions of rehabilitation, tough love, and punishment. It places the burden for violence prevention in schools on students by viewing students as the culprits who must be transformed. To the zero tolerance mind, students must get the message that violence will not be tolerated in school and must fear the consequences that may befall them if they do "act out." At the same time that they are accused, they are responded to as needy: in need of attention, sometimes medication, at times more structure in the form of an institution to replace their dysfunctional family structures, sometimes in need of a violence prevention program, or sometimes just in need of a good, hard lesson in a prison.[32] Zero tolerance is not a complicated idea; it is already so much a part of what we already know and do in regard to welfare reform, incarceration, and international military interventions. In essence, we make people pay for their crimes through actions that are sometimes violent themselves.

That there exist people who may be deterred from a violent act because of an increased threat of punishment is probably true. There are circumstances when the threat of punishment will deter violence. However, there are many times when it will not. In Rosemont and Brandon High Schools, the implementation of their zero tolerance policies did not lead to less fights and other violent behavior; in Brandon High, not a single teacher I interviewed thought that violence had decreased since their implementation of zero tolerance, and there were several teachers who felt that the problem had gotten worse. Records from Rosemont High show no decrease in violent incidents. What often prevents violence are not threats or even behavior modification techniques, but more personal and caring circumstances in the lives of potential offenders.

When I began interviewing inmates convicted of violent crimes, I was interested in what in their lives contributed to the circumstances that led to the act(s) for which they were incarcerated. I had gotten to know the inmates during a twenty-two-hour workshop on violence prevention held at Godwin prison. As a participant in the program, I was awarded a certificate along with the inmates, and spent much time during breaks chatting and having coffee with the men. One inmate, whom I will call Julian, explained to me:

> Personally I feel that anybody can get violent. You put a cat in a corner, he'll get violent. And people who have [are victims of] violence, they may be the first to be violent. But you just got to know how to conduct yourself and where to be and where not to be. The street ain't no good for me, so don't go on the street. So me, a lot of times, what I will do, I walk away. I quit [fighting] because my family is more important to me than being here [in prison] with these guys.
>
> There are a lot of times that you can put yourself in a situation where you be forced into violence. And there are a lot of times, if you use your brain, you can walk away from it. It's a choice left for you to make. I can sit here all day and argue with you. If you don't argue back with me, hey, there is no argument. That's what happens a lot of times. I find people they were being chumps instead of being the bigger man and just saying, "Listen I'm not going to put myself on the line for you."

As a person conducting these interviews, I would ask inmates to explain to me what experiences influenced (or even "led to") their bouts with violence. Frequently, though, they would want to rephrase my question. Sure, family abuse, drugs, and gangs did create environments where violence was seen as an almost natural way to deal with life, but they also wanted to assert their own capacities to "know how to conduct themselves."

Part of this explanation reflects the reality of prison. In prison, inmates must be convinced, or at least convince the parole board that they are convinced, that they are completely at fault for their crime(s) and they have accepted the responsibility to change. Part of it, also, are the inmates' attempts to explain to me that they are not Skinner's white rats blindly reacting to the terrible world around them. The fact remains in almost all of the stories that inmates told me, however, that some people do not even have to worry about "walking away." Some people are not put into corners like cats. Some do not have to worry about staying off the streets. Their streets are safe, and if not, they have parents who would not permit them to hang out on street corners. As in Julian's case, personal circumstances such as having a well-loved family may also prevent violence, for individuals see a purpose for staying out of trouble. While environments did not control their behaviors, most of the inmates I interviewed grew up in predicaments where violent behavior was an everyday part of the neighborhood scene, and to be a part of that neighborhood one needed to participate: a problem that many suburban and middle-class youths do not have to worry about (as much).

The ways the inmates steered themselves through their environments was best explained by one inmate, whom I will call Dan. Dan was born in Puerto Rico, came to the United States when he was five, lived for a while in New York City, then in Hartford, Connecticut. He moved several times in Hartford, and after moving for the third time in three years, returned to Puerto Rico, then came back to Hartford when he was twelve. He can not remember all of the places he had lived or all of the schools that he had attended: "It's just a blur of coming and going, never feeling secure in one place."

Dan was convicted of murder when he was seventeen years old, he spent eight years fleeing the police, and was finally apprehended in Los Angeles in a leather shop that he had been working in for two years, "just when I was getting my life back together." At thirty-five in 1998 when I interviewed him, he had a twenty-two-year-old daughter, a twenty-one-year-old son, and two grandchildren.

Dan began sniffing glue when he was eight years old and soon turned to THC, marijuana, and a variety of psychedelic drugs. He remembers when he started sniffing glue because it was the year that Martin Luther King, Jr., was assassinated, and he felt that "everything in the world was out of control, and so was I. It was the only time I felt that I fit in—being completely out of control like all the *homies* back then." Like other people in his neighborhood, he participated in the looting that followed King's assassination, which was his first experience with serious crime. After this, he would break into trains and steal food that was on board, then he began breaking into cars and apartments; soon he was stealing cars and selling them to chop shops for quick cash.

In school, he remained quiet, kept to himself, and never felt that he had any friends because he moved so much. He was placed in special education classes in the 5th grade: "with all the retards," he explained. School for Dan was a frightening and alienating experience:

> When I grew up in school it was like the teacher was just babbling on and doing his or her thing. Really wasn't taking any interest in myself. I'm sure they had their little couple of kids that they took interest in that they helped, but I never had that. I was illiterate. I didn't know how to read. I didn't know how to write. I had no respect for school because I wasn't learning anything.
>
> I taught myself to read and write when I was a teenager, mostly from reading signs and things like that. I knew how to write my name but that was it. As far as reading and writing, I had a really hard time with that. I was real self-conscious of that. So I sort of stayed in the back of the classroom. You know like when they have you come and read something in front of the class.

I dreaded that. When I knew that day was going to come, I would skip school. I wouldn't show up. Not because I didn't enjoy school. I enjoyed school. It's just that I wasn't getting anything out of it.

These people, they are supposed to teach me, but they weren't really teaching me. There were just too many people in the classroom. I went to too many schools. Every school that I would go to they would put me in the classes with the retards. Sometimes the teachers were more attentive, but at that time, at that particular point, I think it was a little bit too late. I think I was just a little bit too far gone with the drugs at that point to pay attention.

I remember stashing my glue underneath the school. My tubes of glue. I use to hide them under the school. So at break time, lunch time, I'd go underneath the school and drop a tube in the bag and start sniffing away. Boom, I hear the bell, boom, I drop in a mint in my mouth, run upstairs and I'd be gone. I'd be blasted. I'm not trying to concentrate on what's going on. I'm concentrating on getting the hell out of there so I can go back to my bag. That just became a vicious cycle. Then finally I gave up sniffing glue and then I went on to other stuff. I went to Puerto Rico for a period because my mom realized that I had a problem.

Dan's father also had a substance abuse problem. However, not only was he an alcoholic, he was abusive, and on one occasion he beat Dan with a bicycle chain: "I loved that bike, but after that, I wouldn't go near it. That took away my freedom to get away, just ride my bike." Looking back, he explained:

Even before you are conceived, you are already hit because this is what you're coming into the world to. This is it. Then every time that you do something, instead of having your father sit you down and talk to you and help you understand that what you did was wrong and why you shouldn't do it, you get a belt upside your ass, a smack upside your head, and you get gummied up [knocked out]. You get your butt kicked. You are like, "What's going on?" You are a little kid. You don't understand why...and you're looking for love, but you're not interpreting this as love. You're being abused.

So you grow up like that. Then you still love the man because he's your father and it's twisted. It's a twisted kind of love. You love him because he's your dad, but you don't love him because of the things he does. You grow up like that and what do you think? What type of child do you think that child is going to grow up into. It's not just me. My brother's also [in prison]. Everybody at the house, we grew up like that. My uncles, his brothers, weren't any better than he was.

At thirteen, Dan ran away from home. Soon he met the mother of his children, began living with her when he was fourteen years old, and supported them both through odd jobs and theft. He left school when he was in the 9th grade. He was apprehended for a theft and eventually committed to a juvenile detention center: "They throw you in there with a bunch of other kids, some kids with problems more severe than yours. So instead of bettering the situation, it's just being worsened. You don't have anybody calling you to the side and talking to you. Nobody really taking one genuine interest in you."

In prison now, he summed up his past and present experiences simply: "I went through a lot of suffering. I gave it too. The same way I got it, I gave it, and now I'm sorry for the whole damn thing in more ways than one, but there is nothing I can do about it now."

Where does one start to imagine the causes of violence amid such a complicated story of life experiences. Did the violence start because of poverty, because of multiple moves between cities and countries, because of poor schooling, because of domestic violence, because of drug abuse? Was the violence that Dan committed retaliation for the violence that he endured? To try to determine the singular causes of violence is a farce. To suggest that somebody like Dan, if he had been punished more harshly, would not have done what he did, is inhumane. For every individual story I heard, there were multiple circumstances that created the milieu for violence. Violence is always an outcome of circumstances that produce violent situations. As Julian noted, anybody can be violent: Put a cat in the corner, and even the nicest cat rears its back. While there exist problems of violence in middle-upper class and stable communities, today that corner has become many urban centers—and the cats, the urban poor.

Violence and Urbanity

To understand the lives of people like Dan, Julian, and others caught in a web of victimization and victimizing in cities, one must consider their stories within the context and history of cities themselves. While urbanization and immigration to the United States in the 19th century may have led to an influx of poor and troubled kids—incorrigible youths—by the mid 20th century, social policy created the "cat in the corner" milieu in cities.

These post-World War II policies included redlining which prevented the granting of loans and mortgages in city areas, making living there and opening businesses difficult. "Redlining" refers to the now illegal act by banks of marking off in red pen areas considered poor economic risks, which then led to rejection of financial support. In addition, highway expansion that fervently began in 1956 with the National Defense Highway Act favored the lifestyles of the emerging suburbanites. As Jean Anyon noted in her book, *Ghetto Schooling*, "In the postwar period, highway building nationwide received huge subsidies year in and year out, but urban mass transit was starved. Estimates are that 75% of government expenditures for transportation in the United States in the postwar period went for highways and only 1% for urban mass transit."[33]

Federal highway expansion made access to cities simple, and federal housing and mortgage policies, which subsidized and provided low interest rates for new suburban single-family homes, made home ownership outside cities feasible: hence, a important link was secured for the "live in the suburb, work in the city" crowd. The exodus to the suburbs was further propelled by deteriorating schools in cities, the result of lost revenues as middle-classes left the cities, but also due to tax deductions for businesses in cities, which further reduced urban tax bases.

While discriminatory social policy enabled middle-class and primarily white residents to easily move to the expanding suburbs, the population rates of cities did not decline as much as one would expect. While the middle-classes were leaving the cities, poor African-Americans from the south were moving into the more industrial cities of the north, such as those where Rosemont and Brandon High were located, with the hope of finding work in factories. Unfortunately, this movement corresponded with the closing and downsizing of most factories in northern cities.[34] The devastation of all this was described in a litany that included

> economic and racial discrimination; racial segregation and concentrated poverty in deteriorated urban cores; the deindustrialization of cities and movement of manufacturing and service jobs to suburbs; inadequate public transportation systems to enable poor urban residents to reach suburban jobs; the growth of female-headed households, welfare dependency, and minority children in poverty; the deterioration of urban public education; and the destructive impact of crime and violence in these communities on their residents.[35]

We should also consider poor medical attention, lack of insurance, the production and distribution of more lethal weapons, the effects of crack cocaine especially in the 1980s, the mass distribution of other urban drugs, urban riots that left some city areas scarred, as well as high infant mortality rates. Taken together, these circumstances caused devastation to families that contributed to the events that led people like Dan and Julian into their long, violent downward spirals.

To account for these issues in academic circles, urban sociologists and qualitative researchers have put forth ideas revolving around social disorganization and strain theories of violence. The roots of social disorganization theory can be found in the 1943 study, *Juvenile Delinquence and Urban Areas*, by the University of Chicago sociologists Clifford Shaw and Henry McKay. In the book, the authors assert that low economic status, ethnic heterogeneity, and residential mobility causes community disorganization, which leads to high crime and delinquency rates.[36]

More recently, social disorganization has been described to include incidents where there is "anonymity and sparse acquaintanceship networks among residents, unsupervised teenage peer groups and attenuated control of public space, and a weak organizational base and low social participation in local activities"—essentially a breakdown of community.[37] Strain theory is rooted in Emile Durkheim's notion of *anomie*, which describes some social structures as chaotic and lacking in a cohesion that is conducive to the development of positive moral ties, values, customs, and informal codes of behavior.[38] Such a theory was crucial to the development in the 1960s of Patrick Moynihan's notions of a culture of poverty. Both social organization and strain theories are ecological—and sometimes indistinguishable from each other—in that they focus on how environmental plight interacts with young people to create, on the one hand, opportunities that are lacking and sometimes completely blocked, and on the other hand, a general breakdown of morality and caring between people, which ultimately ends up fueling violence.[39]

In the 1960s and 1970s national committees such as the President's Commission on Law Enforcement and Administration of Justice, the National Advisory Commission on Civil Disorders, and the National Commission on the Causes and Prevention of Violence, secured the federal government's role in addressing the problem of violence in cities.[40] Similar to older, progressive notions of reform, the 1960s brought about a time of increased government involvement in social problems and education, highlighted by the Elementary and Secondary Education Act of 1965. However, these newer efforts were characterized not so much by child-saving activities—as in the 19th century—but by social service and Great Society interventions. The difference here is not as great in philosophy as in the magnitude of the bureaucracy attached to the reforms.

What began as a War on Poverty (which eventually led to a War on Welfare in the late 1990s) was a government sponsored attempt to address urban problems associated with poverty and violence with federal aid and the establishment of an enormous social-service bureaucracy funded by tax dollars.[41] While the efforts of such policy did little to change the structural causes of violence they did do much to institutionalize the connection between crime prevention and poverty, and, in time, to secure greater links between the U.S. government, social scientists, juvenile justice, social services, and those in the medical, education, and law professions.

The result has been an elaborate maze of institutional bodies that makes up what can be viewed as the "youth management system"—a combination of systems which include schools, courts, police, non-profit groups, and prisons. The usually caring people who keep the youth management system running maintain a vast bureaucracy that has lost touch with common sense and basic principles of equal educational opportunity and social justice. Zero tolerance, in conjunction with this youth management system, assures the creation of criminals. Like a self-fulfilling prophecy, people are born into savage circumstances, they are labeled savage, treated as such, and when the time comes for them to prove that they are productive citizens, they fail—they act savagely. Each institutional measure to respond to this crisis becomes a downward out-placement into a bureaucratic system, until life is cut short by hopelessness, incarceration, or death.

From Theory to Prevention

Theories of violence and this history of delinquency could remain the sole preoccupation of social scientists if it was not for the fact that they interact powerfully with popular rhetoric about violence, which shape, even today, our national responses to the problem. Like the school social worker who explained violence in terms of kids' poor communities and the school psychologist, who viewed violence as an outcome of inappropriate reasoning, each description is a matter-of-fact way of talking within theoretical and historical frameworks. Such shared, though sometimes contradictory, language set the stage for more recent discussions about school violence.

That kids choose to be violent, that it is their environments that determine their behaviors, that students have to learn to make positive rational choices instead of negative ones, are more than references to theory; they are descriptions by school personnel to explain violent behavior in a language that all people know and can understand. Biological theories of violence may not determine how people respond to students, but certainly biological theories mix with a range of other factors, including the rise of medicine, powerful advertising by drug companies, a strong pharmaceutical lobby in Washington, and the clinical labeling of students, to create a situation that may seem outrageous to some and only natural to others: that the drugging of kids to solve so-called behavioral problems has become so commonplace that expressions have developed in schools, such as "meds" for "medication"—a word used so often that it needs to be shortened.[42]   Students who take daily medications for perceived psychoses are sometimes called "med-heads" by other students.

Zero tolerance policy is the result of many factors. It demonstrates adults' frustrations with youths. It is given legitimacy by a history of delinquency that has included child-saving strategies, eugenic interpretations of criminality, behaviorist models of reward and punishment, and various psychological and sociological theories of violence. It is also a result of what is seen as the failure of "soft on crime" liberalism and progressive education to teach young people a good, hard lesson about their behaviors.

As schools develop closer links with social service agencies and police departments, zero tolerance has become further instituted in schools. Unfortunately, the result has been the creation of an environment where few would like to be and policies that increase (not decrease!) the chances that troubled students will act violently. As criminologist Spencer De Li explained: "Legal sanctions escalate juveniles' involvement in antisocial behavior and diminish their life chances in early adulthood."[43] Must strategies in the name of violence prevention add to the oppressive and controlling qualities of school and be a catalyst for delinquency? Or are there ways of preventing violence that would not only be effective, but would create more caring and warm environments in schools?

The answer to how we move beyond zero tolerance policy and what we take up and adopt in the process are discussed in the following chapters. Starting in the next chapter with an extended field note, the problem of educating city kids born into poverty and truly horrific situations is discussed within the context of urban development, vocational education, and employment. Later, the focus turns to the structure of schools, issues of respect and identity, and the influences of militarism, gun manufacturing, and popular culture. For now, though, the deteriorating circumstances in cities and the problems they cause for youths, is the topic.

Cities do not have a monopoly on poor people and community breakdown—rural poverty and even poverty in some suburbs—is ugly and ubiquitous. In cities, however, poverty is concentrated by the density of people, and violence is often worse because of racial segregation and gangs. In addition, cities were put into a stranglehold in the second half of the 20th century by highway expansion, suburbanization, and the globalization of labor, and the ones who suffered most were those stuck in cities who could not recoup.

In the 21st century, city residents are going to need secure jobs, a better education to obtain them, and security that comes with urban development and social policy responsive to the needs of hardworking, but sometimes desperate, people. Poverty reduction will not automatically solve problems of violence, but serious threats to minority and poor urban youths can be reduced with the creation of communities that are secure, that sustain some degree of economic and political power, and benefit from the financial, educational, and social perks that come with middle-class status. These are topics discussed in the next chapter—after a short trip through a city's downtown.

Chapter 3

City Living and Dying

Rewritten from field notes, October 16, 1999:

As I round the corner past the school and into the parking lot to take the shortcut back to the bus to get out of what is generally referred to as the projects, I am met by a clown. He is sloping up an incline in the sidewalk that enters the parking lot, slouching towards garbage that is piled high next to a shattered chain-linked fence crowned with the remnants of razor wire. The garbage reminds me of complaints by people in the area that sometimes the garbage collectors (or "the City") do not pick up trash in their neighborhood, and the clown reminds me of a nightmarish movie. The clown is carrying an overcoat under his arm, holding his ballooned pants up with one hand. Whether rented or owned, the costume hangs on him like the remains of party streamers. As he comes closer, I notice a limp, a face that seems caved in. When he passes, he glances at me, not friendly, not threatening, a face which seems completely blank and tired. I do not know what to make of the clown; has he just returned from a kid's party, is he dressing early for Halloween? I leave the parking lot and come out onto the sidewalk of a busy street where I see nobody noticing the clown, as I have, but am met with a rush of car horns, stares by a group of boys standing in front of a bodega, and a dog that checks my hands for something to eat.

I hesitate for a moment outside the parking lot and look down both sides of the street, trying to decide which route to take back to the bus stop. Down one side of the street, nearest to me is a group of men, perhaps in their 40s, playing dominoes on milk crates outside an apartment house. They slam the dominoes down on a rigged piece of sheet rock—snap!—pause, sip from their cans wrapped in brown paper bags, and talk in rapid-fire Spanish, which I find almost impossible to understand. They laugh, push each other, and make comments at girls coming back from school. One person standing with his back against the apartment building brick whistles at a girl, and the girl fires back a glance and raises her middle finger at him.

On my other side, there is a group of guys whom I take to be drug dealers. One keeps his eyes on the street where cars slowly pass. The people inside the cars are mostly white in this predominantly Latino area of the city. One guy who has been watching the street lifts his head to some of the cars—a sign, a question, "What do you want?"—he touches the side of his nose, signaling cocaine as well as heroine (which the white out-of-towners more often sniff than shoot up, and the dealers know this). One in the group asks me, "What you want?" It is not an invitation to buy drugs. They do not trust me—white middle-class strollers are not common on the street; they come in cars if they come in at all. I tell the person, who seems only slightly younger than myself, though much bigger and more muscular, that I am going to the bus. The crotch of his pants hang about his knees, which reminds me of students in high school, but his muscle build and his slightly older age, remind me of inmates who spend their days bulking up in prison.

He shrugs and shakes his head as if he has no time for me. They make it clear in their body language and their looks that they do not like me around them. I turn away and pass by the men playing dominoes and glance at the game. I walk in a purposeful way, as if in a hurry, as if accustomed to the area. A student from the high school who lived in this area once told me: "To live there you have to have *juice*"—a mix of power and connections, a public knowledge that you are not one to mess with. I have absolutely no juice and know it but do not feel threatened. People here may want to know what I am doing or what I want; some may even want me out or to show some fear or worry, but that is about it. The people who get hurt here are not white; they are the color of those doing the hurting. I know that I am in less danger in this area of this city than are most African Americans and Latinos, especially if they are male and adolescent.

Interactions between people in this area can be friendly, or can seem on occasion nonexistent, but what seems always prevalent is the interaction that is only seconds away from a fight or confrontation. Drug deals that go wrong, the girls' urge to lash back at harassing men, a prostitute who looks like she has already been beaten, meeting another man who may or may not be violent, groups of boys who pass each other threateningly. Even the patrol cars that swing around corners exude violence. I see police officers who look as if they are fed up and disgusted. I have been stopped here by a cop who wanted to know whom I was buying drugs from. When I explained that I was not buying drugs, I was told that they treat people who protect drug dealers in the same way that they deal with drug sellers. It was the most threatened I have ever felt in the area.

Cars are always stopping in the street, some for drugs, others to make conversations with people on the sidewalks who are walking about, making plans for later, chatting, snapping handshakes that I have seen in the high school. Young and old alike yell their conversations over the thumping salsa and hip-hop that penetrates through the sub-woofer enhanced stereos in some cars. Guys with "juice" have cars that make people turn their heads, if not because of the music, then because of the shine of the body, the decorated antennas, the mag tires, and gleaming chrome. Passing by apartment buildings, doors ajar, I look in and see darkness, stairs that lead up into graffiti-filled hallways and closed doors. There are no lobbies in the buildings. Rarely are there functioning intercom systems and rarely a door that does not show the dented scars of past break-ins. Litter is everywhere, and the smell of urine, when you are passing between buildings, can be overwhelming. Laundry floats overhead, stretched between buildings, and, since it has just recently rained, the sewers are clogged with litter, and in one drain, with pants and a sock.

When I reach the corner, I see a police officer giving the remains of a car a red ticket, which he ties to the antenna. Out of an open window, three stories up, a small plastic bag filled with some liquid comes flying down and smashes in the street at the cop's feet, wetting one cuff of his pants. The cop is startled, looks up at the buildings, does not see anyone, and knows that he would not go inside one of these buildings anyway. He just moves on after affixing the ticket. Across the street some onlookers sitting on a fire escape, nearly fall all over themselves laughing at the officer. I move on. In other parts of the city, I walk with my head up, admiring buildings and trees. Here, I take my footing cautiously, not wanting to step in garbage, trip on the broken sidewalk, or step in dog droppings. It really does not pay to look around much for admiration's sake anyway. There are no trees, no bushes, no flowers; the only vegetation is a rare scraggly bush, and the weeds that come up through the cracked sidewalk. There are large patches of land that are just empty—old parking lots, a place where a fire has done away with a store, vacant lots that would be snapped up for development in a second in another section of the city.

I hear a bus coming up from behind me and since I am only half a block from the stop I turn around to catch the bus driver's eye, toss up my hand, and trot up to the stop. I look ahead to see whether I am going to make it or not and am relieved to see that the traffic light beside the stop has turned red. I reach the bus stop just as the bus pulls up, but it plows through the red light. I decide not to wait for the next bus but to keep walking towards my house. I will catch the next bus at the next stop. I walk and walk, focusing on my footing, a *flaneur* of sorts, slumming, partly interested, partly feeling like an outsider in the city I live in. After six blocks, the neighborhood begins to change. Apartments open up to old Victorian houses, some dilapidated, some

> not. A flower patch with cigarette butts in it, more trees, less garbage, better smelling, I am entering what some call the buffer neighborhood, a mix of working class people, individuals who have moved up out of the projects, artists, and store owners who wish to live near their shops. Here, the bus stops for me. I get on, and it drives farther away from the projects, out of the buffer area, and into a neighborhood where clowns are not so dreary.

Even in 1999, after several years of tragedies involving multiple killings in suburban and rural schools, violence remains more prominent in urban areas and their schools than elsewhere.[1] Consider the issues presented here: destitution, drug dealing and use, harassment of girls by men, unemployment, animosities between police officers and community residents, lack of public services, and crime. While I disagree with Skinner's more deterministic ideas—that environments (or outside stimuli) determine behaviors—individuals are certainly influenced by the neighborhoods in which they live, and youths in this area are sometimes influenced terribly. They make up the bulk of students who are labeled SED, who drop out of school, and who are suspended or placed into alternative schools.

Researchers have provided convincing evidence that poverty plays a far greater role than other factors in determining whether a person is likely either to become violent or to be a victim of violence. As Marcel Soriano, Fernando Soriano, and Evelia Jimenez explained, the conditions of hunger, poverty, homelessness, and other survival threats confronting families become strong indicators of violence in schools.[2] More to the point, criminologist James Short, in his analysis of years of research, identified a litany of issues that are sources of youth violence: "concentrated poverty, residential mobility and population turnover, family disruption, housing/population density, and a variety of dimensions of local social organization (e.g., low density of friendships and acquaintances, lack of social resources, weak intergenerational ties in families and communities, weak control of street-corner peer groups, and low participation in community organizations by residents."[3] His list is in many ways a summary of what life is all about in urban poverty. Dan, Julian, and others would know what he was talking about.

Those who like to question the connection between poverty and violence are fond of pointing out how certain groups of people, who have been or are poor, have, for the most part, avoided epidemics of violence like those in U.S. cities. In one school, a teacher of social studies, who saw herself as a kind of expert in the history of culture, pointed out to me on two occasions that Jewish ghettos of the early 20th century on the lower east side of New York City, while fraught with problems like those of the poor today, never faced the current kinds of crises seen in black and Latino ghettos. Additionally, in a meeting that I attended as a member of a state advisory committee on violence, the lead organizer pointed out, albeit reluctantly, that many poor rural areas in the United States and similar communities in Ireland (she was from Ireland) do not suffer from violence the way U.S. cities do.

While statistics may support these assertions, one must keep in mind that today's U.S. cities are not the Jewish ghettos of yesterday. Nor can one compare U.S. cities to the more rural forms of poverty that plague Ireland and even rural areas in the United States. Although similarities exist between problems faced by rural areas and cities, especially in regard to joblessness, family abuse, substance abuse, and social isolation, one must keep in mind that country areas are not often home bases for drug and gun operations and extensive gang networks and that rural schools do not ordinarily suffer from large schools, high turnover of teachers and students, ethnic heterogeneity, and high population rates.[4] Nevertheless, the teacher and the committee member were correct to a point; poverty does not cause violence. However, poverty, combined with other factors that are predominate in poor urban areas, is a source of violence.

Certainly, people like Dan and others I interviewed in prison might not end up in jail if circumstances in their lives were changed. Even amid poverty, if Dan had not moved so much, if a school had taken a deep interest in him, if his father and uncles had not been abusive, if he had been cured of drug addiction—things might have been different. Violence occurs when multiple factors fall into place, and poverty is the perfect catch-can for them. To say that doing away with urban poverty will create safer streets and schools is a bit naive. Violence in poor urban areas and in ghetto schools is a deeply entrenched manner of acting; from the bully in the hallway to the gang member in the street, these are people who are already a part of the urban fabric. As criminologist Robert Sampson explained, behaviors are cultural ways of acting within "cognitive landscapes," and poverty "provides fertile soil" for criminality that, in time, becomes rationalized and even expected.[5]

To intervene in the life of a youth, we must disrupt the processes that cause factors associated with urban poverty to fall into place and become rationalized. In most school-based mentoring programs, for example, what is most effective for troubled students is a connection with people who act as positive influences—people who help prevent too many negative factors from falling onto the shoulders of students. In one program described by Erin Quillman and David Dupper, students who participated in the mentoring program explained its positive aspects by focusing on their relationships with an older advocate and friend, which provided, "one-on-one attention, friendship, someone to hang-out with, someone who cares about them, someone who helps them not to worry as much, answers their questions, helps with school work, offers encouragement to do well in school, gives exposure to college, gives advice, someone who looks out for them, and someone who stays by their side during school meetings."[6]

Notice that the benefits of the program have more to do with helping, support, and guidance than with manipulation of behavior through teaching and modification techniques. While financial reinvestment in cities and education are crucial to counteract violence associated with urban poverty, any influx of money must accompany community advocacy and the revitalization of families and community networks. Education must be accompanied by a concerted attempt by everyone to show sensitivity and responsibility toward students who have been born into circumstances that are life-threatening and, at times, nightmarish. This is something that zero tolerance policy can never do.

When interviewing poor city students about their lives, several issues seem always to be a part of their experiences. While the more affluent may discuss good times on family trips, yearnings for college, playing sports in leagues, vacations, and other pleasures, the poor city kid tells stories about family abuse, absentee parents, drug addiction, boredom, crime, victimization, gangs, violence, death of friends and family members, and incarceration in prisons, boot camps, or a variety of alternative schools and detention centers. The lives of poor urban students are wrapped up in violence. Their days are violent, they are victimized, they see violence in their homes, streets, and schools, and they often become violent.

To focus on these students without focusing on the context of the problem—the poor neighborhoods themselves and what these neighborhoods produce—is not only futile, it is also demeaning to the kids. It places the onus of the responsibility for change on the poor young person and not also on the adults and circumstances that have created the problem. However, the opposite is also true. To focus only on improving the environment and reducing poverty without focusing on the moral lives of young people assumes that children will automatically react positively to a better environment.[7] It underestimates the long-term effects of poverty and all that it has done to families and communities and, in a sense, views poverty reduction as a violence prevention pill.

If we are to make serious efforts at violence prevention, we must refurbish existing social structures to reflect the needs of those living in poor areas. This way of viewing urban renewal is different from most city gentrification projects, which most often reflect the desires of the upwardly mobile and real estate developers. We must support forms of prenatal, early-infancy, and educational programs that focus on problems associated with poverty, including Head Start, the High/Scope Perry Preschool Project, the Violence Prevention Project and the Family Development Research Program (both at Syracuse University), the Yale Child Welfare Project, and the Houston Parent Child Development Center.[8]

In addition, violence prevention must go beyond simple social planning models that began in the 1960s but continue today in the form of new city civic centers and sports arenas. Major urban renewal projects are too often politically motivated and occur due to a sudden windfall of money from state or federal sources. Often, these large-scale projects disrupt the lives of poor people rather than improve them. The building of large parks that are then left untended and become a kind of dead zone, stadiums that can not be filled, and civic centers that overtake housing and never really attract the entertainment and jet-setters as promised are examples of city planning that in some cases have caused more city devastation than improvement. History has shown us that urban development itself has failed in many cases, and, in some instances, has caused more problems than it solved.[9]

For example, the housing project that I had left when I met the clown on the street was built during a time when architecture and technology were used to construct new "violence proof" buildings in cities. "Skip stop" elevators were meant to cut down on assaults; the use of ceramics, stainless steel, and stucco were seen as a way of diminishing the ubiquity of graffiti and urine; one-way and concave mirrors were installed to enable better vision of hallways; and lights were protected with wire meshing to prevent them from being knocked out in an attempt to darken hallways for an attack.[10] Such architectural engineering parallels devices in schools that attempt to safeguard students through buzzers, mirrors, cameras, metal detectors, automatic locking doors, and the like.

Housing projects, however, in spite of some good intentions, created explosive situations when poverty became concentrated. The building of housing projects attempted to make what was essentially inhumane safer rather than making living conditions for the poor more humane. In the 1961 classic *The Death and Life of Great American Cities*, Jane Jacobs described public housing as a means to "merely shift slums from here to there," a program that added "its own tincture of extra hardship and disruption" and destroyed neighborhoods where "constructive and improving communities existed and where the situations called for encouragement rather than destruction."[11] Jacobs rightly viewed some urban renewal plans as a way of diddling with symptoms while avoiding the causes. If nothing else, they made some areas of the cities more violent.

A View from Nowhere

Many factors have contributed to the destruction of cities and the violence that has been its by-product. Behind the scenes of city blight are realties of political patronage, shifts of power, and funding inequities. When all is said and done, federal aid as a percentage of city budgets dropped 64 percent from an average of 17.7 percent in 1980 to 6.4 percent in 1990.[12] Federal funding for road construction, starting in the late 1950s not only enabled middle-class citizens to leave cities easily, but the new highways split many cities in half. In Brandon City, a major New York highway cuts through the center city, creating poor areas around the roadway and under its overpasses. The same occurred in the city where I live. A major Connecticut highway cuts through the city, and the areas under the overpasses are dark and dirty wastelands. A *New York Post* article of February 1960, at a time when the federal road construction program was taking off, described city hardships and violence in a report about a murder:[13]

> The slaying in Cohen's butcher shop at 164 E. 174th St. Monday night was no isolated incident, but the culmination of a series of burglaries and holdups along the street. . . . Ever since work started on the Cross-Bronx Expressway across the street some two years ago, a grocer said, trouble has plagued the area. . . . Stores which once stayed open to 9 or 10 o'clock are shutting down at 7 p.m. Few shoppers dare venture out after dark, so storekeepers feel the little they lose hardly justifies the risk in remaining open late. . . . The slaying had the greatest impact on the owner of a nearby drug store, which remains open to 10 p.m. "We're scared to death," he commented. "We're the only store that stays open that late."

It is impossible to suggest that we turn back the clock and undo some of the changes that have caused such urban problems. There is little chance that highway systems will be changed, that manufacturing jobs will flourish again, or that businesses will reopen in blighted neighborhoods anytime soon.[14] Our society has changed, and the change has hurt cities. However, cities have not died, they have been transformed; and what is needed is a reinvestment that takes as its starting point these transformations and the needs of people living in these affected areas.[15] Of course, the financing of city revitalization is an important aspect of improvement. Even so, the availability of money does not mean that money is used well. Funding sources, while sometimes offering hope, can also have a negative effect on the outcome of projects when they dictate how money must be spent without an understanding of the people and circumstances involved in neighborhoods.

Often, city funding comes in three forms. The most significant is credit extended by nongovernmental lending institutions, including savings and loan institutions, life insurance companies, and commercial banks. Unfortunately, in recent years the willingness of these organizations to invest in city areas has plummeted. The second form involves government funding—money acquired through taxes and government borrowing. However, since federal support to cities has declined, these monies have become difficult to acquire, causing many nonprofit groups and social service agencies, which rely on federal and state grants, to call their work "the business" and their competition for federal and state grants "turf wars" and "budget battles." The battle against disinvestment is a tough one, even without the budget battles that accompany them.

The third form of funding is a shady area of under-the-table deals. While bordering on criminality, the underworld mortgage market, investment endeavors, and high level loan sharking are means of city management that predate even the muckrakers who brought the practices to the surface at the turn of the 19th century. These financing mechanisms offer money on shaky ground. They are also the foundations of patronage, and, in the case of credit, the cause of some bankruptcy and excessively high interest rates and unjust insurance policies.

Astronomical mortgage insurance charges for city residents are just one example of how lending services take advantage of city residents with one hand while holding out possibilities for revitalization in the other. Not until city improvement is enacted at a grassroots level with all city residents having a greater say in how money is spent, not until funding mechanisms are cut off from high-level corruption and patronage, and not until de facto blacklisting and redlining of city areas is done away with, will substantial improvement be financed properly in cities. In addition, if cities remain poor, they remain violent.

The global transition of cities from manufacturing hubs to information technology and professional centers must be a part of the solution as well. Manufacturing jobs of the past were secured by individuals who did not need a great amount of education, and, for this reason, working-class and less educated people were able to prosper in the manufacturing economy. As William Julius Wilson has explained, current dire conditions in ghettos are partly the result of community isolation from career opportunities. Networks and resources needed to land a well-paying job are nearly nonexistent in city ghettos. Therefore, individuals have a difficult time obtaining jobs, and when individuals have difficulty obtaining jobs, they are incapable of developing the resources and networks needed to pass on job opportunities to newer generations of young people.[16]

If information technology and professional jobs are now the center of city commerce, then, city residents must once again fill these posts. However, in these newer jobs, education is vital. City residents who are very willing to work, to be educated and adjust, must be given the opportunity to learn the skills in mathematics, arts, and technology, science, and language, that they need to acquire these new urban jobs. Unfortunately, though, schools, including vocational education programs, have mostly failed the poor.[17]

Vocational education is too often a holding pen for labeled kids or training grounds for a workworld that no longer exists. In addition, job training programs are often profit-driven or, if publically established, then not well supported with funds. What is needed are long-term efforts to prepare individuals for professional positions. Currently, many businesses rely on suburban workers—those who drive their cars into cities, do their jobs, and then drive out. Businesses, schools, and state and city employers must look to the neighborhoods where they are located for their workers.[18] At the same time, though, workers must be prepared for the jobs. Cities need not lure back the middle classes but should cultivate them through education and job opportunities. As in the past, city businesses can create the middle classes by paying attention to the potential of people who are eager to work but unable to acquire the support that nearly every successful person has received in his or her past.

Educating for Economic Stability

While attention to vocational education has increased in recent years as businesses complain of an inept work force, this form of education has a long history. Current "school to work" programs can be traced back to the National Education Association (NEA)'s 1910 *Report of the*

Committee on the Place of Industries in Public Education and the Smith-Hughes Act of 1917, which provided federal funding to schools to establish vocational education programs. A variety of factors at the time gave rise to these movements, including lingering social Darwinist thought, a push to socialize and Americanize new immigrants, and a need to staff factories with workers. The NEA's report clearly articulated the purpose of vocational education in a way that makes sense to many even today:

1. Industry, as a controlling factor in social progress, has for education a fundamental and permanent significance.
2. Educational standards, applicable in an age of handicraft, presumably need radical change in the present day of complex and highly specialized industrial development.
3. The social aims of education and the psychological needs of childhood alike require that industrial (manual-constructive) activities form an important part of school occupations.
4. The differences among children as to aptitudes, interests, economic resources, and prospective careers furnish the basis for rational as opposed to a merely formal distinction between elementary, secondary, and higher education.[19]

At best, vocational education was—and to some extent remains—a means of supplying the nation with a steady stream of capable workers, providing students with marketable skills to advance economically and socially in life, making the school relevant to the lives of all students, and equalizing educational opportunity by providing instruction for students for whom traditional academic curricula is deemed inappropriate or too demanding. At worst, it is another watered-down curriculum for students in low-level tracks and special education classes. In Brandon and Rosemont High Schools, the vocational education programs had more in common with the second definition than with the first.

However, the separation of students into vocational tracks for the explicit intent of either holding them until graduation or, at best, training them for work was not always the case. The earliest advocates viewed vocational education as an essential part of a general academic curriculum, a program for all students, including those with aspirations for college, that would connect the social and academic through rigorous studies of the applied sciences. This is specifically what John Dewey, an early advocate of vocational education, meant when he explained that "the continually increasing importance of economic factors in contemporary life makes it the more needed that education should reveal their scientific content and their social value."[20] As always, his vision of schooling, including one that was vocational, "would connect with life so that the experience gained by the child in a familiar, commonplace way is carried over and made use of there, and what the child learns in the school is carried back and applied in everyday life."[21] In other words, the curriculum would include challenging studies in mechanics, science, and engineering through real-life and hands-on experiences that would benefit all students intellectually and economically. Unfortunately, today, vocational education is not an academic education; it is training of mostly low-achieving students for bygone jobs.

There are many who may argue that job training for young city residents is abundant. There are, for example, vocational schools, vocational education programs within public schools, federal and state initiatives such as Job Corps, community colleges, and a host of private businesses that offer training in computers, clerical skills, food service, welding, and other trades. This ubiquity, though, is misleading. Unlike Japan and Germany, the United States lacks a formal national system that helps students obtain well-paying jobs.[22] In addition, vocational education in high schools, adult education, and many vocational schools are viewed, usually rightly, by students as "dumping grounds" for the uneducable.

In meetings of the screening committee at Brandon High, I met students who lacked direction in life and were close to dropping out of regular high school. The screening committee, made up of a vice principal, a counselor, a special education teacher, and an afternoon school teacher, who oversaw the vocational education program, was charged with the duty of determining where these students would be placed. Typically the committee recommended that these students, who seemed unable to handle regular high school, attend some form of vocational education program either after hours in the school or during the day in a city program. However, the students were often reluctant to do so. Though they were on the cusp of dropping out, they preferred to take their chances in regular school.

When I asked adults why students were so reluctant to try vocational programs, I received one of two explanations. Some said that students were lazy and feared that vocational education would lead them to a real, full-time job. Others said that students' friends were in the regular high school, so they preferred staying with friends. Though the second explanation seemed plausible (for friends are often the lifeblood of young people, especially for those lacking family), the first explanation did not make sense to me. I have never really met a poor city kid who was more lazy than anybody else, including myself; bored, directionless, tired, yes, but not lazy.

In interviews at Brandon and Rosemont, I asked students about their reluctance to attend vocational programs. The students' explanations were incredibly similar as they described the stigma associated with vocational education and the reality of its inferior design. Gene was an African American student, who, at 16, with only 2½ school credits, should have been a junior but had the school status of a freshman. His father lived in Georgia, his mother worked as a cleaning lady, and his brother had dropped out of school after getting his girlfriend pregnant. I spoke to Gene after a meeting with school administrators and counselors, who had suggested that he attend the vocational education program in the city in order to learn welding. In the meeting, he had refused to sign up for the program, in spite of threats from the committee that he was too old to attend freshman classes.

> I don't want to be in with the knuckleheads. Everybody knows what JVC [the vocation education program] is for. It's for the riffraff, where the school dumps all of us they can't teach or who don't want to learn. I ain't one of them who don't want to learn. I like school, it just takes me more time. And with me moving from Georgia, I got fucked up. They lost all my records. But the thing is that JVC I know 'cause my friends go there. You go there to fuck up and nobody gives you nothing to do. You just sit there, and some guy comes in for two hours and tells you to do something. It's for the dummies, and I ain't no dummy.

Another student at Brandon High had a similar response, this time in regard to the vocational education program in the high school. With a similar background as Gene's, Theresa wanted to graduate and go to acting school but was told by high school administrators that, because of poor grades and persistent absenteeism, she would not graduate if she remained in day school. At first, it was recommended that she get a General Education Diploma (GED), but, when Theresa protested, saying that "GED don't get you nothing," the group recommended the vocational education program. The program ran from 3–5 p.m. each day in the basement of the school. She was also encouraged to attend the adult education program in the city where she could learn "nails." Her response to both recommendations was the same: "No way." She told me:

> I don't want nails. I want to stay in school. I belong in school. I'm still young. They say that they have faith in me, but if they have faith in me, why are they sending me there? I know who goes to those programs, the gang-bangers, the screw-ups. . . like the no-do-gooders. My brother went. That's where he used to go to sleep. He used to come home with sleep in his eyes, and, when my Aunt would ask him how it was, he'd say, "fine, fine," but we all knew what that meant. A fine place to sleep. I don't know why they want to send me there. I'm a good person.

Responses by other students in New York, as well as Connecticut schools, were alike. In Rosemont High, the vocational counselor was a well-intentioned person who attempted to place students in the Job Corps as a last resort before they dropped out. However, as in Brandon High, students were reluctant to go, and, for the most part, fought hard to remain in school, even in stifling self-contained classrooms.

One student, Arnaldo, whose mother wanted to send him back to Puerto Rico to get him away from the gangs in their neighborhood, did not, under any circumstances, want to leave the United States. All his friends were in the U.S., and he felt that Puerto Rico, though he was born there, was a foreign land. Though remaining in the United States depended on his getting a job, which his counselor thought would be best obtained through a job training program such as the Job Corps, Arnaldo did not want to pursue that path, even if it meant going back to Puerto Rico:

> I don't want to go back to Puerto Rico. That's not me anymore. I don't know anybody there, except my father. But my friends are here. But, if it means leaving school and going to Job Corps, I won't do that either. I want something more for myself. The school-to-work programs that you hear about, I know people that went that route and look where they end up. They ain't done nothing with it, because there ain't nothing to those programs that I can see. If those programs were so good, why don't you see any of the general education students going there?

Students in general education go to college; lower class, remedial, and "knucklehead" students go the route of vocational education. This hierarchy is recognized not only in what students say but in the structure of schools.

In Brandon High, the vocational education program was held after school in the basement of the building, along with the GED program and a program for "nontraditional" students (students who were pregnant, worked during the day, or had failed out of regular school). Rosemont High, which consisted of about 2,500 students, was divided into four Houses. The vocational education program was located in

House EL in the "PPT wing" and contained the special education classes, the self-contained classrooms, the noncontent area classes (art and music), and the classes for SED students.

This is an unfortunate reality, especially in light of research that shows that formal channels of employment made possible by schools have had significant positive impacts on the lives of young people. One longitudinal study has found that school contacts lead to jobs that result in long-term high earnings, especially for women and members of minority groups.[23] Another study of low-achieving job seekers in Atlanta, Boston, and Los Angeles has found that the highest paying jobs during the early 1990s were those acquired through formal channels, such as those provided by a school.[24]

That "industrial arts" of the 1970s has been renamed "technology education" or "vocational education" does not do away with the facts behind the euphemisms. The training of students for vocational work often means poor preparation for a work world at the bottom rung of the economic ladder. The United States still needs laborers, tradespeople, and individuals with a strong background in mechanics, building, and technology. However, unless vocational education provides a rigorous curriculum in math, sciences, arts, and technology and makes available opportunities for advancement in a technology-based work sector in a way that would appeal even to high-achieving students, it will remain an undervalued, inadequate, and stigmatized area of study.[25]

Reducing poverty is essential to violence prevention, and there is no better way to reduce poverty than through education that provides opportunities for stable and well-paying work. An academically centered vocational education provides students with not only greater satisfaction with school and feelings of mastery, internal control, and self-competence, but opportunities for meaningful employment.[26] According to one study, those who graduate from high school and have steady work are 6.4 times less likely than individuals who do not have work to become incarcerated.[27]

The best four-year colleges for high-achieving students provide students not only with instruction in their prospective fields but a liberal arts curriculum intended to create well-rounded and educated individuals. Those going into vocational work also need such an education, not just training in their fields. Most vocational education programs are taught by tradespeople, which can be beneficial for knowledge of everyday working skills. However, these trainers must also be educators; they should be people who offer to vocational education students a well-rounded, rigorous, and academic curriculum.[28]

A strong and valued vocational education program for all students would be consistent with the liberal arts values of education in the United States. It would help make schooling for youths beneficial and applicable. An effective vocational education, as described by John Dewey, would be an education that acknowledges the full intellectual and social meaning of a vocation:

> It would include instruction in the historic background of present conditions; training in science to give intelligence and initiative in dealing with material and agencies of production; and study of economics, civics, and politics, to bring the future worker in touch with the problems of the day and the various methods proposed for its improvement.[29]

Vocational education must surpass limited training, which only prepares individuals for specific jobs that are carried out under the control of others. Instead, it should be a liberal education that prepares students for a variety of jobs and means of advancement.

Many might consider a focus on vocational education an odd way to discuss violence prevention, but the fact remains that poverty and its associated factors are major contributors to victimization, especially in urban areas. Whereas Great Society reforms have proven to be a safety net for some, and a policy, such as the Elementary and Secondary Education Act of 1965, has been beneficial in its attempts to address poverty through compensatory programs, the best forms of poverty-reduction are those that empower individuals in two ways: making job opportunities available to them and ensuring an education that enables them to take advantage of those opportunities.

Safety nets and government provisions are crucial even for the middle class, but having work options and control of one's future are necessary so that nets and provisions are not needed or relied upon. Vocational education should provide work options for students as well as formal channels for advancement. After all, the liberal arts curriculum for high-achieving students is also a vocational education; it prepares students for occupations in law, education, medicine, and business and facilitates students' entry into college.

Vocational education is condemned by some as a means of tracking poor and low-achieving students into nowhere jobs, and this criticism is correct, given the current state of most vocational education programs in the United States. However, vocational education must be revamped to reflect its earliest goals of becoming a means for students to obtain steady and well-paying employment in a globalized and deindustrialized economy. Vocational education is not inherently bad, as some critics contend. We already provide a vocational education for those who are not, ironically, in vocational education—for those pursing the professions—and nobody complains.

As Paul Willis explained in *Learning to Labor*, schools and students alike take part in the social reproduction that designates particular classes of people to particular occupations—middle classes to the professions, the poor to menial labor or welfare.[30] If students give up in school too often it is because schools let them give up, and, in some cases, structure the school to ensure their failure. Even the availability of an outstanding vocational education is not going to solve problems of poverty and the violence it produces unless schools quit accommodating students who steer themselves into joblessness, futures steeped in violence, and even prison.

While high school vocational education may prove effective, violence prevention must start much earlier than the 9th grade. Even before high school, we need guarantees of equal educational opportunity for all students. The psychologist Terrie Moffitt described two types of individuals who act violently: what he called "adolescence-limited" and "life-course persistent." "Adolescent-limited" refers to individuals who become violent as teenagers; "life-course persistent" refers to those who act violently from a very young age and continue into high school.[31] In both cases, Moffitt explained that poverty was a major risk factor. For all these children, poverty-reduction is the best form of violence prevention; but, as Moffitt made clear, we cannot wait for students to reach high school to be possibly "saved" by an outstanding education, vocational or not. In Rosemont High, the highest dropout rates were consistently among 9th grade students. These were students who arrived at high school and were already on their way out, destined to fail.

Too often, students arrive at high school unable to manage even the challenges of a remedial education. They come with an eight-year paper trail of files of evaluations, outplacements, suspensions, poor grades, diagnoses, and referrals that prove little more than the failure of schools to help many young people. Students are too often shuffled through schools in self-contained classrooms, are segregated and labeled, and arrive in high school with problems that far exceed what could be achieved through violence prevention and even a fantastic vocational education.

How these students' problems persist is best explained by recognizing the exasperation of many teachers and other professionals who are given duties with truly difficult students and who have all but given up on them. Then, with giving up, many have embraced the popularity of zero tolerance. Rather than insist on an education, children, as young as seven years old, are suspended from school, even arrested, and enter into a juvenile justice system that offers little hope of solving their problems. They arrive back in school (sometimes) with more problems than before. While parents must take responsibility for part of this tragedy, schools, too, must see their part in the problem and take responsibility for being part of the solution. Change must come from within communities and families but also from within schools. My discussion of what must take place in schools in terms of restructuring begins with a short sidetrip into what I have come to see as a place that tells us much about a school's feelings about youths.

A Note on School Bathrooms

Not entirely tongue-in-cheek, I have come to believe that the best indicators of a school's health are found in their bathrooms. In schools, I never used staff bathrooms. They were too often in inconvenient places (inside office areas or teacher lounges) or required a key. So, tromping in and out of students' bathrooms in the last few years, I have come to see them as symbols of what the educational researcher Gerald Grant called a "school's ethos."[32] Their disrepair, lack of basic items (such as toilet paper and soap), broken mirrors, lack of toilet seats and stall doors, tell us something about a school's attention to students' basic needs.

Conversely, the vandalism, the graffiti, and destruction of property by students, tells us something about students and their feelings about school. In the special education wing of Rosemont High, where vocational and self-contained classes were located, the bathrooms were vandalized regularly. In the first three months of one school year, a plumber had to be called on two occasions, and a stall door was replaced by a security guard. In spite of worries about a lawsuit, in November 1999, the school instituted restrictions on when students could use the bathrooms (only during the four minutes between classes). That students do such vandalism, that schools are sometimes slow to repair and stock bathrooms, and that policies that even restrict bathroom use are instituted tell us that all is not well in education.

The activities that go on in bathrooms—the conversations that take place, the comic strip-like pictures of penises, breasts, and vaginas, the smoking, the gang-tagging (writing of gang symbols)—represent a semi-private world where students make public to others different messages and intentions. As Margaret Finders remarked about "hidden literacies" in schools, especially of graffiti and student notes to each other, the acts that take place in bathrooms are examples of not only students' expressions of themselves but of coded messages to other students, adults, and adult society.[33]

In addition, school bathrooms reflect the communities where students live; students who always seem to just hang out in bathrooms are doing the same hanging-out they would be doing in their neighborhoods. A student rips a stall door apart to make the point that he is strong enough to do this, perhaps, or that he is fed up with school. Words that I do not understand appear on walls and, a month later, I find out that two groups have fought because of antagonizing gang-tagging in the school, and especially in the bathrooms.

What is done in bathrooms can often be a means of harassing others as well. In one case, a female student was harassed by another female student (both were honor roll students and, ironically, peer mediators) with bathroom graffiti that called her a "slut" and "bitch." This went on for two months and was only resolved after a meeting with parents, the head of security, and school administrators. School bathrooms are both private places for students, places of reprieve from adult supervision and everyday hassles, and places that reflect the violence and criminality of neighborhoods. One could say that, if neighborhood problems do come into the school, as school personnel are apt to say, the problems always seem to make their way to the bathrooms first.

The disrepair of bathrooms, their abuse and neglect by students, school custodial workers, and administrators alike, and even by teachers who avoid going into them when they know problems are brewing inside, tells us something about schools and the kinds of problems that persist in them. Whereas some school bathrooms are clean and well supplied, some remind me of the street corners I have seen in blighted neighborhoods outside the school: awash in graffiti, urine, and smoke. As with neighborhoods, schools can be places where violence is minimized through efforts that promote sincere attention to basic needs or they can be places that abet violence through neglect. How schools respond to threats of violence is as important as political and economic responses on citywide levels. When we zoom in past solutions that would require a national response to city poverty, education for the professions and meaningful work, and long-term early intervention, we happen upon the school. The school, in conjunction with the community, is the linchpin between young people and society. If schools are going to educate young people to be caring and capable, they must lead the way in creating institutions with the requisite capacities and resources.

Chapter 4

The Prison Model of Schooling

The old axiom that belief fuels action is not entirely incorrect. If school staff believe that youths are out of control, dangerous, and wild, then, young people will be treated as such. Howard Becker made the point decades ago that deviance is not just a state of criminality but also the response by those who label as deviant particular forms of behavior.[1] As students are vilified and held suspect, their every move is viewed as deviant.[2] In one school, to wear a coat in the building (even when the heat was not working well) could lead to suspension. In another school, students could not carry backpacks unless they were transparent. Rosemont High had a policy against PDA, "public displays of affection," or kissing in the hallway.

In these cases, teenage clothing, accessories, and acts of affection are cast as criminal. Certainly there exist legitimate worries about gang clothing, weapons in backpacks, and sexuality, but are we also going to outlaw pockets, purses, and words of affection? Must we turn schools into fortresses?[3] I have had too many students ask me, in the words of one young woman, "Why do schools assume we're bad just 'cause we're teenagers?" One student, whom I had gotten to know through Brandon High's mentoring program remarked, "School is always trying to get us not to be prejudiced, but they are prejudiced all the time against us." It seems that adults are fighting a low-level domestic war against young people, and, the new zero tolerance policy is one step in the escalation of the campaign.

The labels adults affix to students, including those denoting deviance, do more to justify maltreatment of young people than they do to treat students with the care and respect that they deserve. As noted earlier, along with street violence and school violence, there exists systemic violence, a form of institutionalized behavior that has the effect of humiliating, segregating, shaming, and thwarting the life chances of some young people.[4] Many school teachers and administrators are kind, well-meaning, and gentle people. They expect only the best from students. However, to maintain a school ethos that endorses kindness and care, one must institutionalize that expectation. When schools seek creative ways to teach all students in an inclusive manner, when staff have high expectations and show full support for students and insist on respect between students and adults in the building, they institutionalize the basic foundations of a civil society and take a major step in creating schools that are peaceful, enjoyable, and exciting.[5]

Unfortunately, zero tolerance and its associated policies take a different road. They promote hostilities between adults and youths, give fuel to the low-level war against students, and create feelings of mistrust and anxiety that make it very difficult for even the best-intentioned teachers and administrators to be understanding and respectful of students. When all teachers are required to notify security of the slightest infraction of school codes, there is little opportunity for understanding. Instead, teaching becomes policing. Guards become the enforcement arm of schooling, and administrators, like commanders at the helm, oversee the process.

General concerns about violence must take into account all types of violence, including those that are systemic in nature. Meanwhile, it is only fair to maintain a balanced view of schooling and not to judge schools without understanding the extremely difficult jobs faced by the people who work in them. Researchers are renowned for criticizing schools but being virtually silent when it comes to offering support in solving the problems they have identified. This "holier-than-thou" approach is itself unjust. All members of a society are responsible for the state of its public institutions. So, when I discuss systemic violence, I do so knowing that I, too, am responsible for what goes on in schools; knowing, as well, that, while there is systemic violence, there also exist in schools examples of caring and concern for students.

Having said this, I still find it odd that many schools remain places that lack basic necessities for the maintenance of equal educational opportunity and even fundamental civil rights. When students do not want to go to school, when they drop out, when truancy becomes such a major concern, when students fail repeatedly, the school has neglected to accomplish its task. Certainly, some families and students also fail. The question, however, is, "Do schools provide for all students what they need to succeed—challenging classes and high academic standards, inclusiveness, respect, long-term and persistent support, and opportunities for advancement?" If so, then it is unjust to say that the school has failed. In addition, if a school does not provide for all its students what it provides for its best, then the school is not doing its job.

The point is, many schools do not offer for all their students what is needed to advance academically and socially in school and upon graduation. The treatment of students in a school can be vastly different. This is not just differential treatment from individual to individual but from group to group. Entire groups of poor, minority, and labeled students are sometimes written off as uneducable. At the very least, I suppose, one would think that all students needed books to learn. However, in Rosemont High, for example, I often wandered the halls in the area that included vocational education and the self-contained classrooms and wondered why students here did not carry books. Why did I never see books on their desks during class periods? This was quite different from the general education area of the building, where students walked the hallways from class to class with books tucked under their arms. Then, one day, I was interviewing a Hispanic paraprofessional of a self-contained class. She had been a paraprofessional for five years, lived in the city, and could speak Spanish with the predominately Hispanic students in the self-contained classes. I asked her what would be most beneficial for her students. "If they had books," she said. I said, "You mean, had their books in class," and she said, "No, just had books."

As it turned out, the only books in the self-contained classrooms were teacher guides with worksheets, which some teachers copied for students. I had tutored students from the self-contained classrooms, and it was rare that I helped them with some form of work other than worksheets or dittos. However, not all classrooms were completely devoid of books; in some classrooms, students could borrow books, which had to be returned at the end of class. Imagine going through high school without ever having a book, or, at best, never having a book to take home, study, or call your own. What does this say about the school's feelings for these students? What does it say about their treatment?

Not all teachers agreed with such handling of students. During the 1999–2000 school year at Rosemont High, there was talk that the teachers' union was going to file a lawsuit against the school system for its management of the self-contained classrooms. This came up in an interview I had with two union representatives in the school, one, a teacher and the other, a paraprofessional, both of whom taught in self-contained classrooms. One called the situation an outrage, and the other added, "not to mention illegal." Nevertheless, while there were these just voices, most school staff agreed with the management of the self-contained classrooms, or, if they did not agree, they did not give the issue a second thought. Some felt that students in self-contained classrooms did not get books because they would either destroy or lose them; this, they determined, was a good enough reason not to provide them.

Too often, teachers separated themselves from the emotional life of students and failed to see how students' basic educational needs were not being met. School staff rationalize that they are only following guidelines and policies; more often, though, they are following expectations of a school system that has given up on poor and difficult students.

One day, for example, when I was in Rosemont High to observe PPT meetings, the director of the special education program asked me to do her a favor: Could I find out from the social worker in the school's general education area why special education students could not participate in the peer mediation program, neither as mediators nor mediated.[6] The social worker who ran the program assured me, defensively, that there was no policy stating that special education students could not take part in mediation. I reported this back to the director of special education. The school psychologist of the PPT wing happened to be standing nearby and overheard. He repeated, in a knowing way, just what the social worker had said: "There is no stated policy against it." He added, though, "But it's pretty much unwritten that we take care of our own problems in house." "In house" was a reference to House EL, where the self-contained and vocational education programs were located.

With this separation and differential treatment comes the expectation that students placed in special education and self-contained classes will not participate in a valued school program. Though there was no stated policy against it, the PPT wing did not send students to mediation, and the social worker in the main area of the school did not expect that they would. All continued as it had for these students, without books and without mediation.

Being Self-Contained

Violence in schools is sometimes the "striking back" by students against others—what some researchers call "retribution."[7] Teachers know this as well as students. In health classes, when violence prevention is taught, there are often lectures and follow-up discussions about revenge, being disrespected and retaliating, and reprisals in the form of gang-banging. This is true of DARE classes as well. However, rarely do teachers or police officers teaching DARE raise topics of revenge in reference to school, particularly, in terms of students lashing out against school. This involves more than the trashing of bathrooms, though, of course, this is a part of it. Students lash out physically against administrators, teachers, and each other, with pent-up frustrations with classes, relationships with people in the school, and feelings of worthlessness in school.[8]

It is common knowledge among staff that students sometimes come into schools angry because of things that occur at home or in their neighborhoods, and that this is a cause of school violence. However, students also get frustrated when they are treated poorly in school. In these cases, they either turn off completely (becoming nearly invisible and resisting learning) or explode in violent ways.[9] When I asked students in self-contained classes what they would like to change about their school, almost unanimously they said, "Get out of self-contained." Students feel the distancing that is done between them and teachers; they know how they are treated. There was nothing in the past that indicated that students in self-contained classrooms would destroy their books, and yet they were taken from them. There is nothing that warrants self-containment of students because of problems they have in their lives. Students know these things.

The intolerance of delinquent behavior has led to judicial processes associated with detention and imprisonment outside of schools, but, inside of schools, it has given rise to another form of jailing. Furthermore, like confinements in outside placements, self-contained classes in school are touted as beneficial for the jailed. Generally, it was believed by teachers and administrators that, in a self-contained environment, adults could better watch over students with "special needs." In general, self-contained classes are for students with physical disabilities and for those labeled SED (socially and emotionally disturbed) or OHI (other health impaired).

Unlike traditional high school students, these students do not change classes but are taught all subject areas by one teacher in one classroom. To be SED or OHI means that you have a behavioral problem: You act out, get into fights, have brushes with the law, perhaps have been arrested. The differential treatment of these students results from some form of evaluation or testing that is done to warrant the special placement. In addition to the disabled and those labeled with a behavior problem, at Rosemont High suicidal students were self-contained. The separation of labeled students continued even within self-contained classes. Students with physical disabilities were placed in classes separate from SED students. There were subgroups of SED students, as well. Those who "internalized" their anger were kept separate from those who "acted out." The placement and subplacements of students who were labeled "at risk" or a "behavioral problem," and who might be aggressive, were layers of exclusion based not only on behavior, but physicality, race, and class. Students in the self-contained classes were primarily poor, male, and nonwhite. In a study of self-contained classrooms at another school, three researchers examined the placement of what the school called the "socially maladjusted" and found that all of the twenty-four students in the self-contained class they studied were poor.[10] While the researchers did not remark about the students' race, in city schools, linkage of poor and self-contained extends to nonwhite: in Brandon High it was African American; in Rosemont High, Hispanic.

Teachers knew that many of the students in self-contained classes were intelligent, but they sometimes qualified their praises. Though intelligent, they said, these were students who "did not apply themselves"; they "couldn't sit still"; or, they were "just off the wall." Erving Goffman pointed out in his study of asylums that a crucial step in achieving conformity in an institution is to convince people that institutionalization is in the best interest of the institutionalized.[11] The same occurs at schools on the part of both students and teachers. Though students wanted to get out of self-contained classes, rarely did they try; often, they resigned themselves to the diagnoses that supported their placements. Though there was plenty of grumbling about the self-contained classes, and even complaints about harsh treatments of students, many teachers simply took the jobs they had been handed and preserved their work and professions. Students in self-contained classes continued going to self-containment, and, if they did not go, they simply skipped school. In addition, teachers were reluctant to take action against the school district where a close-knit board of education put a lot of pressure on people not to rock the boat.

Self-contained students were not only placed differently; they were treated differently, especially in regard to discipline. With zero tolerance policy has come a greater emphasis on punitive forms of discipline, and nobody feels this more than students relegated to the lower rungs of the school hierarchy. At Rosemont High, it was the poorer and mostly nonwhite students who made up the majority of the 1,019 suspensions during the 1998–1999 school year. At Brandon High, all of the 58 students suspended for fighting during the first half of the 1997–1998 school year were African American.

While the disproportionate numbers of nonwhites and poor students who are suspended and expelled from school reflects high rates of violence and victimization among such groups, the imbalanced rates also highlight inconsistencies in the meting out of punishment.[12] Suspension and expulsion reports do not reveal rates of violence; they state the numbers of people who get suspended or expelled. There is much violence that occurs in schools that never reaches suspension and expulsion proceedings, and, thus, these reports. Whereas nonwhite and poor students are often disciplined according to school zero tolerance policy, and therefore become numbers in reports, white and middle-upper class students often escape harsh disciplinary measures. Paul Kivel, the director of the Oakland's Men's Project in California, noted a similar phenomenon in his work with youths. When a young African American or Latino boy got into a fight, it was often seen as typical of his culture or a mark of long-term pathology or dysfunction. The result: "He will probably be disciplined more quickly and more harshly than his white counterparts."[13]

Differential treatment of students was also a complaint made by some school staff. One teacher, in an interview, complained that, with new discipline policies, there was no longer consistency with discipline. She provided the following story in a faculty meeting during which staff were complaining about the referral system:

> Yesterday, we had two incidents that led to referrals. One involved a student tampering with a fire extinguisher. This is a real offense—I think a federal offense. So, he was referred to his headmaster, and the headmaster gave him a warning and put a report in his file. Another kid was adjusting his belt in the hallway, and when a teacher told him to do it in the bathroom, he said something like, "Hold on a minute," and, just finished doing it in the hallway. Yes, he ignored the teacher so someone should talk to him about having respect. But he was sent down to the headmaster, and the headmaster suspended him for two days. Two days suspension! That doesn't make sense.

However, it does make sense if you consider that the fire extinguisher tampering took place in the general education area of the school and the belt incident in the self-contained area. In another faculty meeting in Rosemont High, one administrator complained that the school had become so strict that he was afraid to send students to their housemasters. He provided the following example in an interview I later had with him:

> You know Juan. He is a pain in the you-know-what. Well, yesterday, he was

getting in my face, just being his usual self. I tried to reprimand him with threats and that didn't work. I took him outside the school to talk to him and that didn't work. He was hostile. So I took him down to the office—to his own housemaster. I told Ms. Jones [the housemaster] that Juan had been oppositional towards me, told her the story, and left it at that. But as I'm walking out of the office, I hear her say to Juan, "You know we can have you arrested for assaulting an administrator." Jesus, he didn't assault me, unless you consider being a pain in the ass an assault.

What fuels differential treatment is not only zero tolerance but attempts to preserve privileges for already privileged students. For example, I attended a discipline meeting involving a dispute between two male students, Jeremy and Stanley, both of whom were in the general education program, honor roll students, white, and middle-class; in addition, Jeremy's father was a high ranking police officer in the city. In school, Jeremy had been harassing Stanley for months, mostly with taunts and graffiti in the bathrooms and on desks. In addition, Stanley claimed that Jeremy shoved him in the hallway on two occasions, one time causing him to fall and bang his head against lockers. The parents blamed Jeremy for mysterious phone calls, sometimes in the middle of the night. In the meeting, which consisted of the two students and their parents, the school police officer, and a vice principal, Stanley's parents insisted that a report be filed with the school district regarding the harassment. They were fed up and wanted to see drastic action be taken. The vice principal steered the conversation away from such measures and suggested that they give Jeremy another chance. In as consolatory a voice as possible, he told the parents that Jeremy was college-bound and a good student, and that he did not want to hurt his future with a blemish in his file. In the end, Jeremy was spared the fate that would have befallen another student who might not have been as privileged. With students in self-contained classes, for example, there is not the same concern for their futures since they are not viewed as individuals with a future.

What happens in the self-contained wing of this high school is not unique. In other schools, in other cities and towns, there are areas or special classes for students labeled SED, OHI, ADHD, hyperactive, even psychotic. These are clinical terms for students who are angry, depressed, feeling hopeless, aggressive, and, in some cases, suicidal. It is no coincidence that in Brandon High classes for such students, as in Rosemont High, were located in the basement of the building. Such differential treatment is not the creation of the school system alone but is the outcome of a history that has condoned, and even supported, institutionalization and reliance on professional diagnoses to quarantine students through various forms of tracking.[14] It also represents the exasperation of school staff who feel nearly powerless to change such an entrenched manner of organizing a school, and who sometimes find themselves at a loss in knowing how to handle particular students who are troublesome. In the end, this tracked and segregated arrangement isolates students, as well as administrators and teachers, and it reproduces social inequities. Furthermore, as Patrick Lee noted in his study of low-achieving students, tracking and the differential treatment associated with it often led to altercations with teachers and staff because students continually felt disrespected in their interactions with adults."[15] When students know that their school regards them as uneducable and inferior to people of greater privilege and advantages, there is no reason for them to respect the school. Tracking does not *lead* to violence, but it is a means of reproducing, in the school, the isolation, differential treatments by authorities, and institutional neglect that characterize violent communities.

De-Tracking Schools

Whether it be self-contained, remedial, or level 2, tracking is the most persistent and accepted form of within-school segregation and one that was built into the very structures of the public schools in the United States. In 1917, the publication of the *Cardinal Principles of Education*, written by specialists in the emerging field of education, proposed that education be based on a social efficiency model of learning; that is, a curriculum that aimed to provide skills in work, family life, and health for students who were not expected to pursue college but to man the urban factories. This was a rebuff to the 1893 report by the Committee of Ten, headed by Harvard University president Charles Eliot, which called for a more liberal education for all students.[16] Not only were charges of elitism aimed at the Committee of Ten, but influential professors, such as G. Stanley Hall, steered the debate to Darwinist notions of adolescence, which seemed to support proposals to create a bilinear system: one tracked for preparation for college; the other, for work.[17]

Unfortunately, the reformers could not combine what was best about each proposal. Rather than provide an academically rigorous education for all students in science, art, engineering, math, mechanics, reading, and social studies for advancement in life and work, the *Cardinal Principles* laid the foundation for tracking and unequal treatment of the poor. According to the historians David Tyack and Larry Cuban, the writers of the *Cardinal Principles* "believed that schools could and should sort out and prepare students differently for their various destinies in life as adults" which "led naturally to the use of intelligence tests and tracking as a form of social engineering."[18] The years that followed saw continued use of a system that segregated and labeled according to perceived abilities and life-chances.

As with self-contained classes, tracking has resulted in the segregation of mostly nonwhite and poor students into classes where remedial work and low expectations are the norm. As Jay MacLeod noted in his study of "hallway hangers," schools do not consciously determine the aspirations of students, but they do "accept and exacerbate already existing differences in aspirations" through structures such as tracking.[19] While proponents of tracking claim that the practice enables students of different abilities to receive instruction that best suits their capabilities and needs, this is only half correct. Those in the upper tracks do receive instruction that usually meets their needs and reflects their professional aspirations. They are given challenging work, the best teachers, opportunities to participate in progressive educational experiences; they are valued and respected and given adequate preparation for college. Unfortunately, though, these students are shortchanged in not having access and exposure to the diverse talents and perspectives of so-called low-achieving students. Worse than this, however, the low-achieving students are left behind in the least respected and lowest performing classes.

The belief that those in the lower-level tracks are given developmentally appropriate instruction and teachers specially trained to educate students with special needs does not hold up in practice. People who believe this theory have not spent sufficient time in lower-tracked classes. Students there are rarely challenged, are often segregated, are presumed incapable by other students and sometimes by teachers, and are asked to do drudge-work mostly made up of worksheets from outdated workbooks.

Educational researcher Nel Noddings has been at the forefront of advocating for greater care of students, but her neutral, if not supportive, take on tracking and her belief that "the arguments against tracking are political and economic, not educational," misconstrues the experiences of those who are shortchanged by the types of education they receive in their low-track classes.[20] As Jeannie Oakes has noted in her decades of research on tracking: "School tracking practices create racially separate programs that provide minority children with restricted educational opportunities and outcomes."[21] By examining students' test scores and other indicators of achievement levels, Oakes has shown that students with the same test scores are placed in different tracks, and that, in fact, students with high test scores are placed in tracks below those of students with lower test scores. To say the least, the criteria used to place students in particular tracks are neither consistently applied nor clearly stated in school handbooks, and yet, such placements have profound effects not only on academic achievement but life-chances in the work world.[22]

Proponents of tracking claim that heterogenous grouping would lead to impossible situations in schools, especially in math classes, but research has shown that math (considered the most difficult class to conduct in a nontracked fashion) taught in an inclusive and creative way can yield positive results for all students at different achievement levels.[23] A host of initiatives, including smaller classes, after-school tutoring, cooperative learning, altering teaching practices to focus on students' multiple intelligences, and, in some cases, summer and intercession classes, have benefited those students who have yet to perform well. Heterogenous groups also benefit high-achieving students, and certainly do not, as has been argued, cause them to be "held back" by "slow learners."[24]

In addition to these pedagogical issues, pro-tracking arguments neglect to account for a basic truth about tracking that has as much to do with civil rights as academics: Tracked school systems lead to greater social isolation of students who are already socially isolated in poor neighborhoods or by life circumstances. Hence, they reproduce the segregated society in which most individuals in the United States live, a segregation as much fueled by prejudice as by policy. While housing, social service, and transportation policies have been the causes of much ghettoization in U.S. society, the policy that has achieved the same outcome in schools has been tracking. Tracking in schools leads to social isolation, and social isolation is one factor—some would say, the most significant factor—that contributes to violence. In other words, perpetrators, as well as victims of violence, are often individuals who are socially isolated, and tracking, which fuels segregation, contributes to this.

Heterogenous grouping is as much an educational as a civil rights issue. Being in a class where expectations are high, and work is demanding, where all individuals are respected, where students are helped to understand new material and are challenged by the thoughts and skills of a range of people is essential to equal educational opportunity. Elijah Anderson, in his book *Streetwise*, made the point that increased violence in urban ghettos is partly a result of de facto segregation which has caused not only youth frustration and blocked opportunities but a lack of social and economic balance.[25] When imbalanced, neighborhoods spiral into a worsening condition of social dysfunction and violence. The same occurs in schools, especially when lower-tracked classes are not only segregated by classrooms but as a unit of the school in particular wings or in basements, as was the case in both Brandon and Rosemont.

Here, to be blunt, ghettos are recreated in schools. Walking from the general education building of both these schools where the low-tracked classes were situated was much like entering the poor neighborhoods I knew outside the schools. Consider, for example, the following field note taken as I entered one school and passed through the general education building and into the low-tracked area where I was conducting my research:

I enter the school and am greeted by the main corridor security guard who, by now, knows me so does not question why I am in the school or require that I get a visitor's pass. The main hallway is clear of students, since most are in class, and the building seems relatively quiet. I pass the security office, the main office, the gym, and several classrooms. Signs about an upcoming dance and a meeting for the National Honor Society are on the billboard outside the main office. Passing by the classrooms, students are either working in groups or listening to lectures by teachers. I pass two students, a girl and a boy, both white, arm in arm. Both are carrying books, and the girl wears a small purse around her neck. She is complaining to the boy that the main office "screwed up" her schedule. The boy explains that it may have been her counselor, since the same had happened to him the year before.

I turn the corner past the gym, where students are playing basketball, and pass posters that signal upcoming elections for Homecoming Queen: VOTE DIAMOND FOR QUEEN, or just a picture of the girl and then written in large letters, YOUR HOMECOMING QUEEN. I recognize the parent of a student I have interviewed, and we talk for a moment. She tells me that her daughter is getting bored with school but is applying for colleges, which excites her. After chatting about her choices among several well-known private liberal arts colleges, we say goodbye, and I take the stairs down to the basement to what is sometimes called the alternative school or special placement section of the building.

I come through the heavy doors and pass by the time-out room. Three Hispanic students sit in the room while a paraprofessional watches over them. Two of the students sit with their hands in their baggy pants pockets. They talk in Spanish to one another. Another is writing on a spelling worksheet. As I come around the corner, I pass several students outside the bathroom and a boy pushing a girl on an office chair with wheels. The girl almost runs into me and tells me, "Cuidado!" Careful. Students who know me, look at me, and sometimes nod to show their recognition. Some students mill around the hallways, but most of them are quiet, since they know that they will be left alone if they do not make a ruckus.

Class is in session, and, though the classroom doors are shut, through their long thin windows, I can see students working individually at their desks. In the three classrooms that I pass, one teacher is helping a student on a worksheet; in the other two, teachers are sitting at their desks with students working individually and quietly. Because the classrooms here are much smaller than those in the general education portion of the building, I can see all the students in the rooms. Most rooms have only about eight students, since most students skip school or leave early. The students in the hall are not forced back to their classes by security staff, since security does not often come down to this section of the school unless called. Unlike yesterday, there is no longer the smell of marijuana at the end of the corridor that leads out of the school.

In general, students in the alternative school section of the building dress differently, speak differently, act differently, and are treated differently from those in general education. The differences resemble those between a middle-class and a poor neighborhood. The lower-tracked classes consist of primarily African American and Latino students. In general, less is expected of them by teachers; their work consists mostly of worksheets since they do not have books, and they are not often forced back to class unless they are causing problems. The students are also mostly male. There are rarely examples of affection shown between girls and boys in this section of the building. Not only are there rules against PDA, and few girls in the area, but boys generally hang out together, as they do in their neighborhoods. In many ways, hallway intersections resemble poor neighborhood street corners; a group of boys at one, another group at another. Hall wandering is endemic, like the wandering around seen in many poor urban areas. The few girls in the area usually stick to their classrooms. Urban clothing, handshakes, the shouting of rap lyrics, goofing off, and an occasional gang tag are typical; discussions about schedules and upcoming events, worries about lost books, and posters about clubs and school elections are not.

Schools make their own ghettos, and students reproduce behaviors, including violent behaviors, that are consistent with segregated and isolated areas. Tracking and the partitioning off of tracked classes from the rest of the school creates situations that even some teachers and administrators describe as "explosive." For example, in a meeting with a group of teachers who taught in the PPT wing of Rosemont High, one clearly stated, referring to the placement of the self-contained classes in one wing of the school: "I don't want this situation to work. Putting all these students together. It isn't equitable, and it's dangerous." After all, the environment is imbalanced: There are few positive role models, few peers who can have a positive influence, and, according to students, few reasons to behave. Students who need help are put together with other students who need help. Tracking is not only an injustice to students; it is an insult to teachers who are inevitably viewed as only capable of teaching students who "don't want to learn."

As I noted earlier, inequity is foundational to most forms of violence. When schools reproduce poverty areas within their buildings, they reproduce the behaviors associated with poverty areas outside school. In order for schools to rid buildings of undesirable behaviors, including those that are violent, they must change the environments that have already proven to provoke violence. If violence is prevalent in partitioned-off communities and in places where most individuals are disadvantaged, schools, at the very least, must not replicate these circumstances. Rather, they must desegregate so that the disadvantaged and advantaged not only mingle but are urged to support one another in an inclusive manner. And, yes, the low-achieving students should be expected to support the high-achieving students with their own unique skills, intelligences, talents, and life experiences. After all, this is the only way high-achieving students will be prepared for an increasingly globalized and multicultural society. We do everyone a disservice—teachers, administrators, and high-achieving students included—when we segregate students based on their perceived abilities, race, and social class. However, most devastating are the effects on those put in the low-level tracks. Here, students are not only prepared for life in poverty, but, more specifically, they are trained for life in containment.

Restructuring for Equity

Certainly, to some extent, proponents of tracking are right to claim that schools would be chaotic and nonproductive if they suddenly de-tracked. While schools should de-track, and, in order to prevent some forms of violence, must de-track, they also need to change those aspects of schooling—self-containment and outplacements, for example—that support tracked systems. Currently, schools are structured to ensure the success of students from middle-class and professional families, a point well made by many critical theorists of education since the 1970s.[26] During the process of de-tracking, schools must also change their ways of teaching, their school environments and structures, and their offerings to students. A good start for restructuring would include smaller classes, rigorous tutoring and mentoring programs, high expectations and inclusive classrooms for all students, and greater reliance on the services of paraprofessionals for academic purposes, not just for baby-sitting and paper-correcting functions.

However, as the smaller size of the self-contained classes makes evident, the restructuring of schools also needs to include a commitment on the part of all school staff to use the restructuring for reasons associated with justice, equity, and the academic care of all students. Decreased class sizes and smaller schools are important changes to make. They would enable staff to know students better so they can help them through crises involving potential violence. Smaller classes and schools, however, do not guarantee such a needed change in relationships. Decreased class sizes, or de-tracked classes, in a school that still treats students poorly and does not act as a check on the environments and behaviors that have proven violent in the past will not lead to peaceful schools, but to "chaos" in smaller classes. To be sure, smaller, de-tracked classes must be part of a larger effort to take advantage of opportunities to know, guide, help, and appreciate the lives of young people.

Consider, for example, the remarks of low-achieving high school students who explained what was needed in their school to improve relationships in the building, and, ultimately, to ensure their success in school and in the workworld. They insisted that teachers needed to:

1. Get to know students on an individual level both inside the classroom and out.
2. Be more encouraging of all students despite what they did in the past.
3. Improve communication with students by asking them if they need more help, why they're having trouble, and how the teacher can help.
4. Provide more individualized attention and tutoring to students.
5. Communicate that they believe in students and that they have the ability to learn.
6. Hold the same expectations for all students, regardless of race.
7. Interact with all students in the same way, regardless of race.[27]

However, the just treatment and respect these students envision can not coexist with the exclusionary methods that school officials often use. School practices, such as tracking, self-containment, expulsion, and suspension structure inequality into the school and, like other activities that label and exclude students, send troubled youths to places (whether in or out of school) where they are in greater contact with those who have also been deemed incapable and a problem. These students develop a combative attitude that becomes structured into their writing graffiti, destroying bathrooms, and challenging teachers and students. They reproduce the violence seen in their own neighborhoods since there is nothing in the school that indicates that the place is different. They see the same alienation, poor services, low expectations, even the same faces. Suspension and expulsion of students, so much the disciplinary rage in times of zero tolerance, leads students back to streets that do a better job of teaching violence than curbing it. Tracking has a similar effect in schools by sending kids to the in-school ghettos.

No violence prevention program or conflict resolution skill is going to solve these students' problems if they are partitioned off from the rest of the school and therefore unable to freely take part in what the school offers. Essentially, schools need to do away with all policies and practices, including zero tolerance, that exclude socially and economically ostracized students even further. Zero tolerance policy, which does so much to ensure labels of criminality and to support exclusionary policy, exacerbates inequality in schools and preserves the social imbalances that create violent environments.[28]

At the very least, schools must support environments that are much different from those that create violence and not mimic the structures of our society that produce dysfunction, imbalances, and isolation. Zero tolerance is not going to do this; and, in some cases, it contributes to the problem by laying the foundation for exclusion. The social isolation of students who are poor, unsupported, and who live in places that are already violent creates situations where violence is naturally transferred to the environment of the school. This happens because the so-called new environment of the school is not really anything new. In essence, it looks much the same to students as their old and violent communities. To structure violence prevention into the school, the old structure has to change. Tracked classes need to be replaced with heterogenous groups where all students are expected to succeed in life and given long-term support to do so. If not abolished, expulsion and suspension of students should only be a last resort, reserved for serious offenders and not for kids who are acting up or on their way to dropping out.

In addition, students who violate rules of behavior must be endlessly encouraged to abide by them. This can only be done under the supervision of those who make the rules: dedicated administrators, not guards. Teachers and school administrators need to recognize the skills and talents of all students and expect that all individuals in school—adults and students—act in ways that are respectful of the great value of each member in the building.

Certainly, there are students who do horrific things to other human beings. However, while we cannot just blame society, neither can we blame students in easy ways that peg them as deviant, dangerous, and criminal. While theorists will forever disagree on the primary causes of violence, most agree on one thing: *Violence* leads to violence. Whether that violence is family abuse, gang violence, or systemic violence in schools, these realities lead to retaliatory responses by students. Students then lash out in frustration, in anger at the world, and with a sadness that is nearly as strong as their anger. While students have a responsibility to be a part of the solution, a topic explored in the next chapter, actions that show that we as a public have faith in young people and will not tolerate the reproduction of social injustice in our public places is also a step toward violence prevention, as well as school equity.

Chapter 5

Being Disrespected

Besides the problems discussed thus far, violence is caused for reasons associated with respect, power, and codes of behavior. The flip side of the urban gang is the suburban and rural clique. Furthermore, though different groups of students may express their violence in different ways, underpinning their actions are what some researchers refer to as accepted codes or scripts that direct interactions among groups. As sociologist Elijah Anderson explained in regard to a "code of the street," such a code requires that a youth be "treated right" and with a certain amount of deference, gained through the unceasing obligation to prove that one is impenetrable and undefeatable.[1] Political scientist Jackson Toby has made the point that youths, and especially men, will go to great lengths, including those that are violent, to gain and maintain respect in the eyes of others.[2]

Codes defining masculinity and social hierarchies among groups of students sometimes lead to gender violence, racial attacks, and even mass shootings. As educational researcher Daniel Perlstein made evident in regard to the 1998 shooting deaths of four girls and a female teacher in a school in Jonesboro, Arkansas, the targets of Mitchell Johnson and Drew Golden's rage were not just other students but girls in particular. Most news accounts ignored this dimension of the killing, even though a fellow student at the school had reported to the *New York Times* that Mitchell "told me yesterday that all the people [the girls] who broke up with him, you know, he's going to come to school tomorrow and shoot them."[3]

When students enter the school, they bring with them their codes, and, as I noted in the previous chapter, since the school can so much mirror students' homes and communities, their codes easily translate over from living rooms and streets to hallways and school bathrooms. These codes are a learned culture, a way of acting within established beliefs about power, control, and respect—what researchers Jeffrey Fagan and Deanna Wilkinson call "procedural scripts children acquire for handling interpersonal conflicts and identity formation."[4] Cognitive psychologists believe that behavior is scripted, and that while people do not ordinarily follow all scripts, individuals do become socialized to act in particular, dynamic ways that are in tune with prevailing ideas about social hierarchies and groups of people. Similar to some of the ideas of Albert Bandura discussed earlier, the notion that youths act within certain codes of behavior is based on the following premises about cognitive "scripts":

1. Scripts are ways of organizing knowledge and behavioral choices.
2. Individuals learn behavioral repertoires for different situations.
3. These repertoires are stored in memory as scripts and are elicited when cues are sensed in the environment.
4. Choice of scripts varies among individuals, and some individuals will have limited choices.
5. Individuals are more likely to repeat scripted behaviors when the previous experience was considered successful.
6. Scripted behavior may become automatic without much thought or weighing of consequences.[5]

There are several problems with the view of behavior as described by these six points. First, that youths follow scripts instinctively, as the above description seems to suggest, is highly questionable; individuals are not automatons with behaviors that "are elicited when cues are sensed in the environment." At the very least, the description misses how race, gender, ability, and other characteristics enter into the decisions people make about their behaviors.

However, the clinical language and other shortcomings should not draw us away from a basic truth to be made about behavior: We are social beings who learn in interaction with groups of others and within a popular culture that shapes beliefs and visions of the world that correspond with certain behaviors, including those that are violent. In the United States, for example, to have complete control of another—to be able to instill fear and to change the way people act, whether a student or another country, and to be positioned toward the top of the prevailing socioeconomic hierarchy—brings respect in many circles. This is true in most aspects of U.S. society and is a premise that shapes not only some school interactions but "strong-arming" international policies.

Meanwhile, though people are socialized to act in particular ways, they also have the ability to resist that socialization. While some researchers have been hard pressed to prove that zero tolerance has benefited schools, others have documented the advantages of interventions that enable students to redirect violent behaviors, or, as John Devine called it, to "code-switch."[6]

Educational researcher James Vigil has made the point that "street culture can be co-opted and redirected but only after key individuals have been converted."[7] He gave an example from a Los Angeles school: A group of local gang members were in the school, and the male principal, who had grown up in the area and knew gang mentalities, approached several gang members and began a series of conversations with them about their behavior and what they wanted from the school. He continued these conversations until he had won the trust of the gang and saw more gang members taking part in the talks. When the group suggested that the school begin a boxing program, the principal obliged. Vigil reports that, within time, many of the gang members were participating in the boxing program and were spending time training and getting in shape. Several adults from the community volunteered in the program by mentoring and coaching the students. In time, the principal began to use the students' participation in the school to have them take part in more conventional school activities. He, along with the gang members and others who became involved in this new organization, developed a "Boys Council," which met weekly to discuss improvement in the school regarding academics, discipline, schedules, and after-school activities and offerings.[8] According to Vigil, who studied this process, the students soon became more involved in all aspects of school, the school became more peaceful, and many of the gang members, newly empowered within the school, shed their gang colors and behaviors for a more appropriate and less threatening demeanor.

It is extremely important to youths that they be respected by adults and other students. Feeling disrespected is a consistent element of most hostilities between students; it is the driving force in fights involving name-calling, acts of revenge, and interracial violence. Students' reasons for fighting, as I have heard explained in peer mediations, counseling sessions, and interviews, have always seemed to involve elements of respect and power. Students who fought seemed to be grasping at the only deed for which they were respected: their power to oppress and control. What Vigil's principal did, in part, was to show these gang members respect and to treat them as people deserving of attention. When a student fights because he has been disrespected, which is often the case, it is a means of "saving face," as some students say, or of showing other people that "you're no chump."

For this reason, it is important for schools to make it possible for youths to gain respect through means other than violence. While many youths will avoid mainstream values, many more may be willing to redirect their codes and seek respect in nonviolent ways if those means are open to them.[9] Through youth intervention programs and the restructuring of schools to enable more nonprivileged people to take part in respected organizations and clubs, including sports, after-school activities, even a "Boys' Council," a group-level change can be made by including students in school decision-making processes and not excluding them. Groups of students may recognize the respect that is earned not through beating down another but through the power gained through political activities in school, involvement in school government, school and community organizing, and sports. It is partly for this reason that new literature has demonstrated the success of peer mediation programs that include as mediators those who would otherwise be violent; not only are the students prone to violence better able to understand particular conflicts, but they take an active role in defining violence prevention in their schools and are rewarded with respect not only from some peers and adults but by college admissions officers.[10]

When violence is a problem involving students who do not participate in school—those who are seen as at-risk, burnouts, gang-bangers, or freaks—active and caring school staff, who have respect for students and the respect of students, must help youths organize, create a consensus of caring for one another, and build solidarity through the same kinds of activities that brought together African Americans during the Civil Rights movement. This would require a change in cultures and institutions; through deed and not just talk, schools must open their halls of privilege to people of little or no privilege. Very few students will turn down opportunities to better themselves, to increase their status in school, and to take control of matters that affect them. When opportunities are blocked, students lash out; when they are open, they struggle hard with themselves to make the most of them.

To some extent, we are dealing here with belief systems, codes and ideological messages about oneself and others that form the basis of a group identity.[11] Middle-class and mostly white individuals have been able to develop identities of self and a respect for one another that comes with professional titles, honors, membership in respected organizations, and through wealth. These advantages are denied to many kids who stand low on the social ladder. Youths need alternatives to fighting as a means of gaining respect and power. Those who are not respected by their peers must be respected by adults. However, the disrespect that some adults have shown children, in both their behaviors and their social policies, is sometimes matched only by the disrespect that some youths show for each other.

In schools, power and respect is gained in many ways. One way, for some students, is through violence. Other ways, though, include involvement with admired groups, teams, and clubs. As in the professional world, power and respect are garnered through titles: "valedictorian," "homecoming queen," "honor student," "peer mediator," "National Honor Society member," "great ball player." Adults have to enable more students to achieve the cultural capital that comes with titles, involvement, and participation in such clubs. As already explained, this can be done by eliminating exclusionary discipline and tracking systems that lead to the inability of some to be a part of the school. Adults must also convince students that these titles and clubs are not just emblems of being "oreo" or selling out, as some students explained, but are a means of advancement within the school and, by extension, within U.S. society. In doing this, we need to convince some social scientists that school organizations and clubs that are participated in primarily by middle-upper class and white students are not just elitist school structures that ostracize poor and nonwhite students; they represent hierarchies that are just as real as the professional delineations of rank, title, and assets that most successful adults strive for. Rather than only criticize such school structures, we should also enable all students to be a part of them.

As I mentioned earlier, the cognitive psychologist's belief in scripted behavior views individuals as without free will and without the power to change circumstances in their lives; in essence, their lives are already "scripted." Even so, we can not write off all aspects of theories that draw upon such notions of behavior. Individuals are socialized to act in particular ways. When boys harass girls, it is not just the individual actions of a boy acting against a random person, it represents the manners (or script) of a patriarchal society that has condoned sexism and even taught boys how to oppress females. What remains unfortunate about this belief in scripts, though, is not only that it sometimes leads to a rather robotic view of people but also that it gives validity to zero tolerance approaches to violence prevention. One of the consequences of the belief that "individuals are more likely to repeat scripted behaviors when the previous experience was considered successful" is the attempt to make previous experiences unsuccessful through harsh punishment. The consequences of using zero tolerance policy to accomplish this result have been briefly explained and will be explored further in this chapter. While efforts to steer students away from behaviors that are violent depend on such interpersonal interactions as those of the principal described by Vigil, zero tolerance policy draws school staff away from such emotional and caring involvement.

A Policy of Interaction and Trust

The irony of zero tolerance is that it incorporates greater surveillance of students at the same time as it results in less surveillance. It pulls teachers away from the emotional life of students and relegates emotional and behavioral problems to guards, police, and the courts.[12] For decades, researchers have made the point that informal sanctions and interventions, and not harsh punishment, made by caring individuals in the lives of youths are the most effective means of preventing delinquency.[13] Unfortunately, teachers, who are urged to make use of new security and zero tolerance policy, often flee the responsibility of overseeing students in a caring way; they do not create the informal bonds that can prevent trouble. The result is that those who are in contact with students the most avoid educating them about their social lives.

On too many occasions I have heard teachers and counselors explain to me that they often chose to overlook taunting and harassment because, in the words of one teacher, "it becomes such a mosh-pit. Kids accusing kids, and you never know what is the truth and what isn't." A teacher in Brandon High told me that she had overheard a male student telling a female student, "Babe, you're looking *hot* today." The teacher took the boy aside and told him that he should not speak to girls that way, and the boy told her that he always talked like that to the girl, who was his cousin. The girl defended the boy and even told the teacher in a roundabout way that she should mind her own business.

I, too, have felt these dilemmas, as the following field note makes evident. At the time, I was outside Brandon High interviewing two female students about the DARE program, which they had just completed. I had come to know them while I sat in on classes observing the six-week program. They had agreed to an interview, and we decided to do it outside, to take advantage of the nice weather and so that one of the girls could smoke a cigarette. The school allowed students to smoke outside, and, during lunch, the front of the school became a kind of get-away for smokers and others who appreciated the outside air.

I stood outside with the two female students as other students milled around, some smoking, most just talking or listening to their Walkmans®, which the school allowed students to listen to outside but not inside the school. I was asking the two girls about the DARE class when, about halfway through the interview, a male student stood beside me and wanted to know what I was doing. I told him I was asking the two students questions about DARE because I was interested in knowing what they thought about it. He nodded and stepped away but stayed close enough to listen and watch, which made me feel self-conscious and seemed to annoy the two girls, especially one who smirked at him. I wasn't sure if they knew each other but sensed that there was some recognition between the two girls and the boy.

The male student stood a little behind me, and I had the distinct feeling that he was either making fun of me or scrutinizing me. I realized that one of the girls I was interviewing kept glancing over my shoulder at the boy. When I turned around, I saw the boy making a lewd gesture at the girl, imitating oral sex. He stopped doing this when I looked. I looked back at the girls. The girls' reactions were neutral, at least on the outside, and I didn't know if the boy was trying to get the girls to laugh during the interview or if he was taunting them. While one of the female students smirked at him (as she had before when he first came over), it seemed that the other was almost grinning. Again, I didn't know if he was making fun of me or taunting the girls. I ended up ignoring him, as the girls seemed to have, and tried to continue with the interview.

Moments later, I saw the girls looking over my shoulder again, and this time I sensed that he was truly annoying them. I was about to turn around to ask the boy to leave us alone, when, suddenly, one of the girls (the one who had been smirking) yelled at the boy, "Fuck you!" In an instant, the other girl (who earlier seemed amused by his antics) stepped across me and walloped the boy across the face with her coat sleeve. The boy stumbled back in an overly dramatic way that was meant to be comical. He acted as if to regain his composure, straightening his collar, patting down his hair, and asked the two female students, "What are you all reacting at—ya'll crazy!" He walked away, chuckling to himself, bouncing side to side, as if he had been dazed by the coat sleeve.

I asked the girls if they were all right, and they just smirked at the boy's back and nodded. I asked them if they wanted to go back inside, and they showed no reaction. One was grinning, pleased it seemed, that she had connected her coat sleeve so well to the boy's cheek. I did not know what to do or say. I fumbled with my words for a moment, then said, "I guess I'll end the interview here." Again, they showed no reaction. They stepped away from me a bit and began talking among themselves, blocking me out. The boy had gone inside the school and became lost in the crowd in front of the cafeteria. I said to the girls, "Do you want me to tell a guard what happened, or the principal?" One looked at me and shook her head. I felt uncomfortable. I did not know what to do or say. I did not want to ignore what happened but didn't want to pursue it if it would embarrass them or if they did not want me to press the issue. I thanked them for the interview and they just about ignored me. I asked them, "Are you all right?" One nodded, and the other mumbled, "Sure." I thanked them again and walked away as the bell sounded, and the school police officer went through the groups urging people to get back inside.

My feelings at the time were very complex. Part of me knew that I should have reprimanded the boy in some way—or at least said something to him—but, at the time, I was not sure what was going on. Part of me did want to do something about the confrontation; but another part felt that the two female students would resent me if I pursued the issue. Regrettably, I let the boy taunt the girls partly because, at the time, I did not know for sure what he was doing and was not quite sure if I should intervene. I also allowed the girl to smack the boy partly because I felt the boy deserved it. In the end, I did not intervene in a situation that was quite common—a low-level confrontation involving harassment and a slap to the face. Meanwhile, in the minds of most school staff, I had acted appropriately. I had witnessed a problem and had offered to call security. While teachers may, at times, discuss their wants to intervene when there are hostilities, most are comforted to know that their only obligation is to notify the guards.

This irony which increases surveillance on the one hand while yanking responsibility from teachers on the other can be seen when two school meetings are contrasted. These Rosemont High meetings occurred within a week of each other. The first was a faculty meeting between several teachers in House EL; the second, a meeting of the discipline committee.

The discipline committee consisted of several teachers and the principal who were charged with defining and, in some cases, altering, discipline policy in the school. In the first faculty meeting, several teachers had decided to get together to discuss problems they were encountering with new paperwork mandated by the state for students referred for special education. In the meeting, which was supposed to focus on the paperwork, the teachers moved into discussions of behavior and discipline, as often happens, and ended up, before moving on to the problem of paperwork, convincing themselves that they should not interfere in students' conflicts:

> The faculty meeting was held in one of the classrooms in the basement of the school and consisted of twenty-one teachers and the two social workers. The

director of special education, who was running the meeting, said, "Let us begin our session."

In the first ten minutes of the meeting, several issues were raised regarding grading, IEP's ("individual education plans" required by federal policy), and the procedures for making a referral. Referrals for testing for special education can be made because of a students' failing grades or because of behavioral problems. But referrals has another meaning: There are referrals to the housemasters because of behavioral problems.

As often happens, the conversation got stuck on the issue of discipline and students' behavior. Though the director of special education had meant to talk about special education referrals for testing, several staff latched on to the issue of referrals for disciplinary purposes.

A business teacher said, "I have an issue with referrals. I have a problem with kids out in the hallways raising all kinds of hell out there. Do I refer them to the housemaster? I have one kid who has been whipping girls with his shirt tail. I know it's just a sweatshirt but a sweatshirt can be a weapon too."

Many faculty members were quick to respond. One teacher said, "You should submit a referral."

An art teacher said, "Nobody reads those referrals anyway, so what's the point? They end up in a pile of paper."

One of the school's union representatives, who taught a self-contained class, said, "You have to document everything you do. Even if the referrals do end up in a pile, in order to protect yourself, you have to write everything down so you have a paper trail to support your action. That way, you don't end up with a problem."

The business teacher still wanted to know, "But what do I do with this kid? I know what to do with the papers."

One teacher asked, "Have you said anything to him?"

The art teacher said, "What do you say? 'Stop that.' I doubt that will work. You need to call security. That's why there are phones in the room."

Another teacher guffawed: "The phones are for them [administration] to get in touch with us, not for us to get in touch with them."

Everyone seemed to be talking at once. The business teacher said, "We are not talking about administration, we're talking about the guards," missing the point that they should have been talking about problems of paperwork, not behavior.

The director of special education seemed to be getting impatient: "That's what we are saying," she said to nobody in particular. "You need to call the guards. But don't use the classroom phone. That goes through to the main office, then to the guards. Forget the main office. Get Penny [the House EL secretary] to call on her walkie-talkie."

The business teacher shook her head. "Now I get the point of the phones in the classrooms. Don't use them. I have an explosive situation, and I'm supposed to leave my room and run down to the office and have the secretary make a call on the walkie-talkie."

Several teachers were nodding. "That's what I would suggest," one teacher said.

"You don't want to get involved at that point," the art teacher said. "Besides, that's what the guards are for. It'll be good to see them get their backs off the wall and come to this section of the school for a change."

The director of special education felt time passing and told the group, "We have a lot on our agenda."

"Yeah," said one teacher. "Let's move on. I have referrals [for suspensions] to fill out."

Consensus seemed to have been reached: When confronted with a student harassing or striking another student, do not get involved. Call security.

The irony of this is made evident when this faculty meeting is contrasted with a meeting of the discipline committee. The discipline committee at the school was formed to discuss problems associated with misbehavior and to spearhead policy and discipline strategies. The chair of the committee, Mr. Ryans, put out a monthly newsletter that was meant to pass on information about discipline to the rest of the school. In this meeting, the issue of students in the hallways was raised. There were seven people on the committee, including the principal, the vocational education teacher, a business teacher (not the same business teacher as in the previous field note), a health, social studies, and two English teachers. Mr. Ryans was a teacher of a self-contained class:

At the discipline committee meeting, all the members sat around a large table in the conference room of the main office. Mr. Ryans mentioned, "Our newsletter just went out. So let's see how people respond." In the newsletter, the committee had issued an article, written mostly by Mr. Ryans, that urged teachers to interact more with students in the halls during class changes. It read, in part: "It is too easy for teachers to stay in their rooms and shut their doors during room changes. But this is the time when teachers are needed most in the halls. Many problems start at these times, and though the hallways are crowded and noisy, the sight of a teacher standing by can make the difference between a smooth transition and a rough one."

Mr. Ryans said, "Everybody is complaining about students' misbehavior and I agree that it is a problem. But we also have to look at what we're doing. Who is out in the hallways while students are changing classes? We should be talking to students, saying 'hello,' seeing if there are problems developing that we can defuse." Around the table people nodded their heads. One teacher said, "I have students come to my eighth period class with their coats on, skirts up to here [points to his thigh], so obviously nobody is saying anything to these students about our dress code."

The principal showed no reaction. He seemed to be thinking. Mr. Ryans looked around the table. He said, "It seems that people know there are problems. The best way to deal with misbehavior is to defuse it, and that is our duty."

Another teacher said, "You are absolutely right, Bob [Mr. Ryans]. We really need to come out of our classrooms more. We can't let the students just take over the hallways."

Mr. Ryans nodded. He turned to the principal and said, "And I know you are very busy, but it would be nice if you tried to break free, like all of us, so that students could see you more." The principal nodded.

An English teacher said, "I think this is a job for all of us. I find myself avoiding the halls just because I don't like crowds. But the students need us out there. We need us out there."

The committee agreed that they would issue another statement in their next newsletter about the importance not only of being in the hallways during room changes but also of interacting with students and intervening in misbehavior before problems escalate. They would also urge teachers, who are free, to monitor the lunch room during any one of the three lunch periods. (Later, in interviews with teachers, they resented the fact that the administration wanted them to use their one planning and lunch period to monitor the students' lunchroom.)

In some ways, the discipline committee was fighting a losing battle. It was following old school policy, prezero tolerance ways of doing things. Ultimately, zero tolerance would cancel out their efforts to interact informally with students. Working against them as well was the structure of the school itself; the four or five minutes between classes is precious time for a teacher to prepare for new groups of students coming in—hardly enough time to get set up for class *and* chat with students.

In the end, the attitudes that dominated the faculty meeting would prevail; teachers would call on the guards to take care of the students.

In spite of the rhetoric and requests of the discipline committee, this is what happened in the school. One may hope that, if zero tolerance must be instated, even against the wishes of some teachers, that school personnel can at least be both zero tolerant and friendly. However, the realization of this concept turns out to be an impossibility. Zero tolerance obtains its power from the adversarial relationship between students and teachers, a relationship that is based on threats and judicial power.

Later in the year, Bob Ryans and others resigned themselves to the fact that nothing had changed in the school. Zero tolerance had been instituted, and, in spite of Ryans's best efforts to convince teachers otherwise, this seemed to suggest to most staff that they throw up their hands and relinquish to guards the duties of developing the character and behavior of youths. Most teachers still stayed in their classrooms, some students still ran wild in the hallways, and calls to the guards remained persistent. In a last attempt to make a change, Ryans asked me if I would write an article for their newsletter. He felt that, if the pronouncement came from an outsider and so-called expert, it might have an effect on teachers. I doubted that it would, but I agreed to write the article. In the months that followed, little if any change had come about in the school.

In another last ditch effort, a later issue of the newsletter under the subtitle, "Some Great Ideas," urged the school to "bring back hallway sweeps." Implementing hallway sweeps (teachers walking down hallways shouting at students to get into their classes) was not the same as talking with students in the corridors, but it was the closest they could get to having a teacher in the hallway.

Public Displays of Power

Besides the problem of getting teachers and other adults to intervene when hostilities arise, the faculty and discipline committee meetings made evident another point. Much violence in school is not hidden.

The problem is not identifying the problem but of knowing how to intervene. This goes from displays of sexual harassment to fights and even to shootings, many of which take place in the most crowded areas of schools. The point of much school violence is to let other people see it. A student who attacks another student does so for many reasons. Often, one reason is to show oneself capable of beating down another, which can only be accomplished by making a public display of the beating. This is because violence is often a means of asserting power, and power must be recognized in order for it to be effective.[14] Sibylle Artz has made the point that violence often "involved some kind of power imbalance: an older, bigger person picking on a younger, smaller person; a teacher picking on a student; a parent picking on a child; anyone hurting an animal."[15] It is "power-tripping." When adults do not intervene, raise a question, or take time to talk to a student about his or her behavior, we legitimize the behavior, support the unjust imposition of power against others, and show not only our powerlessness to make changes but our refusal even to try.

In *The Moral Life of Schools*, Philip Jackson, Robert Boostrom, and David Hansen identified five ways that schools attempted to influence students' beliefs about ethical behavior. They then cited another three ways that schools almost inadvertently influenced the "moralities" of students.[16] The first five included:

1. specific curricular offerings of the kind we might formally call "moral education"
2. the introduction of moral topics into the regular curriculum
3. various rituals and ceremonies of a celebratory and affirmative nature
4. signs and bulletin boards conveying moral messages
5. the spontaneous and often disruptive interjection of moral talk and discussion into the flow of ongoing classroom activities.

The three of a more subtle nature included:

1. classroom rules and regulations that govern interactions between and

among teachers and students

2. commonly held assumptions that undergird and facilitate instructional and curricular arrangements of various kinds (what the authors referred to as "curricular substructures")

3. the expressively moral content of actions, objects, and events in the school.

While the first five may be self-explanatory, the last three are not as clear. The first of the three refers to rules and regulations that instill in students a certain acceptable conduct; for example, the rule that all students must arrive on time to class teaches students punctuality, an acceptable behavior. The second of the three refers to the structure of the hidden curriculum, the incidental knowledges we teach when we divide knowledge into separate disciplines, for example, or focus on the contributions of men in the mainstream content of a history class and then add a separate section (or class period or chapter in a text) that focuses on women. The final point refers to objects, which, in Roland Barthes's words, "act as vehicles of meaning."[17] Security equipment, for example, while having a utilitarian purpose, also legitimizes the moral right of schools to watch over students but not to interact with them. This final point also refers to events, such as football games, which teach patriotism through their own kind of rallying-around-the-school spirit.[18] In all these ways, schools teach students appropriate behavior, the social worth of people, and acceptable manners of interaction with people and even objects such as flags, bells, and chalkboards.[19]

Though I would rather avoid the authors' use of "moral" because of its allusion to conservative attempts to judge people's private lives and to proselytize in school, the points that they make about informal teaching about respect are important.[20] Interactions, rules, objects, expectations, teachers' behaviors, and even simple remarks about what girls are capable of doing, shape students' concepts of right and wrong and the social worth of certain groups of people. School administrators, who are too often overly concerned about academics, testing, covering the curriculum, and other "intellectual" matters, forget the social aspects of education in the development of character. John Devine explained, after his years of work with students in New York City schools: "Students learn behaviors more through an osmotic process of daily interactions than through theoretical talk about ethics."[21]

The informal interactions between students and teachers which Bob Ryans wanted to see are, according to most researchers, the most effective means of preventing violence. Even so, teachers are, too often, reluctant and incapable of spending time in public areas of their schools. The result of zero tolerance policy has been a distancing between students and teachers as staff rely on guards for matters that could be resolved through talk and persistent care and attention.[22] What happens in these cases is that schools attempt to create conditions for bonding and peacefulness at the same time as they condone alienation and the distancing of teachers from students.[23]

To counter violence that is a public display of power, an equally powerful and public reprimand must be made to students who harass, threaten, and bully others. Rather than shy away from such actions, school personnel, in respectful and caring ways that will not humiliate the violator, must make it clear that such behavior is harmful and an injustice. Sometimes, individuals in schools are afraid that they may overreact, but it is better to overreact than to ignore. Any person who works with abused women and children can tell you that, in many cases, tragedies may be avoided if people who suspect abuse intervene rather than take the position that it is not their "place" to interfere. Public displays of power that are enacted through violence occur for two main reasons. First, they occur because they obtain the desired ends: Students who need the emotional and social "uplift" are recognized as powerful. Second, they occur because they are not often discouraged or dealt with in a way that embeds violence prevention throughout the entire school structure and school curriculum.

There must be a middle ground between the teacher who turns his or her head away when students are harassing another and the security officer who stands at the ready to carry out zero tolerance policy. Teachers, students, administrators, custodians, cafeteria workers, and others must decide to move forward in agreeing that they will make it part of their jobs to guide, teach, urge, and demonstrate, by example, behavior that is caring and respectful in nature. This attempt must be as public as the public displays of power that end in violence; they must surpass banners, programs, and posters proclaiming "Just Say No To Violence" (as many DARE programs do). Such attempts must be demonstrated in behaviors that act to change a culture of prejudice in schools. In effect, staff must agree and act to convince students and adults alike that behaviors that hurt, offend, and demean others are, in fact, violent.

I have discussed how codes of behavior often create circumstances that lead to violence; students bring with them into their schools ways of acting that are picked up from families, peers, communities, and the media. These codes are easily transferable from neighborhoods to schools, since schools so often mirror neighborhoods (whether affluent or poor), making the transfer smooth and even logical. Subsequently, the transfer of some of these codes naturalizes hostility, since there is little in school—neither staff interacting informally with students or challenges to exclusionary discipline policy and tracking systems—that disrupts the transfer process.

I have also discussed how violence is often a public performance. This performance is carried out by both the empowered and disempowered. In the United States, even empowered people must always reassert their power, sometimes through violent means. When popular and high-achieving students harass less popular students they are not only acting on prejudice but are reaffirming their dominance in a social hierarchy. Often, these become public performances, for it is expected that people will know of the act. Such performance achieves the goal of letting everyone know of one's ability to beat down another, often viewed as a good thing. When teachers do not intervene, they send a "moral signal" to students; they end up symbolizing the social acceptance of humiliation and harassment in which the humiliated are the disempowered or marginalized.[24]

These issues become significant in regard to another component of school violence: gender. Two prominent issues here concern the violence directed at girls in schools, especially by boys, but also the violence between girls. The imposition of male power over girls is one aspect of gender violence, but so is the powerlessness of girls and their subsequent attempts to act on what boys have always known: Powerlessness can be transformed into power, albeit a fleeting and ultimately destructive power, through physical violence against one another.

Gender and Violence

A 1995 report regarding sexual harassment in schools in Connecticut found that, of a random sample of high school students (308 girls and 235 boys), 78 percent reported experiencing at least one incident of sexual harassment in high school, and that girls were about twice as likely as boys to experience sexual harassment. National studies have reiterated these high frequencies of sexual harassment.[25] The federal government and courts have responded to sexual harassment in many positive ways.

In 1980, the Equal Employment Opportunity Commission issued guidelines that treated sexual harassment as illegal sex discrimination in violation of Section 703 of Title VII of the Civil Rights Act of 1964. In addition, Title IX, a federal civil rights in education law that prohibits gender inequity in schools as an amendment to the Higher Education Act of 1972, states that "No person in the United States shall, on the basis of sex, be excluded from participation in, be denied the benefits of, or be subjected to discrimination under any education program or activity receiving Federal Assistance." The Civil Rights Act of 1991 expanded the rights of victims of sexual harassment, allowing them to receive compensatory and punitive damages for emotional pain, suffering, anguish, and inconvenience caused by harassment. In the landmark U.S. Supreme Court case of *Franklin v. Gwinnett County (Ga.) Public Schools*, in a 9–0 decision, the court decided that schools could be held liable for damages if they failed to intervene in persistent incidents of sexual harassment in their buildings.[26]

In court cases, sexual harassment has been defined in two ways: as quid pro quo and hostile environment. "Quid pro quo" refers to threats that one must submit to sex in order to remain employed or, as a student, remain within the good graces of school personnel. "Hostile environment" refers to sexual behaviors that create in schools and workplaces feelings of intimidation, danger, and offensiveness.[27] Most often, school sexual harassment cases fall under the hostile environment definition. The Office for Civil Rights (OCR) of the U.S. Department of Education states in regard to hostile environment:

> To find that a hostile environment exists, OCR must find that the alleged victim was subjected to verbal or physical conduct imposed because of the victim's gender, that the conduct was unwelcomed, and that the conduct was sufficiently severe, persistent or pervasive as to alter the conditions of the victim's education and create an abusive environment. In case of student-to-student harassment, an educational institution will be liable for hostile environment sexual harassment where an official of the institution knew, or reasonably should have known, of the harassment's occurrence and the institution failed to take appropriate steps to halt the conduct.[28]

While strides forward have been taken to address domestic violence and some abuses against girls, sexual harassment remains merely a whisper in schools.[29] In spite of the lofty language of policy, educational researcher Nan Stein has pointed out that, "although sexual harassment among K-12 students is now recognized as a form of sex discrimination and the rush to litigation has begun in earnest, sexual harassment is still not considered to be violence."[30] As not "violent," it often falls outside the parameters of most violence prevention efforts in schools. Too often, as well, teachers are afraid of confrontations of a sexual kind, or, due to ignorance or their own propensities to harass, avoid action even when harassment takes place in public.

The girls themselves, who are harassed, do not always take action either. In interviews, they claimed, sometimes rightly, that school personnel would not take their charges seriously and that the administration was afraid of the publicity a sexual harassment case could bring to the school. The girls also felt that other students would alienate them for causing trouble and aligning themselves with school administrators and disciplinarians. Not only do girls have to deal with the direct threat of sexual harassment, they must contend with the public humiliation associated with it. In addition, they are often labeled as sluts for being sexually harassed, especially when they are not good students, have a reputation for dating boys, or choose to dress provocatively.

To prevent violence associated with harassment, a silence must be broken about the issue. First, school personnel and individuals in society must be forced to recognize that sexual harassment is not "natural" playfulness between the sexes. It is a form of humiliation that is violent in nature. While this point has been partly made through communications such as school newsletters, workshops, in-services, and signs or billboards that warn against sexual harassment, solutions must go beyond the merely rhetorical and didactic. Teachers need to feel encouraged and empowered to intervene when they see sexual harassment. While some teachers refuse to get involved because of their own sexism, there are other teachers who do not know how to intervene. For them, the school needs to distribute clear guidelines. These guidelines must start by listing various forms of sexual harassment in very concrete terms (including sexual taunting, bra snapping, pinching, and so forth) and then outlining a course of action to respond to each form of harassment. Such action might include a talk with the student after class, a reprimand, or, if the offense is serious enough, a referral to administration. Once these guidelines are established, teachers who do not follow them must be treated as if they were ignoring school policy. Throughout the process, the seriousness of sexual harassment and the respect of all people involved must be emphasized.

In addition, students need to be reminded that they, too, are responsible for the welfare of other students in the school and that they, also, have a responsibility to report incidents of harassment. School staff should make it clear to students that anyone who reports an act of violence will be treated with respect and care. If necessary, serious efforts should be made to prevent retaliation against people who report harassment. Administrators must show themselves open to complaints by being advocates on the behalf of victims as well as those who take on the responsibility of coming forward and speaking out on potentially difficult incidents. Clearly, to prevent the problem, we must alter an entire school culture—and perhaps an entire U.S. culture—that has tolerated, and even instigated, sexism, that has accepted violence against women, and that has justified, as a natural part of masculinity, the oppression and humiliation of females. Too often, those who intervene in incidents of sexual harassment are viewed by others as fanatics, whistle blowers, and alarmists. Sexism in the wider society is a double-edged sword. It motivates people to harass girls in school and is the catalyst for the inept responses that follow in the wake of many harassment incidents.

The other issue concerning gender and violence revolves around conflicts that are committed by girls against other girls, and sometimes against boys. When I have gone into schools to conduct research on violence, I have often been directed toward the girls with statements by administrators claiming that "girls are the worst" when it comes to fighting and that "girls are the ones who are the most violent."[31]

There have been many theories put forward to explain why girls have appeared to become more violent in recent years. Sibylle Artz has given a clear overview of these theories.[32] They include, "biological theories" that assert that girls' disposition towards violence is caused by an excess of male chromosomes, premenstrual syndrome, and their natural inabilities to control their emotions. Gender role theories of female violence assert that women have been socialized to be passive and caring, and, in recent years, they have managed to break out of these typical roles. The result has been greater violence, as girls fight back against male patriarchy and begin to understand what males have known all along: that violence is at times a means of gaining respect as well as economic advantages. Another theory of female violence asserts that girls have become more masculine in recent years because of their efforts to take on traditionally male roles, the women's movement, and their greater participation in the work force. They have been recently socialized, like males before them, to be assertive, aggressive, and even violent. Partly a backlash against the women's movement, this theory suggests that girls today are being raised differently than they were years ago, and the consequence of this new socialization process has been girls acting more like boys.

Theories that account for female aggressiveness often take the position that girls are almost programmed to act violently either because of biological, instinctual, social, or economic causes. What is often left out of the picture is the notion that females act violently as a response to violence in their own lives. Gini Sikes has pointed out that girls in violent gangs are as much victimizers as those who are victimized by abusive boyfriends, fathers and mothers, stepparents, and even older brothers and sisters.[33] Similar to what Freire has noted about "oppressed group behavior," girls often act violently not toward boys but toward people of equal or lower social status.[34] A response to victimization has been to victimize back, but, unlike boys, the marginalization of female victims makes them the target of violence from both girls and boys. When boys are victimized, they respond by victimizing people of lower social standing, which may include boys or girls, disabled students, gay students, or anybody of minority status. When girls retaliate against people of lower social standing, their actions are directed almost exclusively at other girls. It becomes a kind of "cat fight" on the scrap pile of the school hierarchy.

In her study of violence by girls, Artz pointed out that girls are victimized much more than boys, and this adds fuel to their own frustrations and impulses to act violently. Through their own victimization, they also come to understand that a means of obtaining might, advantage, and dominance is through the physical assertion of power over others.[35] In the girls' households, which were the subject of Artz's study, conflict quickly became ugly and abusive "because the perspective in which righteous action is grounded is one that endorses the use of power over others and construes others as the source and cause of one's feelings."[36] In other words, conflict becomes not a positive means of making a compromise or understanding another person's feelings but a way of asserting power over another and casting blame onto the victims, who are most often girls and women.[37] Girls sometimes respond by emulating the males who victimize them; they share the successes of victory and enact the power they see being used against them. In addition, in some cases, boys not only find girl-fighting fun to watch, but sexually stimulating, especially when girls are fighting over boys. Furthermore, as Artz has pointed out, some girls fight to oblige boys' desires to watch them do so.[38]

To intervene in this form of violence, a school must work at different levels; one would advocate and support girls and victims of abuse, another would address gender equity in the school itself, and a third would challenge paternalism and sexism in society. We must see behind the violence and understand the circumstances of some girls' victimization and how they have become emboldened by access to weapons, girl gangs, and general disorganization in many communities. Violence prevention programs, typically gender neutral, if not focused solely on boys, must include explicit strategies that are specific to these circumstances of girls.

Changes in attitudes are needed if we hope to reduce the forms of violence discussed in this chapter. Sexism, acceptance of violence, and prejudices fuel types of violence that are a result of power imbalances and desires to control others. In order to prevent such violence in school the larger culture must be altered—no doubt a monumental task for a country steeped in paternalism, militarism, and other forms of prejudice and unjust impositions of power. However, schools can initiate the change by becoming a check on social inequities, rather than a mirror image of them. As Jackson Katz noted in his research on sexual harassment, "Sexual assault is best understood as occurring in a socio-cultural environment that promotes rape-supportive attitudes and socializes men to adhere to them."[39]

Violence prevention programs that focus only on students and do not account for domestic abuse, the role of prejudice and power, and issues of respect and control are doomed to failure. While such programs may be beneficial in a localized way—to prevent two students from fighting each other on a particular day—long-term violence prevention must sustain and be part of a larger transformation of U.S. culture. This is the subject of the next chapter.

Chapter 6

Gun Manufacturing, Popular Culture, and Militarism

When a question arises about the connection between school violence and other forms of violence in U.S. society, a debate often ensues about influences, especially the influence of gun production, militarism, and popular culture on youths. While different issues arise when we speak of each of these three topics, they are connected in that they comprise what I have come to see as a military-economic complex. They have influenced the creation of a U.S. society that is, in part, militaristic and supportive of corporate forces that have made the country a leader in gun manufacturing, firearm possession, and the production of an extremely violent popular culture.

The previous chapters have attempted to look beyond individual students in order to view violence prevention within the context of communities and school structures, and in relation to codes of behavior, power, gender, and respect. However, violence prevention must surpass even these issues. Because youths do not have a monopoly on violence, prevention must take into account violence that is enacted by the adult power brokers. This is exactly what zero tolerance policy does not do.

Violence is also initiated in halls of defense, in the manufacturing of weapons that enables violence to be more violent, in lobbying efforts that promote access to weapons designed to kill other human beings as efficiently as possible, and in a popular U.S. culture enamored of the visceral power of media violence. The zero tolerance view of violence cannot account for the more informal means through which violence becomes familiar in U.S. culture because it diverts attention away from economic, military, and media violence, focusing instead on the behaviors of youths.

The issue of whether there exists a connection between youth violence and more far-flung forms and representations of violence is not new. As I mentioned earlier, since the 1960s, researchers have been studying the effects of media on children, and the worry about television violence has existed since the first mass distribution of TV sets in the 1950s.[1] Throughout the history of U.S. attempts at gun legislation, debates and research have abounded regarding links between gun ownership, firearms manufacturing, and youth violence.[2] Concerns about militarism and youth violence are heard in passing conversations and editorials and reflect political beliefs and worries about increased military activities by the United States since World War II and their effects on society.[3] For example, at a national education conference in 1999, a keynote address was given about school violence. After the address, a member of the audience raised the issue of the unprecedented violence at Columbine High School by noting what he saw as an irony: that, at the time of the high school shootings, U.S. war planes had begun the bombing of Kosovo, while Bill Clinton in public speeches was lamenting the violence that had seemed to overrun the nation. The point was made, and, with knowing nods of the head, some in the audience showed their agreement that aggression in school is just one part of a more nationwide violence. Many felt Bill Clinton had missed the boat when he did not recognize his own connection to the problem.

Though there was some agreement by the essentially liberal crowd at the conference about the connection between shooting sprees at schools and international violence, the "influence" argument becomes a controversial point of view for two reasons. First, it upsets patriotic mentalities, for it defines as essentially violent a nation that has prided itself on democratic principles of peace. Second, it becomes contentious because there is no "scientific" way to truly gauge how the military and economic forms of violence associated with gun manufacturing and popular culture influence students' behaviors on the streets and in schools.

There exist few studies that examine connections between militarism and youth violence. The correlation is more often argued on the theoretical grounds that there occurs a kind of trickle-down effect with violent attitudes, whereby militaristic mentalities spread through the country as we socialize younger generations to accept violence as a logical way to deal with conflict.[4] On the other hand, although many studies exist that examine the influences of gun manufacturing and firearm possession on incidents of violence, their conclusions are often contradictory. While many studies claim the lax gun laws and enormous productions of firearms, which have pumped over 200,000,000 guns into our country, exacerbate violence, other studies show that there is no such correlation. A well-known study echos NRA logic by claiming that increased distribution and possession of firearms actually lead to less crime.[5]

In regard to popular culture, there have been thousands of studies measuring the effects of media violence on youths, and, though most have recognized a positive correlation between the watching of violence and incidents of violence, there still exists much controversy regarding the exact effects of media on youths, especially as new media forms are sold, including first-person shooter video games.[6] In general, there is a lot of controversy about the effects of militarism, gun manufacturing, and popular culture on the behaviors of youths. Do militaristic countries create a violent society, or are people capable of separating international behaviors from social behaviors? Does gun manufacturing exacerbate violence or deter it? Are violent video games and movies pure fun or desensitizers that do all but teach students how to pull the trigger?

The point of this chapter is not to prove that economic and military forms of violence are sources of school violence but to examine the topic with the knowledge that a connection exists. People not only live in the world; they interact with it. Decades of research on "socialization" and "informal education" have shown us that we learn behaviors through our interactions with other people and objects, through our interpretations of the media, and through imitation of what we see other people do. While there exists much in the United States that "teaches" us to be kind, respectful, and peaceful, there is much—road rage, militarism, some sports, and some aspects of corporate culture, for example—that teaches us to be cutthroat, if not violent. Certainly, not all people just soak up these messages and then transform them into their own violent behaviors. People are capable of resisting socialization that paves the way for aggression through supportive and positive families, living arrangements, peers, and other kinds of constructive influences.[7] However, we do not want to underestimate the enormous power of the military, popular culture, and corporatism to shape our thoughts and behaviors.[8]

The "Influence" Argument

In the prevention of school violence attention must be given to the experiences of young people and how those experiences are interpreted by them. These experiences should include those in the community and school and with others but also experiences that students have with their popular culture, with the military (including JROTC organizations in high schools), and their knowledge of easy access to weapons. Cultures are created in neighborhoods, families, and states, and within a national context. What is easily accepted in the United States, what is produced and used, how individuals view themselves in relation to others, all add up to define U.S. culture; who Americans are as a people. If U.S. society continues to support militarism, to tolerate the mass manufacturing and distribution of weapons that have caused what health experts call a national health crisis in the country, and to patronize needless violence in the media, then, those who take part in such activities continue to produce a culture that is partly defined by violence. This violence may, if other factors fall into place, lead to youth and school violence. Reiterated by school staff and many educational researchers in relation to families and communities is the common saying that "school violence is just one part of violence in the rest of society." This is mostly true. However, to follow through on this belief, we must see "the rest of society" not only in homes and neighborhoods but also in places of work, in institutions, government bodies, corporations, and the military. These, too, are a part—an especially prominent part—of society.

While the problem of school violence is considered in many ways by researchers and the popular press, too often, the experiences of students in school are not recognized and taken seriously. Researchers, enthralled with clinical studies, surveys, measurement instruments, and statistics, and sometimes possessing a general disregard for the views of youths, have forced the perspectives of students to the sidelines of most school policy. Youths tell us what the problems are all the time. They even have solutions. Their sometimes subtle comments and critical questions reveal to adults their take on the issues. However, when the problems or solutions they propose are threatening to adult society, they are ignored.

Most adults want students to blame themselves, to fall into lockstep with zero tolerance thinking. Take, for example, a health class I observed. It is but one example of how issues of economic and military violence enter into discussions about violence and how such perspectives are sidestepped in favor of perspectives that blame students. During an eight-day unit on violence prevention, the teacher of the class, Mr. Darien, had been describing to students different ways to avoid violence. Toward the end of the unit, after introducing the topic of avoiding violence, he wrote on the board: "Ignore the Situation." As soon as he wrote the words, several students in the lively class raised an uproar. The following field note shows the complexities of talking about school violence, but, more importantly, demonstrates its connection to "influences," in this case, military influence. In spite of the students' perceptive thoughts, they were overridden with a rebuff.

> After writing on the board, Mr. Darien said that all situations can be ignored and that students had the responsibility to walk away from potential hostilities. One student said, over others who were shouting out similar kinds of sentiments, "You can't just ignore it. You gotta do something." Mr. Darien acknowledged the point by shaking his head. Though he did not hear it, another student sitting next to me turned to her neighbor and said, "I think you can ignore it, but eventually you'll have a blowup." One student shouted over the rest, "You got to deal with the problems you got!"
>
> Mr. Darien interpreted the students' remarks to be advocating violence. When the student said, "You can't just ignore it," Mr. Darien felt that the student was saying that you had to fight. But the student, who explained himself later, was saying that it was impossible to ignore conflicts because they will inevitably escalate. As the one student said, "Eventually you'll have a blowup." For a moment, Mr. Darien got angry with the students and said that he didn't approve of their "macho attitude." He saw himself as doing the right thing, challenging what he interpreted as their insistence on fighting. He said, "This is no place to be putting on your macho fronts. Nobody has anything to prove here, so just leave the macho talk outside and use your brains."
>
> The boy who had said, "You can't just ignore it," raised his hand, and Mr. Darien called on him. He had to quiet the class and, when the room was less noisy, the student said, "What we're saying is that you have to deal with the problem or it'll just get worse. I know that I can't just walk away from it, because then I'll be thinking about it all night, and, eventually, I'm going to see that person, and *boom*, we're going to get down [fight]."
>
> Mr. Darien acknowledged the point and seemed to understand the mistake he had made. He said, "Okay. So what are the kinds of things that make it difficult to ignore?"

Another student shot up her hand and said, "Because everybody knows you just can't ignore it."

Mr. Darien nodded, but he wanted to dig deeper. "Okay, okay, but why? I'm asking *why* can't you ignore it?"

As so often happened in the class, suddenly, the attention was shifted a bit. A male student sitting in the back suddenly asked, "What about our country? You want us to just walk away, but we never walk away from anything."

Mr. Darien understood what the student was saying, and he tried to quiet the class again as they had all started remarking about the comment, mostly to their neighbors or people behind them.

A female student, sitting closest to the teacher, said, "Just look at the wars we're in; it's ridiculous. My brother went to the Gulf War."

Another student said, shouting across the room, that his older brother went to the Persian Gulf as well. The teacher added, "I, too, know people who have gone."

It seemed that the class was waiting for Mr. Darien to say more about who had gone, but he didn't. For a second there was quiet, then, a male student who had been quiet during most of the discussion, said, "It's just the way I was brought up." Mr. Darien nodded and finished the thought, "By your family," and the boy said, "And my country."

People began talking again, commenting on the thought. One student yelled out, "Look what they did to Diallo," referring to the West African immigrant who had been shot down by white police in the Bronx. "That's how we take care of business in this country," a female student said.

Mr. Darien shook his head and waved his hands. He began erasing the board, signaling that the conversation was over. While erasing, he half-turned to the class and said, "I don't accept that. You can't be blaming other people for your behaviors." After erasing, he came forward and told the students that they had to move on to the next topic in the text.

Often, adults do not accept the points that students make, especially when they aim criticism at adult institutions, such as the military. In true zero tolerance fashion, adults would rather cast blame at youths. Many would write off the students' comments about our country and wars as naivete, or their way of casting blame elsewhere and not taking responsibility for their actions. Adults accept what students say about violence when students blame themselves.

In another health class, students were asked to list on the board different types of gangs. The teacher in this class, as in the other, was mostly receptive of students' comments and even seemed to enjoy lively discussions. However, as so often happened, he had his own strong opinions about violence and expected students to share them. While he expected students to list the names of well-known youth gangs (the Bloods, Crips, Latin Kings, and so on), students added their own ideas. In addition to the explicit gang names, he also received NEPD (New England Police Department) and NATO. At the time, the World Trade Organization was meeting in Seattle, accompanied by mass protests, and one student added the WTO. In a different school, a similar exercise had spurred one student to state that the U.S. Army was also a gang. Social workers and others who work closely with young people acknowledge students' preoccupations with forms of military-economic violence. When I asked one school social worker what he thought were the problems that created violence, he told me:

> You got the usual things. Peer pressure, gangs, depression, poverty, all that. You also got video games and everything else we hear about. These kids spend a lot of time in front of video computers and televisions. On one hand, I only know what students tell me and what I know from books on the topic. I often hear about families in both places. We are all aware of the social crisis, single-parent families, broken homes, all that. But students also have a deep nihilism, like a void. Sometimes I interpret that void as spiritual, but that's because of the type of person I am. It is also deeply psychological, I think. It comes from years of knowing that we are only a button away from self-destruction, that many adults don't care about them, that we keep beating people down, and that, in general, adults have built a world that does not look so rosy. We keep telling kids that the U.S. is great, but they look around and they don't see it. I have kids come in here and tell me that they're suicidal or they're going to do something, something violent, and when I tell them that they shouldn't, they want to know, "Why the hell not?" They have this attitude that nobody cares, and they have all this proof from society. They say, "Look at the wars, look what we do to Puerto Rico and Panama (and other countries where some of them come from). The whole country is going to hell in a handbasket, it isn't just the kids." It's like they know that they are just one part in a wheel or something. Everything around them is violent, and it just doesn't end with their families and communities.

Forms of violence seen in schools are part of a continuum of violence that extends outside the school, through neighborhoods, families, institutional bodies, corporations, and paramilitary organizations. Part of the problem with studying "school violence" is that one reifies the notion that violence in school is a particular problem that is unique unto itself. In reality, school violence is one form of the violence that is enacted within a violent U.S. culture. When gangs fight over turf, wear bandanas and beads like uniforms, make use of automatic weapons, have particular signs that designate membership to the group, and demand a commitment to the group that is hierarchical and at times fanatical, they reenact military strategies of organization, behavior, and warfare. The battlefields for gangs are not the deserts and jungles of the world but the parking lots and streets of neighborhoods.

Likewise, sexual harassment in school is a reenactment of the larger sexism in U.S. society. Violent video games not only desensitize; they train the mind and hand for warfare.[9] School violence has broader parameters than is ordinarily thought. Who can deny the connection between sexual harassment and popular culture's violence toward women? In one case, World Wrestling Federation (WWF) action figures that included the severed head of a woman were sold in Georgia. In the advertising picture accompanying the figures, a maniacal looking Al Snow, a popular WWF personality, is shown carrying a woman's head in his hand. That products such as these can be manufactured and distributed is as much a reflection on the wrestling organization as it is on U.S. society. In what kind of country can figures such as these be produced, sold, and bought? Interestingly, the products were pulled from Wal-Mart shelves after a teacher and store manager in Georgia protested against them. This incident marks the easy acceptance of violence in our society, in this case, a gruesome violence against women; but it is also an example of individuals taking steps forward to challenge the production of violence in the United States.

School violence can not be partitioned off from a discussion about the apparent U.S. acceptance of weapons and aggression in many aspects of U.S. society. For a country that has always prided itself on its role as defender of the individual and as the great world stabilizer, it is hard for many to accept that the United States is a violent nation. It is also hard for people to accept that it is not just youths doing the violence. As early as 1968, the National Commission on the Causes and Prevention of Violence determined that cities in the United States were among the most violent in the world when compared to other "modern stable democratic nations."[10]

Since World War II, the United States has become the nation most willing to use worldwide military force against enemies and is the leader in the sale of armaments to the rest of the world.[11] The country is a world-leader in suicide, homicide, and other forms of social violence.[12] In addition, our production of violent video games, film, music, and toys can hardly be matched by any country. Perhaps the concerns expressed by a friend of mine, who had moved with his family to the United States from France for work, explains it best. When I asked him what one of his greatest concerns was when he moved to the United States, he told me, "I was afraid we'd be shot somewhere and then wouldn't have health insurance to be treated." Not entirely tongue-in-cheek, my friend's concern was based on the impression, shared by others in the world, that the United States is violent. Some time later (after he had been in the country for nearly a year and had received health insurance), I asked him again if he still felt the same way about the United States. In total seriousness, he told me that he had been wrong when he had first explained his concerns. "Actually," he said, "the health care problem isn't really as bad as I thought." He could not say the same about the violence.

Gun Making

Rarely are adults seen as responsible for school violence. Either we blame the students, or we blame dysfunctional and poor families.

Rarely do we recognize how violence and other social problems result from middle to upper class preoccupations in adult society. For example, while many focus on individuals who use guns, few focus on those who make guns or on those who are so obsessed with guns that they view any form of gun control as an infringement of their constitutional right to bear arms. Whether gun restrictions will reduce incidents of violence is a hotly debated topic, but the fact remains that people would not die from gun shot wounds if guns were not available. Because of the lethality of guns, especially newer higher caliber and automatic weapons, when guns are available, violent incidents are more likely to end in death than when guns are not available.[13]

The NRA and other gun enthusiasts will often remark that guns protect individuals from crime and can actually act as a deterrent. However, when one considers that the vast majority of homicides involve people who know each other (usually family members, acquaintances, lovers, and, more recently, schoolmates), the "protection against strangers" argument does not hold up.[14] As researcher Diane Zuckerman explained, "Gun ownership offers no apparent protection against being murdered, even in cases involving forced entry into the home."[15] While it may be utopian (and some would say, downright un-American) to hope that guns would be nonexistent in the United States, legislation that prohibits gun purchases by individuals with felony convictions has been determined effective in curbing violence.[16] Criminal background checks now prevent handgun purchases by nearly 80,000 individuals each year. According to one research report, this decreases the likelihood of later criminal activity by 20 to 30 percent.[17] A California law that preceded the Brady Bill, which required a waiting period and background check, reportedly prevented the sale of 11,000 handguns to convicted felons, including 71 convicted murderers in 1991–1992.[18]

Some research and polls indicate that individuals in the United States are becoming more intolerant of the mass production and distribution of handguns and the violence that they create in streets and schools. Some hopeful signs have begun to emerge to suggest that individuals in the United States are truly weary of violence in rural, city, and suburban schools and communities. After years of trying to change laws, usually unsuccessfully, gun opponents are targeting firearm producers for the destruction that their products do. As noted earlier, in 1999, several cities, including New Orleans, Miami, Chicago, and Bridgeport, Conn., attempted to sue gun manufacturers for their production of handguns. In particular, these lawsuits cited the practices of oversupplying states where gun laws were lax (notably in the South) and cutting costs by not including the most advanced forms of safety devises.[19] New Orleans mayor Marc Morial, who organized the first suit against gun manufacturers, was, in 1999, leading a lawsuit against fifteen manufacturers of handguns.

While such suits are often seen as a way of keeping lawyers rich and as copycat cases mimicking tobacco suits, they also highlight a reality that others battling health crises and social problems in other areas have recognized: that entrenched injustices in the United States can only be fought through protest and the courts. The political elite are too indebted to big business, and, in this case, NRA lobbyists, to expect radical changes from that quarter. For example, in 1999, Atlanta filed suit against fourteen manufacturers of handguns. Unfortunately, the NRA had financed many politicians in the state, including Georgia Governor Roy Barnes, so legislators bedded with the NRA and other progun groups. The state senate passed the first bill in the nation designed to block lawsuits against gun manufacturers, and the NRA expects to add another twenty-five to thirty states to its roster in the next year.[20]

No matter how much we like to blame students and community dysfunction for violence, we must also recognize how the despicable acts of politicians and lobbyists (who are concerned with their own private interests and money, seemingly, not the lives of young people) readily accept the production and sale of weapons that have no other purpose than to maim and kill other human beings. Even a conservative public figure like George Will, who supports the production and sale of handguns, notes that in the United States about 80 million individuals own between 200 million and 240 million guns.[21] However, rather than use these figures to argue that our society is flooded with weapons, Will uses them to note that *only* several hundred children are accidently killed each year by handguns. This is a pathetic argument and proves once again the uncaring attitude that many adults have toward children. Just as drug dealers are partly responsible for the destruction and deaths that their products cause—even accidently—so are gun dealers partly responsible for the deaths and destruction that their guns cause.

One cannot separate the selling of weapons from the use of weapons, especially when gun manufacturers have increased production of more deadly and higher caliber weapons to compensate for lagging sales of lower caliber guns.[22] However, many in the United States refuse to believe that the nation uses what it produces. When objects are mass-produced in the United States, whether they be SUVs, computers, or guns, what is produced is used. Individuals have tried to convince themselves that guns are not made for fighting. While collectors exist who may never fire a gun, most guns are bought explicitly to be used for their intended purposes: to be concealed and then fired at another human being. Rather than see the connection between the production, sale, and use of guns, individuals would rather shift the blame onto those who are not careful with guns or who use guns for unintended purposes, as if the purpose of an easily concealed instrument that fires high caliber bullets were not to conceal and shoot it.

Education has always been a means of socializing children, a way of transmitting cultural values from one generation to another. So when the NRA decided to develop a gun safety course for elementary schools, the Eddie Eagle Gun Safety Program, we may well wonder what cultural values were being transmitted. More importantly, are these the values we would like elementary school children to share? The Eddie Eagle Gun Safety Program entails representatives from the NRA coming into schools to teach students how to handle a gun appropriately, and, most importantly, to make clear that they should not touch guns until they are old enough to do so safely. What cultural value is being instilled here? First, that handguns, as well as all forms of war weapons, including AK-47s and Uzis, the production and ownership of which the NRA also supports, are acceptable items to own. Should we also teach children that drugs and bombs are also acceptable if used safely? Instead of teaching gun safety, why not teach students the truth? Handguns and automatic weapons are responsible for tens of thousands of deaths each year and should be avoided. In fact, they should not be owned. Those who manufacture weapons introduce into our society a highly destructive item which affects us all, even those who do not own guns. Why not teach students that guns are "bad," and, that all who own handguns and automatic weapons are potentially dangerous, even if, under most circumstances, they are ordinary law-abiding citizens? Any of the *only* 100 or so children killed accidently each year could tell you this.

In a newspaper editorial, a member of the NRA, who supported the Eddie Eagle Gun Safety Program, noted the following, "Legislators can make laws telling us to lock our guns up, put trigger locks on them or child-proof them, but there will always be people who do not obey. Moreover, as far as child-proofing guns, I think it is impossible. Any child with enough determination can, and will, figure out how to overcome these intended safeguards." The writer's solution: Teach children to leave the gun alone, and, in time, to know how to use the gun safely. Once again, we deflect responsibility away from adults and put the burden on children. Children must learn to deal with the callousness of adults. When another child is killed accidently by a gun, whose fault is it? The fault rests with the single individual who did not take precautions—not all individuals who own or advocate the ownership of handguns—and, of course, with the school system that did not have an Eddie Eagle Gun Safety Program.

Gun manufacturers escape blame for the devastation that their products do because they are members of corporate America. Linked to a powerful lobby (the NRA), they support politicians hungry for donations and are endowed with the power to profit from their own national policies. If most street drug dealers were middle-upper-class and white, linked to a powerful lobby, and supported politicians with millions of dollars, we would also see a change in thinking and policy regarding drug dealing: Individuals who use drugs inappropriately would be blamed and not the dealers. As criminologist Michael Tonry explained, "America has the highest rates of gun crime of any developed country . . .the problem lies not in underlying rates of crime but in underlying rates of gun ownership. The long-term solution lies not in sentencing policy, but in gun control policy."[23]

For too long, though, the crackdown on violence has accompanied the expansion of the U.S. prison system and the mass incarceration of mostly poor and nonwhite citizens. Middle-upper-class society has been relatively free of blame and in many ways has prospered economically through gun sales, the privatization of the U.S. prison system, international gun dealing, and other businesses that are supported by, and hence support, violence.[24] Violence is profitable for many. Where would crime policy analysts, prison guards and wardens, police officers, and gun manufacturers be if it was not for violence? The profitability of violence is seen as well in the media industry, where violent entertainment is explained away as mere fun.

Popular Culture

As discussed earlier in regard to Albert Bandura and other "media effects" researchers, there have been many individuals who have shown how youths, under certain circumstances, will imitate what they see in the media. This is a troublesome thought when we take into account the most common form of media in the United States—the reality of television programming:

1. By the time the average American child finishes high school, he or she will witness on television 40,000 murders and 200,000 other acts of violence.
2. Although prime-time television features on average five violent scenes an hour, there are twenty-five violent acts an hour on Saturday morning cartoons, which are mostly watched by children. That's only network television; many more cartoons shows are on cable.
3. A survey by the Center for Media and Public Affairs determined that on one day in 1994, a look at all programming including cable in one city tallied 2,605 acts of violence.
4. The body count of motion pictures continually rises to impress a youthful audience that has become almost inured to violence. The first *Die Hard* movie had 18 deaths, while *Die Hard 2* had 264. The first *Robocop* had 32 deaths; the second, 81.[25]

It is nearly impossible to keep up with media advancements. While television was the culprit in the 1960s and 1970s the problem became increasingly charged with issues of race in the 1980s when a national concern was raised over gangster rap lyrics, and music distribution kicked into high gear with the advent of compact disks. Later, the debate turned to violent video games, especially as mass shootings that seemed to resemble the homicidal rages of video games began to occur in suburban schools.[26] Concerns about television and rap lyrics seem almost quaint in comparison with today's worries about first-person shooter video products and computer games that feature slaughters and exploding bodies.

Since the advent of mass communications in the early part of the 20th century, there has been sustained concern about the influence of media entertainment on young people; concerns today are similar, but the products have changed. The young people I have met in school do play a lot of video games, especially the boys. Even so, in spite of the exploding body parts in *Quake II* and the homicidal rages of *Postal* and the brutalizing of women in *Night Trap*, few students I spoke with felt that video games actually caused violence. However, many were able to name people they knew who seemed to get more violent after playing or would make threats against other people using references to video games they played.

Although there has been research that attempts to prove that popular culture and, more specifically, violent Hollywood movies, television, music, and video games, have a negative effect on the behavior of youths, most often this literature addresses the topic in an explicitly "cause and effect" manner. Students are right. It is not that violent media and video games cause violence. Rather, under certain circumstances, and with some youths, the violence they watch and the video violence they do collaborate with other issues to create increased likelihoods of serious violence in their lives. As Daniel Derksen and Victor Strasburger explained in their article about media violence, U.S. television, music videos, movies, and video games are the most violent in the world, "the effect [of which] is subtle and ingrained over time by repetition of images and stereotypes that offer children distorted information about gender roles and violence as an acceptable means of conflict resolution."[27]

However, not all children will react the same way to violent media imagery, and information about gender and violence is interpreted differently by different students. How students make sense of media depends, in large part, on their circumstances in life. For some students the violent media will be one more negative component of their lives that, along with a slew of other negative influences and circumstances, will increase the likelihood that a conflict will turn violent. In her journalistic account of girl gangs Gini Sikes watched as girl gang members repeatedly "hyped themselves up for violence by snorting coke and watching gang movies."[28]

Whenever I asked cops about the genesis of San Antonio's gang wars, their opinion could be summed up in one word: *Colors*. Although it seemed absurdly simplistic to blame a city crisis on Dennis Hopper's 1988 movie about L.A.'s Crips and Bloods, I heard this from kids, too, who'd seen it fourteen and fifteen times. Though *Colors* is ultimately a morality tale, the children most influenced by it chose to identify with the power of the shooters.

Along with poverty, child-care responsibilities, abuse by boyfriends and fathers of their children, and other factors, drugs and media contributed to gang fighting by girls. Not everybody who watches a gang movie, though, heads out into the street to shoot somebody. Japan's movies are as violent as those in the United States, but the country has a murder rate among the lowest in the world. Violent media do not cause violence. However, violent media in association with isolation, depression, misguided power, drugs, alienating circumstances in schools and in families—all this and more—combine with the realities of gun availability to produce explosive situations in the streets and schools of the United States.

In an elementary school where I conducted research, one teacher spoke of a troubled 2nd grader. He had been suspended from school after he had scratched the face of another child with classroom scissors. "He was imitating some program, doing all these Ninja-like moves, and got another kid in the face with the scissors," the teacher told me. "I think he didn't mean to cut the other student, and it wasn't really a bad cut, but the kid was clearly out of control. But then again, he's got so many problems." Later, the teacher told me that the student was always watching the most violent movies. He would come into school talking about them. She also told me that he was allowed to watch the violent programming ("and pornography," she added) because his mother worked late and his father did not live with them. It is not that the television programs he watched caused the violence but that they became a part of his experiences, along with family and social problems, to make him the kind of kid who would get up in the middle of a class and start swinging scissors at people.

Regardless of protests against media violence and support for the notorious V-chip, violent Hollywood movies, television programming, and music and video games continue to bring in billions of dollars a year, attract multitudes of consumers, and create legions of media killers who are sometimes emulated in school hallways and in the streets.[29] It is this production of violence and its acceptance by producers and consumers alike that infuses our culture (and not specifically the imaginations of young people) with violence and even the attractions of gang membership. In their study of St. Louis gangs, for example, criminologists Scott Decker and Barrik Van Winkle explained that movies, clothes, and music provided a symbolic reference point for gang antagonisms: "In this way, popular culture provided the symbols and rhetoric of gang affiliation and activities that galvanized neighborhood rivalries."[30] The authors pointed out that characteristics of Los Angeles gangs (2,000 miles from St. Louis), and not Chicago gangs, which were only 300 miles away, came to dominate St. Louis gangs, because "Chicago gangs lacked the means of transmission for their beliefs and practices found in popular culture."

In addition to research and journalistic accounts, the success of advertising is proof of the power of the media to influence the way people act. However, some students are disgusted by violent forms of popular culture—especially girls, most of whom have little interest in video games. There are also many boys who are not terribly interested in video games. Adults, as well, are influenced by the media, and even television programming that is not explicitly violent can shape thinking about violence. For example, in her research on the viewing of crime dramas, Margaret Reith found that many white men who enjoyed crime dramas were especially aggressive toward people who threatened law and order and tolerant of those who represented established law and order.[31] In her account, crime dramas support zero tolerance thinking and to some degree, acceptance of police infractions, if the purpose of breeching the law is imposition of order. For boys, media that are both sexually and violently explicit can have the effect of increasing acceptance of violence toward women, and lowering compassion for victims of sexual aggression.[32]

While there exist many boys (and, especially, girls) who are not interested in such media, there are many young people who are. After all, the entertainment industry is a multibillion dollar business. Among these people, there are some who have few things in their lives that work to counterbalance the negative power of violent television programming, movies, or video games. Though some researchers may take issue with the clinical nature of the research done by Bandura and his associates, few will deny the fact that people do respond to outside stimuli (though they do not all respond in the same way and are not controlled by it).[33] With all its advertising, financial, and lobbying forces behind it, the entertainment industry has spread mindless violence through youths' forms of entertainment and soaked our popular culture with aggressive musclemen and military killers. In many ways, such popular culture has been a form of free advertising for the military elite, nourishing the easy acceptance of violence as a means of conflict resolution.

Like education, popular culture transmits beliefs and values. One could say that popular culture must be seen as a verb, not just as a noun. Popular culture is not just the music video, teen magazine, movie, but the interactions that individuals have with these products and the dynamic and complex behaviors that result from them. The products create powerful visceral reactions, they shape beliefs, socialize, stimulate, and sometimes desensitize. They occupy the minds and bodies of individuals for hours a day. They produce strong feelings of enjoyment, rage, and even fantasy.

In spite of the problems with media violence, censorship is not the answer. What is called the "third-person effect" refers to the censor's belief that he or she must protect others (some "third person") and not himself or herself from offenses in the media.[34] It is a morally superior point of view that assumes that people are not capable of screening content for themselves. It opens floodgates for the censorship of other materials besides those deemed violent by government bodies. Also, we must be wary of the claim that violent images easily translate over into violent actions. We should also avoid demonizing entertainment and people's desires for fantasy and emotional highs.

Individuals act in partial accordance with beliefs and worldviews and always within a context of certain life circumstances. There are many factors that come to shape people's worldviews, circumstances, and behaviors. Violent popular culture is but one factor, but it is a strong one during a time when technology, media, and other forms of telecommunications are becoming increasingly pervasive in life.[35] Violence is *popular*, an integral part of frontier mentalities, imperialist drives, movie plots, many moneymaking machines, fame and fortune, great world movements, uprisings, and militarism. It is a kind of cultural reference point for Americans.

Military Might

Since at least the time of Sigmund Freud, individuals have pondered people's natural tendencies to become violent. Many have argued that there exists in human beings an instinctively violent dark side. "After all we are animals, we used to be cave-dwellers," people will say, "and though we have become more civilized, we cannot simply leave behind our primordial pasts." However, numerous writers have countered this argument by pointing out that, while there exist people who seem naturally murderous, "natural born killers" in effect, there exist many pacifists and opponents to war; while there have been soldiers, even enthusiastic soldiers, there have been thousands of conscientious objectors.

If there exist innate violent tendencies, there also exist innate peaceful tendencies, it seems. Howard Zinn addressed this topic in an insightful book, *Declarations of Independence*, in which he wrote that it was illogical to believe that violence was instinctive when there was so much in the United States that prepared, educated, trained, and propagandized youths for violence and war.[36] In her popular book, *Blood Rites*, Barbara Ehrenreich made a similar point: "War is too complex and collective an activity to be accounted for by a single warlike instinct lurking within the individual psyche. . . instinct does not mobilize supply lines, manufacture rifles, issue uniforms, or move an army of thousands."[37]

The degree to which schools prepare students for war and violence depends on the school; certainly, military schools are specifically designed to produce a steady stream of military officers and service personnel. However, even the comprehensive public schools have always had a propagandizing function. We see this, for example, in both the curriculum (in some social studies and civic classes) and in extracurricular activities, such as the singing of patriotic songs at school sporting events, or, during morning rituals, when classes stand, salute, and pledge allegiance to the flag. In some cases, school-sponsored patriotism has crept into a subtle form of militarism, represented, for example, in school uniforms and severe regimentation and in the marching band and some sporting events. It arises in more extreme instances, such as programs that sponsor the hiring of retired military personnel to teach in city schools, new protective gear and weaponry used by riot police at some after-school events, surveillance cameras, the use of armed officers to patrol halls (like peacekeeping troops), and perhaps most pointedly, JROTC troops in high schools.

In some of these ways, schools socialize students for a militaristic society, and, especially in regard to JROTC, specifically train students for the military. To counteract this growing trend, Jack Gilroy, an activist, writer, and educator for over thirty years, has proposed the development of public diplomacy schools—schools that would prepare students for a more globalized and international society through the teaching of languages, world culture, interpersonal communication, politics, and diplomacy. The curriculum would be rigorous and grounded in peace studies, international relations, and political science.[38] It seems insane to train students for warfare but not for peace; to have military schools but not diplomacy schools.

While some may view military influence as nonthreatening and even beneficial, there are those in the field of peace studies who see a clear link between such militarization and more localized forms of youth and school violence. This strand of violence prevention research veers away from traditional sociological and psychological orientations and aligns itself with human development, community studies, and even spiritualism, and, in so doing, turns its focus on general values and qualities that have made our society cynical, splintered, materialistic, and overly competitive. Linda Forcey and Ian Harris have remarked in their writing that "Role models who say that they want the world to be a better place have to recognize that the competition inherent in racism, materialism and militarism cannot lead to peace."[39] The values and qualities that need to be reexamined are not the traditional ones made famous by moralists of the 1980s but are those that have supported militarism, competition, materialism, and prejudice.

Certainly, a great many people are negatively affected by warfare, and both military training and the psychological effects of war on children and adults alike have created fresh cadres of aggressive, devastated, and deranged people.[40] So what does this say about the role of the military in schools? Eugene Carroll, a retired Navy Rear Admiral, had this to say about the JROTC:

> JROTC is an abomination. It is just absolutely unconscionable to start teaching thirteen- and fourteen-year-olds about military science, how to handle a gun, that wearing a uniform with an insignia on it makes you an important person, and so on. It is the inculcation of immature people, immature personalities. And that training affects you for the rest of your life. And that's why JROTC is an abomination and unconscionable. It's absolutely immoral. But it's true: they come out with a knowledge of firearms and with some sense of organizational discipline. They can put together a drug gang and arm it and operate it more effectively. I'm not saying the military trains them to do that, but they can apply that training. The whole idea of trying to

teach a child that wearing a uniform and shooting a gun is patriotic—that this makes you a patriot, to kill somebody—is obscene.[41]

The Department of Defense has pursued a goal of doubling the number of JROTC programs in the country. In several public schools in Washington, D.C., it is mandatory to serve for one year in the JROTC. Since the enactment of the National Defense Act of 1916, which established the JROTC, the organization has grown to about 1,200 programs in schools nationwide, and, according to the JROTC commander in Rosemont High, another 200 programs were being developed during the 1999–2000 school year. While viewed as a means to a future by some students, the JROTC was developed by Congress during a time of world tensions. In tune with the militaristic high that World War I produced, combined with the dread that so many could be massacred so efficiently, JROTC was for the military what vocational education programs were for the factories: a means of increasing the ranks.

At Rosemont High, the organization is given administrative recognition with a spot in the trophy case next to sports memorabilia and plaques. Here, a photograph shows JROTC students marching down a main street in the city: it reads, "FIRST CLASS OF JROTC 1995." By 1999, the number of students participating in JROTC at Rosemont High had soared from 25 to 120. In spite of these national and local efforts, many school personnel do not give the JROTC much thought. Outside schools, many people do not know that military training takes place during class time. They do not know about the incessant military recruitment that goes on in schools. One teacher described the military recruiters who regularly came into the school in the following way: "They strut around here like fashion models on the make. They are cool identity types for kids, and they pursue high school juniors and seniors like basketball scouts target star athletes. The problem is the objective is not sports, but war."

With the JROTC and army recruiters, the militarization of school becomes accepted, and supported by a culture that considers force a means of conflict resolution and accepts military training in lieu of education. Another teacher summarized the major points given by many school personnel who saw JROTC as a good disciplinary mechanism and provider of future employment. In an interview, the teacher explained:

> I know a lot of people look at JROTC and think "military," that we shouldn't have the military in the school, the kids walking around in uniform and all that. But it also gives students a structure. Some kids coming into school have absolutely no structure in their lives. They do not know what it means to follow orders, to listen, to obey, to be someplace at a certain time, to respond positively to people. The JROTC gives people some structure. It works with certain students who need that.

The "certain students" referred to are those who are considered low-achievers and are locked in the bottom tracks of schools; they are minority students, mostly male, and usually from poor or working-class families. For these students, JROTC brochures cloak their aims in character development and a paternalistic "civilizing" process that harks back to the forced Americanization of immigrants.

One brochure read:

Cadets will gain:
1. Understanding of the ethics, values and principles that underlie good citizenship.
2. Practical experience in leadership skills with the ability to live and work with others.
3. Ability to think logically and communicate effectively both orally and in writing.
4. Appreciation of the importance of physical fitness in maintaining good health.
5. Knowledge of the dangers of substance abuse as well as techniques for resisting pressures to try drugs.
6. Development of mental management techniques, including goal-setting, visualization and positive self-talk.
7. Familiarity with the history, purpose and structure of the military services.

8. Knowledge of educational and vocational opportunities, and how to make the most of them.
9. Understanding of the importance of high school graduation to a successful future.

Though we may not take issue with attempts to show students the importance of high school graduation and to give knowledge about future opportunities—for what school should not do that?—we may wonder what citizenship means to military trainers or what perspectives will be taught when the purposes of the military are discussed in classes. One researcher found that JROTC curricula tout military successes against Native Americans, present military might as inevitable and desirable, regard war as a technical (not human) endeavor, and caution cadets about "subversives" and the dangers of free speech.[42]

On one side, individuals claim that students need the structure and discipline which a military training can provide. On the other, those of a more critical perspective claim that students are socialized into an abusive military mentality that supports aggression and injustices associated with warfare, jingoism, and violence against women and homosexuals. I suspect the truth is somewhere in the middle. What must be accounted for is the desperation of youths who view the military as their only means to a future. It took a chastisement by a student to make me realize the significance of the military for poor and nonwhite youths. I had met one student in Brandon High who had told me that he planned to join the military and, when I suggested that he consider an alternative career path, he told me in no indirect way that he did not have a chance in college, that he was not interested in college, and that it would be impossible for him to get a job in the rundown city. There was nothing else he could do, he explained, except of course end up like his derelict and lazy friends. In many ways, he was right.

Regardless of what one thinks about JROTC, one must accept that the militarism of education, like the professionalization of education before it, will introduce a system of beliefs and acceptable behaviors into the school. What will be the result of militarizing schools? Is this a new model to replace the factory model, which has long been the most popular paradigm among school leaders? Now, however, will it be that "military strategy"—with its commanders, technology, strategies, and organizational schemes—will replace the old "scientific management" business-way of running schools?[43] In the years to come, will we be saying goodbye to the managers and escorting in the officers?

A Note on School Policing

Beyond the training of students in JROTC, the trend toward militarization includes basic military-like strategies in schools, many of which have been supported if not introduced by zero tolerance policy. The incorporation of school police officers is the most blatant example of this. John Van Maanen, who studied the training of police officers, explained that police training is "traditional quasi-military" in nature.[44] School security forces are in many ways the peacekeeping troops of schools. They make a militaristic response to school violence seem normal, which, along with tracking and expulsion, further distances school staff from the emotional lives of children, since it ends up being the guards, not the teachers, who intervene when students are troubled or in trouble.[45]

While military drilling in the school's courtyard may provide some kind of structure that is missing in students' lives, it also instills military behaviors associated with blind obedience to authority, physical might, and warfare. In a similar way, school policing may at times be a means of informally interacting with students in caring ways—which is true some of the times—but it is also a way of upholding unjust judicial and punitive responses to discipline problems. Moreover, while the military and police may offer hope to youths for employment, like tracking, they target the low-achieving for their work. For the most part, school police officers are friendly, but they also have jobs to do, and, in true military fashion, they have been trained to perform their jobs to the letter of the law. The police officer who banters about sports with a hall wanderer one day will, if necessary, arrest the student the next day for a violation of school policy or of the law.

What makes the militarization of education so natural, and, for some, so appealing, is that it represents the same kind of "get tough" responses to violence that are at the center of zero tolerance. School police officers are the enforcement arm of zero tolerance policy—the step before juvenile court and the step after professionals have determined the student unfit for school. One would hope that JROTC programs, with all their focus on discipline and structure and potential for employment, would channel students away from a route down to criminal court. I have no doubt that it has had this effect in some cases, just as the military has had this impact on thousands of low-income kids during the last century. At the same time that it holds out these opportunities, though, it trains students for warfare and in some cases slaughter—just as it has throughout U.S. history.

The school interests of professionals, business elites, and, now, the military will always be a double-edged sword. The JROTC provides handouts touting its value for employment and structure, but it is also the recruiting arm for the United States military. Such programs as JROTC feed both ends of zero tolerance, providing bodies for enforcement and tracking students with few options to military recruitment stations. It is also a means of incorporating into a student's education the ideals of militarism, including logic that sometimes inverts moral reasoning.

Chapter 7

Where the Kids Are

It is hardly controversial to say that individuals constantly act in a world that is partly structured by beliefs, relationships, hierarchies, organizations, and systems of governance, and that, in everyday activities, individuals take part in determining what that structure will look like. When our activities are philanthropic, caring, and part of a process that is constantly protesting against injustices, we take part in the creation of a culture that is peaceful. Gun manufacturing, the production and consumption of demeaning and violent media, the militarization of education, intolerance, segregation, inequity, oppression—all this and more take part in creating a culture that is violent in ways that are both symbolic and actual.

While a gun does not cause violence, when guns are readily available in a country, violence becomes more lethal. Mass shootings at schools are committed by enraged kids, but they are made possible by mass produced automatic weapons that are designed not just to fire but to spray bullets. In some cases, first-shooter video games add to the fray, for they do not only entertain but also provide a common reference point for how killing should be carried out. While video games and other forms of violent media will not cause violence, they do provide for youths a model for how one should channel rages. When we heap on top of this, everything else, from isolation and inequity to the militarization of education, we create an environment that is almost guaranteed to be violent.

It seems cruel, then, to raise kids to be violent—or at the very least, to accept violence—and then to "zero tolerate" them when they perform as would be expected. U.S. intolerance toward crime, popularized in "get tough" and zero tolerance policy, is a sham. It berates the young, creates injustice, and comes down hard on people who would be as nonviolent as anyone who has grown up in a violence-free and caring environment that offers hope and encouragement.

Violence is an integral part of the United States for a very real reason: It has benefited the country immeasurably. Through the Revolutionary War, the massacre of Native Americans, slavery, and all forms of Western and worldwide expansion, the United States has come to be a great world power. Violence was, and remains, an essential part of this plan; it is how the country achieved and maintains its position economically, politically, and socially. We cannot change interactions that are violent by simply flipping off a switch or providing a violence prevention program, because violence in the United States, even in schools, is wound up with the entire culture and governance of the country.

When guns are manufactured, people, including students, will use them. There is no item in the United States that is mass-produced and not used; we produce items to use them. When we create and support forms of violent and demeaning media, we further entrench sexism and other forms of violence. These forms of media are yet another influence on people, another aspect of the culture that is violent. The military training of students and the establishment of military schools will have the effect of inserting into school pedagogy the beliefs and acceptances of military thinking, including those which Dave Grossman, a veteran who teaches military science, described as training that subverts one's natural inclinations not to kill another person.[1]

To ban the military, violent forms of popular culture, and the production of guns is highly unlikely in the United States, to say the least. To put a stop to further increases in their influence on youths is not. However, this goal can only be achieved by protest. First, individuals must become outraged, tired, and so fearful of what we have become as a nation that we put aside special interests and take some time out of busy lives to take action in ways discussed in this book. It is hardly any use to convince youths in school not to be violent when adults support (and students know this!) violence through our institutions, policies, politics, and mass productions. Banning guns may be impossible at this point in our history but not buying one is not. Doing away with forms of mindless, demeaning, and violent popular culture is unlikely, given the stranglehold the telecommunications industry has on the country. But boycott is not. Only through actions, advocacy, and protest do changes in culture occur.

In an interview, I asked a high school social worker, who worked with students with the most severe behavioral problems, what he felt was the cause of violence among youths in the school. He explained that students often did not have secure family arrangements that showed a lot of caring: "Of all the kids I deal with—over a hundred—maybe two of them have a family that I would say is the kind of family that I had. What's the difference between me and kids who come in here? That's simple . . .what they have in their home." Students who live lives of poverty, family dysfunction, transience, and hopelessness act violently. "They lash out at the world, even against innocent people." The social worker added, as well, that students felt that the world was at its end. "Even things like war, all the murders, all the guns that are out there, they look at the world and say, 'It's screwed up.' That's what they tell me."

Youths enter into the world and see before them the world the generation before them has created. The nihilism and alienation that many youths feel is not something they are born with, and it is not caused by the music that they listen to, as many adults like to think. However, their music, videos, knowledge of violence in the world both domestically and internationally, life circumstances and experiences in school all provide stimuli for their feelings and behavior. Amid this is the culture, the society, which adults have created for youths. In the words of one student I interviewed who had been suspended several times and then finally expelled for fighting: "I don't look forward to anything. I look around me and think, even if I could make it in this world, who would want to?" If youths are alienated—economically, socially—it is because they have been alienated.

With violence prevention, we can tweak the structure without changing the culture. We propose a program, implement a new curriculum, add new police to hallways but often leave intact the beliefs and cultural arrangements that create violence. A society that values peace, and neither tolerates violence in social nor international matters, will be a culture less violent than the society that accepts it. There is nothing truer than the simple fact that violence causes violence. Certainly, all kinds of factors have an influence on a person's behaviors, and there is much in the world, including caring people, supportive environments, everyday friendliness, that can counteract influences that create violent circumstances. Unfortunately, in many areas, we as a society are losing those counterbalances. When families are not there to steer a child through poverty, when examples of peace are drowned out by images of violence and destruction, when society accepts crushing inequities and prejudices, violence—with all its ugliness, sufferings and fears—will become part of our everyday lives.

Where We Go from Here

Daily strategies to deal with violence in communities and schools do not just drop from the sky. They are shaped by policy that is enacted by law and through the money made available to fund violence prevention.

Zero tolerance in schools has its foundation in Section 1031 of Public Law 103–227, the Gun-Free Schools Act. As Title VIII of *Goals 2000*, which President Clinton developed to reflect George Bush's *America 2000*, the act addressed violence with a focus on expulsion and with a goal of developing closer bonds between schools, police departments, and the juvenile justice system. As I noted earlier, it mandated that schools expel students for not less than one year when it was determined that the student had brought a gun to school. Passed by Congress in 1994, along with the Safe Schools Act, the guidelines were summarized by the National School Boards Association:

1. Private schools are not subject to the act.
2. In order to be eligible for Elementary and Secondary Education Act (ESEA) funds, local school districts must have an expulsion policy consistent with the required state law.
3. The one-year expulsion requirement does not allow school districts to waive the due process rights of students.
4. State law must allow the chief administrative officer of each local school district to modify the one-year expulsion requirement on a case-by-case basis.
5. In its application to the state for ESEA funds, each local school district must include in its policy a requirement that students expelled for weapons violations be referred to the criminal justice or the juvenile justice system.
6. The requirement for the case-by-case exception may not be used to avoid overall compliance with the one-year expulsion requirement.
7. The term "weapon" in the federal law does not include knives or common fireworks, though a state law implementing the federal act may use a broader definition of weapon that does include knives. The federal definition of weapon does include guns, bombs, grenades, rockets, and missiles.[2]

The policy uses the withdrawal of funds distributed by the Elementary and Secondary Education Act of 1965, which provides monies for compensatory education and poverty reduction, to force schools into compliance. In short, while the Gun-Free Schools Act did not make available funds in the way other legislation has, as an amendment to the

Elementary and Secondary Education Act, it required that federal funding be withheld from a school in the event that it did not conform to the mandate. While the initial legislation focused only on firearms, states and school districts have added their own requirements, tacking on a variety of offenses that would be dealt with in a zero tolerance fashion. The result has been expulsions and suspensions of students from schools for violations ranging from possession of drug paraphernalia and toy guns to fighting, truancy, and, even over-the-counter medicines.[3] During the 1999–2000 school year Rosemont High and other schools in the district added to their zero tolerance policies not only drug violations but persistent absenteeism.

A fundamental problem with zero tolerance policy is that it does not address the causes of violent and destructive behavior. It dismisses students who may be better served with attention, not segregation. Another outcome of the policy has been a shift in focus regarding school control. While literature about classroom management and inclusion has shown the effectiveness of creating humane school environments, schools in recent years have taken an alternate approach. They have become more rigid and inflexible, coming down hard on students even when their infractions are minor. They do this to benefit from federal funding but also to march in lockstep with national initiatives to get tough on crime and increase the power of police forces. They do this, as well, to show the public that the school is in control, that it is not being "taken over" by unruly kids.[4] The result has been expulsion of mostly nonwhite and poor students, who often return to school with greater anger.

Consider, for example, the description by a young prison inmate, Gabriel, about his high school experiences. I had met Gabriel during a violence prevention workshop in Godwin Prison and interviewed him more formally a month later. I asked each of the inmates I interviewed about their experiences in high school. Gabriel told me in the interview:

> I liked to fool around in school, but I also liked school. But then I fooled around too much and got put in a program for kids who got tutored at this Child Guidance Center or something like that [a city-run program for "at-risk" students]. Like two hours a day, I got tutored, but I hated it. I didn't see my friends, and my parents didn't care. They thought it was great that I had a tutor, even though the tutor would just give me this shit work that I had already, like these exercises on paper. Then when I got back to school, the teachers were like, I hope I learned my lesson. And I did. I learned that they didn't give a crap. I knew the slightest thing I did, I'd be booted. So I was pissed. I mean really pissed. I didn't think schools could do that, and they didn't think I would be bad again, but I was worse. And look where it got me [prison].

I think Gabriel might have been wrong to think the school expected that he would not be "bad" again. Students like Gabriel are targeted by school staff; it is mostly for them that zero tolerance policy was put into effect. In recent years, schools have been organized to facilitate the removal of these students; the zero tolerance policy is in place, surveillance has increased, and police officers stand at the ready. Complaints like Gabriel's were common among students who felt that schools steered them out through discipline policy. We might write off such grievances as overreactions if it were not for teachers and some administrators who also criticized zero tolerance, and in some cases refused to enforce it.[5]

Like national attempts to get tough on crime, the implementation of zero tolerance is not going to reduce school violence; and, if it does, it will only be after turning schools into lockup facilities. With zero tolerance in full force in national as well as school contexts, already we see rising rates of violence in cities such as New York. Not only did crime rates begin to fall in 1991 before the implementation of zero tolerance (which means that zero tolerance had nothing to do with the decreasing crime rates) but zero tolerance proved incapable of keeping the rates down. At the very best, zero tolerance may temporarily exclude from school a kid who is potentially violent, but, inevitably, that student will return and will do so with a vengeance. If he or she does not return to school, or is placed in an alternative program, then the problem persists, albeit becoming somebody else's problem.

This is not a method of violence prevention; it is a method of violence creation. To address violence, one must focus on creating more humane environments, not less. Respect for students and the development of sustained support for their achievements does not mean that we show them pity and give them a hand as we lead them to the door under the red exit sign, sometimes in handcuffs.

In a Harvard University report entitled, *Opportunities Suspended: The Devastating Consequences of Zero Tolerance and School Discipline Policies*, not only do the authors agree that zero tolerance policy has "spun totally out of control," they comment on the schools that have not succumbed to its stranglehold.[6] Schools throughout the country have recognized the debilitating effects of zero tolerance and have turned their attention to effective and humane ways of dealing with violence, misbehavior, and troubled kids. These schools have in common, according to the report, the following characteristics:

1. A shift away from disciplinary practices designed to rid schools of "the problem" toward a more inclusive model that is a schoolwide effort, heavily promoted by the principal and "bought into" by the majority of teachers and staff.
2. Specific strategies are devised for providing students and teachers with opportunities to develop strong bonds. This often means that large schools are broken into smaller units in order to allow personal relationships between teachers and students to flourish.
3. There is frequently a concerted effort to provide teachers with training and workshops focused on positive classroom management techniques and on helping teachers understand the root cause of disruptive behaviors.
4. Discipline is focused on preventing and diffusing potentially disruptive situations before they erupt, and specific, well-understood strategies for addressing crises are in place. In addition, many schools employ a parent coordinator or interventionist. This individual, who is neither a teacher nor a school counselor, is available to the students during the day, often providing a safe haven for students who may "lose their cool." Funds to pay such an individual often come out of Title I or fundraising money.

5. Student sanctions are considered on a case-by-case basis with input from students and parents.
6. Parents, community members, mental health and juvenile justice professionals, business leaders, and others are welcomed into the daily life of the school, and there is a particular emphasis on engaging parents in school activities.
7. Explicit efforts are made to show students that they are respected and valued members of the school community, and that, as such, they are expected to adhere to high behavioral and academic standards.
8. The school implements a wide range of programs, including peer courts, conflict resolution programs, early interventions, mentoring, mediations, and character education programs that promote a mutually respectful and collaborative school climate, and teach students and teachers how to handle and resolve conflict in appropriate ways.
9. Schools frequently transform the physical environment into a more welcoming and friendly space.

Many adults do not understand that young people want the same things that adults want: to be challenged, to feel valued, to have feelings of accomplishment, to get ahead in life, and to sense that people regard them as intelligent and worthy of praise. Zero tolerance does none of these things, and, in many cases, sends the complete opposite message: that students are not wanted, that they are not worthy of schooling, and deserve to be segregated and alienated—that they are *criminal*. While I do understand the frustration and fear that has led to zero tolerance, fear and frustration are not the right principles on which to base a nationwide policy.

If there is one thing that most educators, criminologists, and researchers of school violence can agree upon, it is this: The student who is valued and respected, who recognizes, and actually has, a future that looks bright, and who is academically challenged in school, that student is not ordinarily violent. Certainly, neighborhoods, home lives, and family backgrounds can contribute to the problem. But schools cannot blame families and students' backgrounds for what is lacking in the schools. While the community-level causes of violent behavior are valid, schools, too, are communities, and these communities can either be hotbeds of aggression and unruliness or places where peace and respect is part of everyday events and interactions between people, young and old. In short, peace and respect are created and maintained when students are challenged and supported by adults, and when youths support those adults who are trying to help them. On the other hand, violence becomes endemic to schools when placements, and hence treatments, end up being hierarchical and unfair.

Undoing Zero Tolerance

When a student gets into a fight in a cafeteria, he or she is at fault for fighting. However, when he or she is suspended or expelled from school, that student is hurt by the punitive policy in a way that is not deserved. To criticize a "get tough" policy does not mean that one is excusing the behavior of those who act violently. Violence has sources that exceed the behaviors of youths, and those who create and enforce policy must recognize this fact. As criminologist James Short explained, "Sources of violence, such as residential instability, the concentration of poverty and family disorganization, attenuation of social networks, the decline of 'old heads' that care for the young, and the breakdown of local law enforcement, are all influenced by policy decisions and actions of public officials."[7] Zero tolerance neither urges nor teaches students to act nonviolently; nor does it address the behavioral and structural causes of violence. It is a policy based on fear, frustration, and a notion of violence prevention garnered from a U.S. history that has supported the institutionalization of youths, behaviorism, and all forms of social and political violence.

Zero tolerance policy joins a rising choir of moralists and traditionalists who abhor "soft on crime" politicians and tout the sensibilities of "new disciplinarian" public figures such as John Rosemond, whose syndicated column, which appears in about 150 newspapers, extols the virtues of paternalism and authoritarian rule over young people in the household. It finds company with those who have supported a range of social "wars"—war on drugs, war on immigration, war on welfare. The United States has gone to great lengths to prove that it knows how to get tough on foreigners, the poor, addicts, and young people, and zero tolerance is another step in that direction. It institutes at policy level the continued neglect of young people.

Michael Tonry has written that American social welfare policies, notably Medicare and Social Security, have greatly improved the lives of older Americans, who vote; yet the "story concerning children, who do not vote, is not so encouraging."[8] This applies to crime control policy as well. Young people have little say in the process of how adults attend to their problems. They have little control over how adults view their problems and how they should be treated when their frustrations boil over. Zero tolerance tells kids they are criminal; it treats them like rejects. Meanwhile, students' own understandings about the problems that create violence are sidelined.

There are several injustices here. First, popular understandings about violence and policy aimed at youths often blame the youths themselves for violence, and, if not blaming them directly, see them as the locus of the solution. To change *them* is to solve the problem. Second, laws and school policy penalize mostly poor and nonwhite youths, students whose school days are made nearly intolerable by drudge work and low expectations. These are often students who lack support at home and in school, students whose chaotic and boring home lives are reproduced in self-contained and lower-tracked classes. Third, through all this, middle-upper-class and mainstream society escapes responsibility and even well-deserved blame. Generally, when crime rates go down, adults pat themselves on the back and tout their policies and their efforts. However, when they begin to rise, the same people do not see failure in their policies and efforts; they see failure in young people. For adults, it is a win-win situation; for youths, it is quite the opposite.

One of the unfortunate outcomes of our fixation on crime statistics is the tendency to go into a panic when reports show increases in violence, and then to congratulate ourselves when rates take a dip. After years of rising crime, in the early 1990s violent crime rates began to decrease. Then, in the new century, there has been growing concern about increases in rates of violent crime, especially homicide. The endless panics and the back-patting that accompany these turns are both inappropriate. The more appropriate reaction would be a steady and eternal feeling of disgust to think that the United States, with all its greatness, has become one of the most violent countries in the world by many measures, even when crime rates are at all-time lows.

There is a whole sector of violence that is a direct outcome of circumstances involving U.S. poverty and its associated problems of victimization by prejudice, alienation, blocked opportunities, lack of health care, and multiple forms of abuse. Poverty in the United States is enmeshed with forms of family, street, and school violence and is produced by a society that has accepted severe destitution and segregation, especially in cities and some rural areas where the power of its citizenry is nearly nil. The unbounded wealth that characterized the end of the 20th century has not benefited all and has, in fact, caused greater class stratification. At the same time that newspaper headlines boasted the benefits of the bullmarket and individuals grew rich, the poorer grew more impoverished in the United States. Worldwide, globalized, and highly powerful corporations and their stockholders cannot continue to rake in unimaginable sums of money without a price being paid by those left out of the loop.

In his discussion of the mismanagement and sheer neglect that has been school funding policy in the United States, Bob Peterson, founder of the newsletter *Rethinking Schools*, a teacher, and co-chair of the National Coalition of Education Activists, turned his sights on the Milwaukee school system:

> For a period of time Milwaukee had a progressive mayor, county executive, and school superintendent. But there was little money to do what needed to

be done. A consultant group said it would take $500 million to rebuild the run-down schools in our city and to increase the number of classrooms so class size could be reduced, full-day kindergarten could be provided, and every school would have an art room, music room, and library. Five hundred million seems like a lot—but in fact it's less than the cost of one B-2 bomber, those low-flying offensive jets that military people say are going to be ineffective. And the Congress, which itself is bulging with millionaires, has ordered the construction of 132 such mechanical death birds.

In addition to the B-2 bombers that Peterson speaks of, new "stealth" aircraft, which were developed by the military to fly undetected by radar, have not only proven ineffective but cost the United States about $2 billion to build. That's $2 billion for each ineffective air craft. Peterson made the point that Congress could establish a National School Reconstruction Fund, and, just with the money saved by not building the B2s, could spend $500 million—the amount needed to reform Milwaukee's schools—on the 132 largest cities in the United States.[9]

Certainly, the money collected by a National School Reconstruction Fund (or any initiative that would lead to equity in funding) would need to be used wisely. However, there are enough descriptions of "effective schools" by successful school principles, researchers, and educators to know that the money must be used to create schools with small and heterogenous classes that require nothing less than the best from all students. As Linda Darling-Hammond explained, policy and funding "should foster the development of heterogenous and democratic classrooms that offer students more opportunities to learn about and with one another, about reaching goals in concert with others, and about gaining knowledge from others who are different from themselves."[10] These would-be schools are friendly and caring and support and involve parents and the community in decision-making processes; such schools have high expectations for all students and are never, ever satisfied with a student failing out.

Although a school cannot change the national policies and

movements that have led to severe deindustrialization in cities and downsizing throughout the country, it can prepare students for a world that has drastically changed. Students need to develop a deep, intellectual foundation in academics, physical education, the arts, and technology and engineering. They must become free and critical thinkers, talented speakers, individuals who have skills to learn, take up new challenges, and solve problems. They must know their talents and have developed them; and they must know how to use these talents to persist in a world that can be overly competitive and inequitable.

With these skills, even students from dire circumstances may achieve economic stability in a world that is increasingly technology-driven and lacking in truly full-time and stable jobs. Deborah Meier made the point, in reference to her work in running schools, that it is fine to accept an academic tradition that does not justify itself by its "usefulness," but added: "But we can't then simultaneously insist that all young people spend twelve years devoted almost exclusively to its demands."[11]

Schools have to be worth a student's time. If they are not, students will react as many adults would: They will become frustrated, revengeful, hateful, and, in time, all these feelings may boil over. In spite of multiple reforms, the influx of billions of federal dollars, and the construction of new buildings, too many schools remain remnants of 19th-century warehouses that sorted students for futures based on their sex, life circumstances, race, social class, and perceived abilities. Too many schools are crowded, lack proper windows and ventilation, are uncaring and alienating places, and fail to treat young people with the respect they deserve.

How is it that schools are unable to produce the delight and power that education in the United States should be? There is absolutely no reason why the wonder of learning and experiencing should degenerate into drudgery, neglect, segregation, and violence. Learning should not demean, hurt, or bore students to death. There is no reason why what often begins in elementary school with wonder and joy should end in high school with a rush to "get the hell out" on graduation day or simply dropping out.

One can hardly teach peace when we as a society permit the creation of circumstances that are sources of violence. Poverty, racism, and inequities in schools persist because we allow them to persist. We profit from and support never-ending wars, we remain a supplier of weapons for both domestic and international markets, and we sustain industries that stand by the mantra that "violence sells." Intervention must include youths but address, specifically, economic disparities, prejudice, inequitable school structures and organizational features, unjust hierarchies, and the culture we create at large.

The problem with zero tolerance, ultimately, is that it does not even come close to doing any of these things. It exacerbates the problem through its own forms of hard justice and lashings. In some ways, the United States is incapable of peacefulness. In spite of our best attempts, we have not been able to be the people we say we are.

Notes

Introduction

1. See, for example, Joan McCord, "Placing American Urban Violence in Context," in Joan McCord, ed., *Violence and Childhood in the Inner City* (78–115) (Cambridge: Cambridge University Press, 1997); also, James Fox, *Trends in Juvenile Justice: A Report to the United States Attorney General on Current and Future Rates of Juvenile Offending* (Washington, D.C.: Bureau of Justice Statistics, March 1996); Michael Tonry, "Why Are U.S. Incarceration Rates So High?" *Crime and Delinquency* 45 (1999): 419–37.

2. Boot camp chant cited in Daniel Hallock, *Hell, Healing, and Resistance: Veterans Speak* (Farmington, PA: The Plough Publishing House, 1998), 34.

3. These incidents and the one involving the peanut-throwing on the school bus were described in the Report by the Advancement Project and The Civil Rights Project (2000). *Opportunities Suspended: The Devastating Consequences of Zero Tolerance and School Discipline Policies*. Cambridge, MA: Harvard University.

4. Cited in John Nichols, "The Beat," *The Nation* 270 (January 31, 2000): 8.

5. Mary Pattillo-McCoy makes this point in *Black Picket Fences: Privilege and Peril among the Black Middle Class* (Chicago: University of Chicago Press, 1999).

6. For an overview of qualitative and participatory-action research methods and theories, see Robert Bogdan and Sari Knopp Biklen, *Qualitative Research in Education: An Introduction to Theory and Methods* (New York: Allyn and Bacon, 1998); John Van Maanen, *Tales of the Field: On Writing Ethnography* (Chicago: University of Chicago Press, 1988).

7. Bruce Jacobs, *Dealing Crack: The Social World of Streetcorner Selling* (Boston: Northeastern University Press, 1999), 6.

8. Gaining access to schools can be a frustrating experience for researchers. More than frustrating, though, gaining access to prisons can prove impossible. Virginia, California, and other states ban reporters from routine interviews with inmates.

9. Paula Rabinowitz, *They Must Be Represented: The Politics of Documentary* (London: Verso, 1994), 218.

10. Mike Featherstone, *Undoing Culture: Globalization, Postmodernism and Identity* (London: Sage Publications, 1995), 151.

Chapter 1. The Kid Crackdown

1. Reviews of these large-scale studies can be found in David Anderson, "Curriculum, Culture, and Community: The Challenge of School Violence," in Michael Tonry and Mark H. Moore, eds., *Youth Violence* (317–64) (Chicago: University of Chicago Press, 1998).

2. Public Law 103–382. (1994). *Safe and Drug-Free Schools and Communities Act.* SEC. 4001, 20 USC 7101.

3. Public Law 103–227. (1994). *Safe Schools Act.* SEC. 701, 20 USC 5961. Public Law 103–227. (1994). *Gun-Free Schools Act.* SEC 1031, 20 USC 2701.

4. Public Law 101–647. (1990). *Gun-Free School Zones Act.* SEC 1702, 18 USC 921.

5. Public Law 99–570. (1986). *Drug-Free Schools and Communities Act of 1986,* SEC 4101, 20 USC 4601.

6. Public Law 103–227. (1994). *Gun-Free Schools Act.* SEC 1031, 20 USC 2701.

7. Peter Elikann, *Superpredators: The Demonization of Our Children by the Law* (New York: Plenum Publishing, 1999), 107–14. Elikann discusses the panic that surrounded the brutal killing of Janet Downing in 1995 that led to the passage of a Massachusetts law requiring that juveniles accused of murder be transferred to adult courts and hence adult prisons. For an insider's perspective on the Massachusetts Experiment which led to the controversial reforms in juvenile justice prior to the 1995 revisions, see Jerome Miller, *Last One Over the Wall: The*

Massachusetts Experiment in Closing Reform Schools (Columbus: Ohio State University Press, 1990; 1998). Jerome Miller was head of the juvenile justice system in Massachusetts. A 1995 Connecticut law made automatic the transfer to Superior Court juveniles 14 or older charged with a major felony.

8. Elikann, *Superpredators*, 41. Federal court oversight of prisons began in the 1970s when it was determined that cities and states needed to be forced to maintain humane conditions in prisons. Several states, including Washington, Florida, and Arkansas have ended court supervision of their prison system, which human rights activists believe will lead to greater inhumane treatment of inmates.

9. Michael Tonry, "Why Are U.S. Incarceration Rates So High?" *Crime and Delinquency* 45 (1999): 419–37. The United States is not the only country that treats its inmates poorly. Even democratic countries that pride themselves on their civility, such as France, have been criticized for their inhumane treatment of prison populations. Veronique Vasseur's muckraking book, *Chief Doctor at La Sante Prison*, exposed horrendous prison conditions in Paris. Among other injustices, she noted in her book that nearly half of the country's 55,000 prisoners have never been convicted in courts of law.

10. Prison conditions in the United States have long been horrendous. The settlement in January 2000 for $12 million to victims of the Attica Prison uprising and assault is one recognition of the inhumane treatment of inmates. In 1971, when lawyer Haywood Burns surveyed the result of the assault by state troopers on Attica, which left 32 inmates and 11 corrections officers dead, he reported to Congress that the assault represented a national disgrace that ranked with My Lai. Governor Rockefeller, who ordered the assault, was the originator of the draconian drug laws that started the swelling of prison populations in the United States. In 1995, prison rebellions throughout the nation over mandatory sentences, lack of basic necessities, and abuse by guards, caused over $39 million in damages. Abuses of inmates continue to increase. In March 2000, for example, six teenage boys were removed from a prison run by the largest for-profit prison operator in the world—Wackenhut Corrections Corporation—after it had been discovered that they had been repeatedly brutalized by guards, kept in solitary confinement for months for no reason and deprived of shoes, blankets, education, and medical care.

11. William J. Sabol and James P. Lynch, "Crime Policy Report: Did Getting Tough on Crime Pay? *The Urban Institute Document* (1997): 1–19. One must wonder as well whom we are getting tough on. Most reports on the prison population state that as many as 70 percent of prison inmates are illiterate and that perhaps 200,000 suffer from serious mental illnesses.

12. Michael Tonry, *Malign Neglect: Race, Crime, and Punishment in America* (New

York and Oxford: Oxford University Press, 1995), 24–29.

13. Tom Tyler and Robert Boeckmann, "Three Strikes and You're Out, But Why?" *Law and Society Review* 31 (1997): 237–65. "Get tough" policies have also led to an increase in the use of capital punishment to such alarming levels, and in such irresponsible manners, that even leaders who have traditionally supported capital punishment have called for an end—or at least moratorium—on the death penalty. For example, Governor George Ryan, in February 2000, was the first governor to call for a temporary halt to the death penalty in the state after it had been discovered that innocent individuals had been sentenced to death, that death row inmates had been represented by lawyers who had been disbarred or suspended from practice, and that many death row inmates had been convicted partly on testimony made by jailhouse informants, who are usually considered unreliable sources.

14. Rebecca Jones, "Absolute Zero," *The American School Board Journal* October (1997): 29–31.

15. Tonry, "Incarceration Rates," 432.

16. David Johnson and Roger Johnson, *Reducing School Violence Through Conflict Resolution* (Alexandria, VA: Association for Supervision and Curriculum Development, 1995).

17. See, for example, Vicky Dill and Martin Haberman, "Building a Gentler School," *Educational Leadership* February (1995): 69–71; and Morton Deutsch, "Conflict Resolution and Cooperative Learning in an Alternative High School," *Cooperative Learning* 13 (1993): 2–5.

18. Laurie Stevahn, David Johnson, Roger Johnson, Anne Marie Laginski, Iris O'Coin, "Effects on High School Students of Integrating Conflict Resolution and Peer Mediation Training into an Academic Unit," *Mediation Quarterly* 14 (1996): 21–36.

19. John Devine, *Maximum Security: The Culture of Violence in Inner-City Schools* (Chicago: University of Chicago Press, 1996), 76.

20. Reported in *The Herald*, (Wednesday, September 15, 1999), A4.

21. See Kevin Bushweller, "Guards with Guns," *The American School Board Journal* January (1993): 36.

22. David Tyack and Larry Cuban, *Tinkering Toward Utopia: A Century of Public School*

Reform (Cambridge, MA: Harvard University Press, 1995).

23. Deborah Prothrow-Stith, with Michaele Weissman, *Deadly Consequences: How Violence is Destroying Our Teenage Population and a Plan to Begin Solving the Problem* (New York: HarperCollins, 1991).

24. These figures were cited in James Mercy & Mark Rosenberg, "Preventing Firearm Violence in and Around Schools," in Delbert Elliott, Beatrix Hamburg & Kirk Williams, eds., *Violence in American Schools* (159–87) (Cambridge: Cambridge University Press, 1998), 161–64.

25. Louis Harris and Associates, Inc., *The Metropolitan Life Survey of the American Teacher 1999: Violence in America's Public Schools: Five Years Later*, (New York: Louis Harris and Associates, Inc., 1999), 132.

26. Tonry, *Malign Neglect*, 200.

27. See, for example, Fox Butterfield, "To Rejuvenate Gun Sales, Critics Say, Industry Started Making More Powerful Pistols," *New York Times* (National Report, February 14, 1999), 16. In spite of stark differences between gun proponents and advocates, James Brady, a board member of Handgun Control, Inc., who was White House press secretary in 1981 when he was shot and paralyzed during an assassination attempt on Ronald Reagan, and Wayne LaPierre, executive vice president of the National Rifle Association, joined forces over the passage of Program Exile. Program Exile, which was piloted in Richmond, VA, and now operates in several other states requires that states use federal courts rather than state courts to prosecute gun crimes. It is suspected that the greater supply of federal prisons and stricter federal sentencing guidelines will deter crime.

28. Paul Kingery, Mark Coggeshall, and Aaron Alford, "Weapon Carrying by Youth: Risk Factors and Prevention," *Education and Urban Society* 31 (1999): 309–33.

29. Joseph Sheley and James Wright, *High School Youths, Weapons, and Violence: A National Survey* (Washington, DC: National Institute of Justice, 1998).

30. David Kennedy, Anne Piehl, and Anthony Braga, "Youth Violence in Boston: Gun Markets, Serious Youth Offenders, and a Use-Reduction Strategy," *Law and Contemporary Problems* 59 (1996): 147–96.

31. Valerie Besag, *Bullies and Victims in Schools: A Guide to Understanding and Management* (Milton Keynes and Philadelphia: Open University Press, 1989). This was one of the first books to take seriously the damaging effects of bullying and harassment in schools.

32. Ron Avi Astor, Heather Ann Meyer, and William J. Behre, "Unowned Places and Times: Maps and Interviews about Violence in High Schools," *American Educational Research Journal* 36 (1999): 3–42.

33. Melba Coleman, "Victims of Violence: Helping Kids Cope," in Allan M. Hoffman, ed., *Schools, Violence, and Society* (199–224) (Westport, CT: Praeger, 1996).

34. Besag, *Bullies and Victims in Schools*.

35. Jeffrey Haugaard and Margaret Feerick, "The Influence of Child Abuse and Family Violence on Violence in the Schools," in Allan M. Hoffman, ed., *Schools, Violence, and Society* (79–100) (Westport, CT: Praeger, 1996). One only needs to consider the attention that surrounded the shootings in Columbine High School in 1999, where it was reported that the two students committed the killings partly because they had been perpetually harassed by athletes in the school. They were troubled students, no doubt, whose shift from trouble to violence was caused by a number of circumstances, being teased being one of them.

36. For some examples, see Jean Anyon, *Ghetto Schooling: A Political Economy of Urban Educational Reform* (New York: Teachers College Press, 1997); Allan Block, *I'm Only Bleeding: Education as the Practice of Violence against Children* (New York: Peter Lang, 1997); Juanita Epp, Schools, Complicity, and Sources of Violence. In J.R. Epp and A. M. Watkinson, eds, *Systemic Violence: How Schools Hurt Children* (1–23) (Washington, D.C.: The Falmer Press, 1996).

37. Jeffrey Fagan and Deanna L. Wilkinson, "Social Contexts and Functions of Adolescent Violence," in Delbert S. Elliot, Beatrix A. Hamburg & Kirk Williams, eds., *Violence in American Schools* (55–93) (Cambridge: Cambridge University Press, 1998), 56.

38. Robert Sampson and John Laub take a "life course" approach to understanding delinquency, which focuses on major events and turning points in the life of a person that either leads him or her to delinquency or conventional behavior. Robert Sampson and John Laub, *Crime in the Making: Pathways and Turning Points Through Life* (Cambridge, MA: Harvard University Press, 1993).

Chapter 2. From Child-Saving to Zero Tolerance

1. See, for example, Sibylle Artz, *Sex, Power, and the Violent School Girl* (Toronto: Trifolium Books, 1998); Richard Lawrence, *School Crime and Juvenile Justice* (New York: Oxford University Press, 1998); and John H. Laub and Janet L. Lauritsen,

"The Interdependence of School Violence with Neighborhood and Family Conditions," in Delbert S. Elliot, Beatrix A. Hamburg & Kirk Williams, eds., *Violence in American Schools* (127–158) (Cambridge: Cambridge University Press, 1998). Each of these readings explain in detail different theories of violence, including those with a psychological, sociological, criminal justice, psychoanalytical, and health care, focus.

2. David Johnson & Roger Johnson, *Reducing School Violence through Conflict Resolution* (Alexandria: Association for Supervision and Curriculum Development, 1995).

3. Rational choice theory is sometimes referred to as deterrence theory; the belief being that deviant behavior can be controlled or *deterred* by legal punishments. Jeffrey Fagan and Deanna L. Wilkinson, "Social Contexts and Functions of Adolescent Violence," in Delbert S. Elliot, Beatrix A. Hamburg & Kirk Williams, eds., *Violence in American Schools* (55–93) (Cambridge: Cambridge University Press, 1998), 64.

4. Structural theories of delinquency have a history that date back to at least Frederic Thrasher's *The Gang: A Study of 1,313 Gangs in Chicago* (Chicago: University of Chicago Press, 1927), and Clifford Shaw's, *The Jack-Roller: A Delinquent Boy's Own Story* (Chicago: University of Chicago Press, 1966), originally published in 1930.

5. For an interesting examination of eugenics in connection to photography, see David Green, "Veins of Resemblance: Photography and Eugenics" *The Oxford Art Journal* 7 (1985): 3–16.

6. Interactionist theories are put forth by a number of phenomenonologists and qualitative researchers in the social sciences. See, for example, Bradley Levinson, Douglas Foley, and Dorothy Holland, eds., *The Cultural Production of the Educated Person: Critical Ethnographies of Schooling and Local Practice* (Albany: State University of New York Press, 1996).

7. Elliot, Hamburg, & Williams, *Violence in American Schools,* 64.

8. Vicky Schreiber Dill and Martin Haberman, "Building a Gentler School," *Educational Leadership* February (1995): 69. See also David W. Johnson and Roger T. Johnson, "Why Violence Prevention Programs Don't Work—and What Does," *Educational Leadership* February (1995): 64.

9. Albert Bandura, *Social Learning Theory* (Englewood Cliffs, NJ: Prentice-Hall, Inc., 1977), vii.

10. Joseph Kett, *Rites of Passage: Adolescence in America 1790 to Present* (New York: Basic Books, 1977), 132.

11. Michel Foucault, *Discipline and Punish: The Birth of the Prison* (New York: Vintage, 1977; 1995), 23.

12. Barbara Finkelstein, "Reading, Writing, and the Acquisition of Identity in the United States: 1790–1860," in B. Finkelstein, ed., *Regulated Children/Liberated Children: Education in Psychohistorical Perspective* (114–139) (New York: Psychohistory Press, 1979), 121.

13. Sterling Fishman, "The Double-Vision of Education in the Nineteenth-Century: The Romantic and the Grotesque," in B. Finkelstein, ed., *Regulated Children/Liberated Children: Education in Psychohistorical Perspective* (96–113) (New York: Psychohistory Press, 1979), 102

14. From Wordsworth's poem, *The Prelude*, cited in Judith Plotz, "The Perpetual Messiah: Romanticism, Childhood, and the Paradoxes of Human Development," in B. Finkelstein, ed., *Regulated Children/Liberated Children: Education in Psychohistorical Perspective* (63–95) (New York: Psychohistory Press, 1979), 65–66.

15. Christopher Lasch, *Haven in a Heartless World: The Family Besieged* (New York: Basic Books, 1977), 5.

16. Barry Feld, *Bad Kids: Race and the Transformation of the Juvenile Court* (New York: Oxford University Press, 1999), 49

17. Erving Goffman, *Asylums: Essays on the Social Situation of Mental Patients and Other Inmates* (New York: Doubleday, 1961), 43.

18. Feld, *Race and the Transformation of the Juvenile Court*, 49

19. Nancy Lesko, "Past, Present, and Future Conceptions of Adolescence" *Educational Theory* 46 (1996): 460.

20. Nathaniel J. Pallone and James J. Hennessy, "Tinderbox Criminal Violence: Neurogenic Impuslivity, Risk-Taking, and the Phenomenology of Rational Choice," in R.V. Clarke and M. Felson, eds., *Routine Activity and Rational Choice: Advances in Criminological Theory*, vol. 5 (New Brunswick, NJ: Transaction Publishers, 1993), 128; see also Fagan and Wilkinson, "Social Contexts and Functions of Adolescent Violence."

21. Sol Cohen, "In the Name of the Prevention of Neurosis: The Search for a

Psychoanalytic Pedagogy in Europe: 1905–1938," in B. Finkelstein, ed., *Regulated Children/Liberated Children: Education in Psychohistorical Perspective* (184–219) (New York: Psychohistory Press, 1979).

22. B. F. Skinner, *The Behavior of Organisms: An Experimental Analysis* (New York: Appleton-Century-Crofts, Inc., 1938), 5.

23. Cited in Bandura, *Social Learning Theory*, 203.

24. Patrick McQuillan, *Educational Opportunity in an Urban American High School: A Cultural Analysis* (Albany: SUNY Press, 1998), 84.

25. Jacqueline Jones, "Back to the Future with *The Bell Curve*: Jim Crow, Slavery, and G," in Steven Fraser, ed., *The Bell Curve Wars: Race, Intelligence, and the Future of America* (80–93) (New York: Basic Books, 1995), 80–81.

26. Bandura, *Social Learning Theory*, vii.

27. Bandura, *Social Learning Theory*, 22.

28. Albert Bandura and Richard Walters, *Social Learning and Personality Development* (New York: Holt, Rinehart, and Winston, Inc., 1963), 47; Gladys Reichard, "Social Life," in Franz Boas, ed., *General Anthropology* (409–86) (Boston: Heath, 1938).

29. Douglas Fry, "The Intergenerational Transmission of Disciplinary Practices and Approaches to Conflict," *Human Organization* 52 (1993): 182–83.

30. Albert Bandura and Richard Walters, "Adolescent Aggression: A Study of the Influence of Child-Training Practices and Family Interrelationships," (New York: The Ronald Press, Co., 1959), 355.

31. Bandura, *Adolescent Aggression*, 356.

32. The United States imprisons more people than any other country in the world—about a half a million more than Communist China. California's prison system is 40% bigger than the Federal Bureau of Prisons. The state holds more inmates in its jails and prisons than do France, Great Britain, Germany, Japan, Singapore, and the Netherlands combined. See Eric Schlosser, "The Prison-Industrial Complex," *The Atlantic Monthly* 282 (December 1998): 51–77.

33. Jean Anyon, *Ghetto Schooling: A Political Economy of Urban School Reform* (New York: Teachers College Press, 1997), 81.

34. William Julius Wilson, *When Work Disappears: The World of the New Urban Poor* (New York: Knopf, 1996).

35. Feld, *Bad Kids*, 87.

36. Clifford R. Shaw and Henry D. McKay, *Juvenile Delinquency and Urban Areas* (Chicago: University of Chicago Press, 1942).

37. Robert J. Sampson, "The Embeddedness of Child and Adolescent Development: A Community-Level Perspective on Urban Violence," in Joan McCord, ed., *Violence and Childhood in the Inner City* (31–77) (Cambridge: Cambridge University Press, 1997), 38; See also, Janie V. Ward, "Cultivating a Morality of Care in African American Adolescents: A Culture-Based Model of Violence Prevention" *Harvard Educational Review* 65 (1995): 175–188.

38. Emile Durkheim, *The Division of Labor in Society* (New York: Free Press, 1953).

39. William Julius Wilson, *The Truly Disadvantaged: The Inner City, the Underclass, and Public Policy* (Chicago: University of Chicago Press, 1987). See also, Artz, *Sex, Power, and the Violent School Girl*, 2–5.

40. Joan McCord, "Placing American Urban Violence in Context," in Joan McCord, ed., *Violence and Childhood in the Inner City* (78–115) (Cambridge: Cambridge University Press, 1997).

41. Michael Katz, *The Undeserving Poor: From the War on Poverty to the War on Welfare* (New York: Pantheon Books, 1989).

42. Pharmaceutical companies have gained economic power, as well, since 1997, when the Food and Drug Administration enabled drug manufactures to advertise drugs on television directly to consumers.

43. Spencer De Li's research pointed out that judicial convictions especially at ages fourteen to sixteen had a strong negative effect on status achievement and an overall positive effect on antisocial tendency and delinquency. Spencer De Li, "Social Control, Delinquency, and Youth Status Achievement: A Developmental Approach," *Sociological Perspectives* 42 (1999): 320.

Chapter 3. City Living and Dying

1. Beth Warner, Mark D. Wister, and Amy Krulak, "Risk Factors for School Violence," *Urban Education* 34 (1999): 52–68.

2. Marcel Soriano, Fernando Soriano, and Evelia Jimenez, "School Violence Among Culturally Diverse Populations: Sociocultural and Institutional Considerations," *School Psychology Review* 23 (1994): 216–35.

3. James F. Short, Jr., *Poverty, Ethnicity, and Violent Crime* (Boulder, CO: Westview Press, 1997), 49. In spite of a strong economy in the 1990s, the gap between the poor and rich continues to grow. For example, incomes of the poorest fifth of families in the United States declined in eighteen states between the late 1970s and the late 1990s. In six states, including New York, the decline was very steep: $2,000 per family. While average real income of high-income families grew by 15%, average income remained the same or declined for the lowest-income families and grew by less than two percent for middle-income families. Connecticut and New York were among the top ten states in which income inequality grew the most.

4. Carol Stumbo, "Teachers and Teaching," *Harvard Educational Review* 49 (February 1989): 87–97.

5. Robert J. Sampson, "The Embeddedness of Child and Adolescent Development: A Community-Level Perspective on Urban Violence," in Joan McCord, ed., *Violence and Childhood in the Inner City* (31–77) (Cambridge: Cambridge University Press, 1997), 42.

6. Erin Quillman and David R. Dupper, "School-Based Mentoring Programs for At-Risk Youth," *School Social Work Journal* 22 (1998): 19.

7. Janie V. Ward, "Cultivating a Morality of Care in African American Adolescents: A Culture-Based Model of Violence Prevention" *Harvard Educational Review* 65 (1995): 175–88.

8. For an overview of these initiatives, see J. David Hawkin, David P. Farrington, and Richard F. Catalano, "Reducing Violence Through the Schools," in Delbert S. Elliot, Beatrix A. Hamburg, and Kirk R. Williams, eds., *Violence in American Schools* (188–216) (Cambridge: Cambridge University Press, 1998).

9. Even after decades of "urban renewal," the number of high-poverty neighborhoods—defined as census tracks with 40% poverty or higher—have increased. Paul Jargowsky estimated in 1997 that the number of poor urban

neighborhoods in the United States has more than doubled in the last two decades. In addition, the number of people living in those poor neighborhoods has also doubled. Paul Jargowsky, *Poverty and Place: Ghettos, Barrios, and the American City* (New York: Russell Sage Foundations, 1997).

10. William J. Mackey, Janet Fredericks, and Marcel A. Fredericks, *Urbanism as Delinquency: Compromising the Agenda for Social Change* (Lanham, MD: University Press of America, 1993), 3.

11. Jane Jacobs, *The Death and Life of Great American Cities* (New York: Vintage Books, 1961), 271.

12. Jean Anyon, *Ghetto Schooling: A Political Economy of Urban School Reform* (New York: Teachers College Press, 1997), 167.

13. Cited in Jacobs, *The Death and Life of Great American Cities*, 260.

14. Some have felt that corporate cutbacks were the result of a recession in the late 1980s, and expected that businesses would hire back those who were downsized. However, this was not the case. Even in 1991, one company, Eastman Kodak, that fired thousands of workers which caused a city crisis in Rochester, New York, explained that downsizing was not just the result of a recession. A spokesman for the company explained:"The recession was a lot worse than we thought, and it triggered this round of cutbacks. But if it were just the recession, we would be hiring these people back again. And we aren't going to do that." Cited in Lillian Rubin, *Worlds of Pain: Life in the Working-Class Family* (New York: Basic Books, 1976), xxvii.

15. Anyon, *Ghetto Schooling*, 165.

16. William Julius Wilson, *The Truly Disadvantaged: The Inner City, the Underclass, and Public Policy* (Chicago: University of Chicago Press, 1987). In spite of the booming economy in the 1990s and a low unemployment rate, nearly 30% of workers were employed part-time, as temporary workers, on-call laborers, and other types of nonstandard jobs. It was determined by the Economic Policy Institute in 1997 that such nonstandard workers were paid less, were less likely to receive health insurance or a pension, and had less job security than workers in regular full-time jobs. Low unemployment rates can be misleading when nearly a third of the jobs are insecure and/or do not provide a salary to boost people out of poverty.

17. See, for example, Carol Camp Yeakey and Clifford Bennett, "Race, Schooling, and Class in American Society," *Journal of Negro Education* 59 (1990): 3–18; Jay

MacLeod, *Ain't No Makin' It: Aspirations and Attainment in a Low-Income Neighborhood* (Boulder, CO: Westview Press, 1987); Paul Willis, *Learning to Labor: How Working Class Kids Get Working Class Jobs* (New York: Teachers College Press, 1977).

18. To hire within the city is especially difficult as globalization causes the flight of businesses to not only suburbs but to other countries. This has not only been a problem faced by the northeast of the United States, but in cities throughout the country. Between 1978 and 1982, over 200 Los Angeles-based firms, including Hughes Aircraft, Northrop, and Rockwell, left the city for suburbs such as those in the San Fernando Valley, border towns with Mexico, including Tijuana, Ensenada, and Tecate, and into Mexico itself. The result: "Such capital flight, in conjunction with the plant closings, has essentially closed off to the residents of South Central Los Angeles access to what were formerly well-paying, unionized jobs." Cited in Melvin Oliver, James Johnson, and Walter Farrell, "Anatomy of a Rebellion: A Political-Economic Analysis" (117–41), in Robert Gooding-Williams, ed., Reading Rodney King, Reading Urban Uprising (New York: Routledge, 1993), 122.

19. Cited in Jeannie Oakes, *Keeping Track: How Schools Structure Inequality* (New Haven, CT: Yale University Press, 1985), 30.

20. John Dewey, *Democracy and Education* (New York: The Free Press, 1916; 1966), 200.

21. John Dewey, *The School and Society* (Carbondale: Southern Illinois University Press, 1980), 54.

22. James E. Rosenbaum, Stefanie DeLuca, Shazia Miller, Kevin Roy, "Pathways into Work: Short- and Long-Term Effects of Personal and Institutional Ties," *Sociology of Education* 72 (1999): 179–196.

23. Rosenbaum et al., "Pathways into Work."

24. James Elliot made the point that where informal contacts are nonexistent or lead to low-paying work in ghetto areas, formal contacts and networks are necessary, especially for minority groups. He also concluded from his research that jobs with predominantly white workers are higher paying than those made up of predominately non-white workers, and formal networks were needed to enable minorities to break into these predominately white, higher paying occupations. James Elliot, "Social Isolation and Labor Market Insulation: Network and Neighborhood Effects on Less-Educated Urban Workers," *The Sociological Quarterly* 40 (1999): 199–216.

25. Examples of vocation-oriented schooling with high academic standards do exist. Though it may be unfortunate that the method of education is not a part of a traditional high school, the Aviation High School in Queens, NY, blends rigorous academic and vocational course work to prepare students for work in aviation or higher education. Though more than half of the students in the school qualify for the free or reduced-price lunch program, more than 90% of graduates pass the FAA certification examinations and about 80% of graduates go on to two- and four-year colleges.

26. Richard Arum and Irenee Beattie, "High School Experience and the Risk of Adult Incarceration," *Criminology* 37 (1999): 515–39.

27. Arum and Beattie, "High School Experience," 528.

28. My own father who owned a construction business was fond of complaining that most young individuals applying for jobs he offered did not know the basic math and engineering to do the plumbing required of them. I have heard him say on more than one occasion that when he went to school to learn the trades he had classes in science, machinery (the technology of the day), and especially math. During my summer jobs working with carpenters and plumbers I heard the same complaint. As one foreman was fond of saying: "They can swing a hammer but that's about it."

29. Dewey, *Democracy and Education*, 318.

30. Willis, *Learning to Labor*.

31. Terrie Moffitt, "Adolescence-Limited and Life-Course-Persistent Antisocial Behavior: A Developmental Taxonomy," *Psychological Review* 100 (1993): 674–701.

32. Gerald Grant, *The World We Created at Hamilton High* (Cambridge, MA: Harvard University Press, 1988).

33. Margaret Finders, *Just Girls: Hidden Literacies and Life in Junior High* (New York: Teachers College Press, 1996).

Chapter 4. The Prison Model of Schooling

1. Howard Becker, *Outsiders: Studies in the Sociology of Deviance* (New York: The Free Press, 1963).

2. Sue Books, "Speaking of and Against Youth," in Sue Books, ed., *Invisible Children in Society and its Schools* (183–99) (Mahwah, NJ: Lawrence Erlbaum, 1998).

3. There have long been comparisons between prisons and schools, but the comparison has reached newer levels with more recent forms of security in schools. In one school that I know of, the in-school suspension room is locked and padded and students can be heard screaming and slamming their bodies against the padded walls while they are in suspension. Another school has automatic locking doors: not only do teachers need keys to get into their classrooms, but also to get out. In another school, a red line was drawn down the middle of the hallways, and students were required to walk in single file on the right side of the line. The principal told me that he implemented the plan after hearing that it had been an effective means of crowd control in a nearby prison.

4. Juanita Epp, "Schools, Complicity, and Sources of Violence," in J. Epp and A. M. Watkinson, eds., *Systemic Violence: How Schools Hurt Children* (1–23) (Washington, D.C.: The Falmer Press, 1996).

5. For an overview of the rich array of positive and creative changes that can be made in a school, see Shelley Harwayne, *Going Public: Priorities and Practice at the Manhattan New School* (Portsmouth, NH: Heinemann, 1999).

6. This is the same incident described in the intoduction. Later, I found out that the director of special education did not just want me to do her the favor. The director and social worker did not get along very well, so the director used me as a intermediary. However, more than this, the director wanted me to know about this situation—which she saw as an injustice—and felt that the school would do something about the situation when they found out that an outside researcher had been questioning the "policy."

7. What is sometimes called "retributive violence" can be perceived by the perpetrator as a kind of moral behavior in pursuit of justice—a means of "righting a wrong." See Jeffrey Fagan and Deanna L. Wilkinson, "Social Contexts and Functions of Adolescent Violence," in Delbert S. Elliot, Beatrix A. Hamburg & Kirk Williams, eds., *Violence in American Schools* (55–93) (Cambridge: Cambridge University Press, 1998); also, Laura Moriarty, Patricia Grant and James Hague, "Victims and the Church: Model Approaches to Building Support," in Laura Moriarty and Robert Jerin, eds., *Current Issues in Victimology Research* (153–162) (Durham, NC: Carolina Academic Press, 1998).

8. Young people also lash out violently against injustices in their own neighborhoods, and not just in their schools. An extreme case is the Los Angeles rioting that followed the not-guilty verdict of the police who beat Rodney King. None of the

civil disorders of the 1960s, including the Watts rebellion in 1965, was as extreme as the violence that ensued in 1992 in Los Angeles. Not only did the rioting require the deployment of the full forces of the LAPD and the Los Angeles County Sheriff's Department, but also 10,000 National Guardsmen and 3,500 military personnel. The fire department responded to about 500 fires, 4,000 businesses were destroyed, fifty-two people died and 2,383 people were injured. This is an extreme case of violence which is a result of people lashing out, in the only way they see possible, against grave injustices. See Melvin Oliver, James Johnson, and Walter Farrell, "Anatomy of a Rebellion: A Political-Economic Analysis (117–141)," in Robert Gooding-Williams, ed., Reading Rodney King, Reading Urban Uprising (New York: Routledge, 1993), 118.

9.   The psychologists Linda Camras and Sol Rappaport made the observation in their research that students who are treated poorly not only retaliate in violent manners, but many withdraw, fall into silence, and resist interactions with others. Linda Camras and Sol Rappaport, "Conflict Behaviors of Maltreated and Nonmaltreated Children," *Child Abuse and Neglect* 17 (1993): 455–64.

10. William J. Mackey, Janet Fredericks, and Marcel A. Fredericks, *Urbanism as Delinquency: Compromising the Agenda for Social Change* (Lanham, MD: University Press of America, 1993), 133.

11. Erving Goffman, *Asylums: Essays on the Social Situation of Mental Patients and Other Inmates* (New York: Doubleday, 1961).

12. Criminologist Michael Tonry noted that scholars sometimes differ on how much more involved nonwhites are in crime, but generally the disagreements are about extent, not about the existence of the higher levels. Even in Brandon High, where black and white students were split almost evenly, observations of fights and school reports showed that many more nonwhites fought than white students. Why nonwhite and poor students become violent has a lot to do with social and economic disadvantages. Those social and economic disadvantages are a part of school as well, where students are relegated to poorly funded and inept programs, and sometimes to poorly funded schools. Michael Tonry, *Malign Neglect: Race, Crime, and Punishment in America* (New York: Oxford University Press, 1995).

13. Paul Kivel, *Boys Will Be Men: Raising Our Sons for Courage, Caring and Community* (British Columbia, Canada: New Society Publishers, 1999), 62.

14. Educational researcher Douglas Biklen noted the same kinds of exclusionary practices, and its connection to history, in reference to students with physical disabilities. He wrote, "In the late nineteenth and early twentieth centuries there were states and provinces and school districts in the United States and Canada that

systematically segregated students with disabilities in order to hide them from public view; they were considered abhorrent. Schools have a choice: to perpetuate the disabled-as-unsightly-freak perspective or, as many families have done, to transform their notions of who is acceptable." Douglas Biklen, *Schooling Without Labels: Parents, Educators and Inclusive Education* (Philadelphia: Temple University Press, 1992): 15–16.

15. Patrick Lee, "In Their Own Voices: An Ethnographic Study of Low-Achieving Students within the Context of School Reform," *Urban Education* 34 (1999), 228.

16. More specifically, the Committee of Ten was made up of college presidents and professors, headmasters of private schools, superintendents and representatives of teacher training institutions.

17. G. Stanley Hall, *Adolescence: Its Psychology and Its Relations to Physiology, Anthropology, Sociology, Sex, Crime, Religion and Education*, 2 vols. (New York: D. Appleton, 1905).

18. David Tyack and Larry Cuban, *Tinkering Toward Utopia: A Century of Public School Reform* MA: Harvard University Press, 1995).

19. Jay MacLeod, *Ain't No Makin' It: Aspirations and Attainment in a Low-Income Neighborhood* (Boulder, CO: Westview Press, 1987), 115.

20. Nel Noddings, *The Challenge to Care in Schools: An Alternative Approach to Education* (New York: Teachers College Press, 1992.), 40.

21. Jeannie Oakes, "Two Cities' Tracking and Within-school Segregation," *Teachers College Record* 96 (Summer 1995): 682.

22. Jeannie Oakes, *Keeping Track: How Schools Structure Inequality* (New Haven, CT: Yale University Press, 1985).

23. Jennie Oakes and Amy Stuart Wells, "Detracking for High Student Achievement," *Educational Leadership* (March 1998): 38–41.

24. This point was demonstrated by Michelle Fine, Bernadette Anand, Markie Hancock, Carlton Jordon, and Dana Sherman, in the documentary-like film, *Off Track: Classroom Privilege for All* (New York: Teachers College Press, 1998).

25. Elijah Anderson, *Streetwise: Race, Class, and Change in an Urban Community* (Chicago: University of Chicago Press, 1990).

26. See, for example, Paul Willis, *Learning to Labor: How Working Class Kids Get Working Class Jobs* (New York: Teachers College Press, 1977); Henry Giroux, *Theory and Resistance in Education* (South Hadley, MA: Bergin and Garvey, 1983); Douglas Foley, *Learning Capitalist Culture* (PA: University of Pennsylvania Press, 1990); Michelle Fine, *Framing Dropouts: Notes on the Politics of an Urban Public High School* (Albany: State University of New York Press, 1991).

27. Lee, "In Their Own Voices," 238.

28. This point was made in Gary D. Gottfredson and Denise C. Gottfredson, *Victimization in School* (New York: Plenum Press, 1985); see also Arnold Goldstein, *The Ecology of Aggression* (New York: Plenum Press, 1994).

Chapter 5. Being Disrespected

1. Elijah Anderson, *The Code of the Street: Decency, Violence, and the Moral Life of the Inner City* (New York: W.W. Norton & Co., 1999). See also Anderson's, "Violence and the Inner-City Street Code," in Joan McCord, ed., *Violence and Childhood in the Inner City* (1–30) (Cambridge: Cambridge University Press, 1997).

2. Jackson Toby, "Everyday School Violence: How Disorder Fuels It," *American Educator* Winter (1993): 4–9; See also Howard Pinderhughes, *Race in the Hood: Conflict and Violence Among Urban Youth* (Minneapolis: University of Minnesota Press, 1997), 133; Ervin Staub, "Cultural-Societal Roots of Violence: The Examples of Genocidal Violence and Contemporary Youth Violence in the United States," *American Psychologist* 51 (1996): 117–32.

3. Daniel Perlstein, "Saying the Unsaid: Girl Killing and the Curriculum," Journal of Curriculum and Supervision 14 (1998): 88–104. In 1997, in West Paducah, the three students killed were also girls, shot by Michael Carneal. Even when girls are not the victims of the violence, boys are almost always the perpetrators.

4. Jeffrey Fagan and Deanna L. Wilkinson, "Social Contexts and Functions of Adolescent Violence," in Delbert S. Elliot, Beatrix A. Hamburg & Kirk Williams, eds., *Violence in American Schools* (55–93) (Cambridge: Cambridge University Press, 1998), 80.

5. Cited in Fagan and Wilkinson, "Social Contexts and Functions of Adolescent Violence," 78.

6. John Devine, *Maximum Security: The Culture of Violence in Inner-City Schools* (Chicago: University of Chicago Press, 1996).

7. James Diego Vigil, "Streets and Schools: How Educators Can Help Chicano Marginalized Gang Youth," *Harvard Educational Review* 69 (Fall 1999): 280.

8. Obviously, the focus of the intervention is on boy gang members. However, similar strategies can be used with girls and nongang members.

9. See, for example, Signithia Fordham, *Blacked Out: Dilemmas of Race, Identity, and Success at Capital High* (Chicago: University of Chicago Press, 1996); also Douglas Foley, "The Silent Indian as a Cultural Production," in Bradley Levinson, Douglas Foley, and Dorothy Holland, eds., *The Cultural Production of the Educated Person: Critical Ethnographies of Schooling and Local Practice* (Albany: State University of New York Press, 1996).

10. I make this point in "The Benefits of Peer Mediation in the Context of Urban Conflict and Program Status," *Urban Education* 35 (September 2000): 326–357.

11. Pinderhughes, *Race in the Hood*, 155.

12. Devine, *Maximum Security*.

13. Travis Hirschi, *Causes of Delinquency* (Berkeley: University of California Press, 1969).

14. Michel Foucault made this point in *Discipline and Punish: The Birth of the Prison* (New York: Vintage Books, 1977) in his discussion of the "spectacle" of public torturing and executions. The point of the spectacle, in part, was to demonstrate to all people the power of those in charge to mutilate and torment.

15. Sibylle Artz, *Sex, Power, and the Violent School Girl* (Toronto: Trifolium Books, 1998), 121.

16. Philip W. Jackson, Robert E. Boostrom, and David T. Hansen, *The Moral Life of Schools* (San Francisco: Jossey-Bass Publishers, 1998).

17. Roland Barthes, *The Semiotic Challenge* (Berkeley: The University of California Press). Barthes, the semiotician, wrote (p. 182): "The paradox I want to point out is that objects which always have, in principle, a function, a utility, a purpose, we believe we experience as pure instruments, whereas in reality they carry other things, they are also something else: They function as the vehicle of meaning. In other words, the object effectively serves some purpose, but it also serves to

communicate information."

18. The French sociologist, Pierre Bourdieu, referred to events—various kinds of rituals—as symbols and "instruments of knowledge and communication" which define social orders and hierarchies. He wrote that "symbols...make it possible for there to be a *consensus* on the meaning of the social world, a consensus which contributes fundamentally to the reproduction of the social order." In *Language and Symbolic Power* (Cambridge: Harvard University Press, 1991), 166; for more about the culture of school football, see Douglas Foley, *Learning Capitalist Culture* (Philadelphia: University of Pennsylvania Press, 1990).

19. The teaching of patriotism in school was not only the intent of civics and social studies classes but also the aim of rituals that revolve around the American flag, including the saying of the Pledge of Allegiance and the use of the flag in school marching bands. In order to socialize students to the factory schedule and to maintain order, bells were introduced to schools, which, along with the division of knowledge into subjects and the efficient management of time, prepared 19th century children for industrialized labor. Even the introduction of chalkboards was a significant educational reform, which not only made instruction easier but secured the placement of a "all knowing" teacher at the head of the class. See David Tyack and Larry Cuban, *Tinkering Toward Utopia: A Century of Public School Reform* (Cambridge: Harvard University Press, 1995); also David Tyack, *The One Best System: A History of American Urban Education* (Cambridge: Harvard University Press, 1994).

20. My concern about the use of "moral" in discussions about student behavior and violence arises from some reactions to school shootings. When discussion turns to morality too often a conservative-Christian ethos takes over. Violence is interpreted as a lack of religion on the part of young people, a "relativistic" secular society is blamed, and there erupts, as was the case in the late 1990s, calls to post the Ten Commandments in school lobbies and to incorporate teaching from the Bible.

21. Devine, *Maximum Security*, 164.

22. It should be noted as well that union representatives in schools indicate to teachers that they should avoid involvement in arguments between students—that they should call guards. Meanwhile, guards in Rosemont High complained that teachers called them for trivial reasons. In one class I attended, a teacher called a guard because a student was falling asleep in his class.

23. J. David Hawkins, David P. Farrington, and Richard F. Catalano, "Reducing Violence Through the Schools," in Delbert Elliott, Beatrix Hamburg & Kirk Williams, eds., *Violence in American Schools* (188–216) (Cambridge: Cambridge

University Press, 1998), 194.

24. See, for example, Laura Elisa Perez, "Opposition and the Education of Chicana/os," in Cameron McCarthy & Warren Crichlow, eds; *Race, Identity and Representation in Education* (268–79) (New York: Routledge, 1993).

25. Permanent Commission on the Status of Women, "In Our Backyard: Sexual Harassment in Connecticut's Public High Schools" (1995); see also American Association of University Women Educational Foundation and Louis Harris Associates, *Hostile hallways: The AAUW Survey on Sexual Harassment in America's Schools* (Washington, D.C., 1993).

26. Though laws have been instated to protect heterosexual individuals from harassment, gay and lesbian men and women have found very little national sympathy for the endless harassment that they endure. In 1998 and 1999, State Representative Ed Murray of Seattle introduced a bill that would add lesbian and gay students to a law that forbids sexual and malicious harassment in schools. However, it has been defeated twice mostly by House Republicans. In Orange, CA, a group of gay students wanted to hold weekly lunch-time meetings in an empty classroom but was banned by the board of education. Threatened with a lawsuit charging discrimination since other clubs are allowed to meet in the school, the Orange Unified School District moved forward to ban all 38 extracurricular clubs from convening in the school just to keep the gay students from meeting for lunch.

27. Bernadette T. Muscat, "Sexual Harassment: A New Look at an Old Issue," in Laura J. Moriarty and Robert A. Jerin, *Current Issues in Victimology Research* (195–208) (Durham, NC: Carolina Academic Press, 1998).

28. Domestic violence remains a serious problem and is a leading source of violence in school. However, attention has been given to the problem, and there exists some institutional support for victims of domestic violence. In Rosemont city the Prudence Crandall Center for Women housed and supported battered women. See, for example, Jeffrey Haugaard and Margaret Feerick, "The Influence of Child Abuse and Family Violence on Violence in the Schools," in Allan Hoffman, ed., *Schools, Violence, and Society* (Westport: Praeger, 1996).

29. Nan Stein, "Sexual Harassment in School: The Public Performance of Gendered Violence," *Harvard Educational Review* 65 (1995): 146.

30. Stein, "Sexual Harassment," 149.

31. There is actually little evidence that girls are more violent now than in the past.

Sibylle Artz (see following note) claimed that increased focus on girl violence may not be a result of greater incidents but of greater attention to it, fueled by gender studies and more women doing work in the area of criminology.

32. Sibylle Artz, *Sex, Power, and the Violent School Girl* (Toronto: Trifolium Books, 1998).

33. Gini Sikes, *8 ball chicks: A Year in the Violent World of Girl Gangs* (New York: Dell Publishing Group, Inc., 1997).

34. Paulo Freire, *Pedagogy of the Oppressed* (New York: Continuum, 1970).

35. Artz pointed out that girls who are violent have reported in surveys the highest rates of fear of, and experiences with, physical abuse. Often the perpetrator of violence in families is the father, uncle, boyfriend, or stepfather, and the violence in her case studies was enacted in ways that were physically, emotionally, and sexually abusive.

36. In some ways, Artz adopts an interaction of gendered and cognitive theories of violence to explain girls' behavior. Girls end up repeating what they have learned from their own families: They not only learn abusive behavior but learn to blame those who are victimized. There develops the feeling that people who are victimized deserve the blame. As the victimized girls internalize their own worthlessness and begin to accept that they are the cause of their own victimization they expect others to do the same. The outcome is one where violence is enacted upon another sometimes with the mutual understanding that she who is victimized is the cause of the violence.

37. Artz, *Sex, Power, and the Violent School Girl*, 169.

38. Boys' voyeuristic experience of watching girls fight can have an explicitly sexual component. This is true in schools, and it is the driving force behind the popularity of scantily dressed women tearing at each other's clothes and bodies in professional women wrestling.

39. Jackson Katz, "Reconstructing Masculinity in the Locker Room: The Mentors in Violence Prevention Project," *Harvard Educational Review* 65 (1995): 166.

Chapter 6. Gun Manufacturing, Popular Culture, and Militarism

1. Congressional investigations on television violence began in the 1950s, and in the 1960s media violence was a priority of the Commission on the Causes and Prevention of Violence.

2. See, for example, Mona A. Wright, Garen J. Wintermute, and Frederick Rivara, "Effectiveness of Denial of Handgun Purchase to Persons Believed to Be at High Risk for Firearm Violence," *American Journal of Public Health* 89 (1999): 88–90.

3. Of the 24 countries which experienced at least one major armed conflict in 1997, the United States sold arms or provided military training to 21 of them. With statistics like these, it is difficult to say that the United States is a promoter of peace in the world.

4. This point is made in Dave Grossman, *On Killing: The Psychological Cost of Learning to Kill in War and Society* (New York: Little Brown & Co., 1996).

5. John R. Lott is a proponent of the position that gun control actually increases crime, which he highlights in his provocatively titled book, *More Guns, Less Crime: Understanding Crime and Gun-Control Laws* (Chicago: University of Chicago Press, 1998).

6. Not only are young people inundated with thousands of murders, rapes, and assaults each year on television, but they are bombarded with advertising that encourages the purchase of war toys and weapons. Toy guns alone are a $100 million per year industry in the United States. In the 1990s the War Resisters League in New York City made a campaign against the selling and buying of war toys a top priority. The advertising industry itself is a $233 billion a year business. That is the equivalent of six U.S. federal education budgets. For more about the effects of media on children and an overview of major literature, see Daniel John Derksen and Victor C. Strasburger, "Media and Television Violence: Effects on Violence, Aggression, and Antisocial Behavior in Children," in Allan Hoffman, ed., *Schools, Violence, and Society* (61–78) (Westport, CT: Praeger, 1996).

7. What John Fiske stated about popular culture may apply to gun manufacturing and militarism: "Popular texts are inadequate in themselves—they are never self-sufficient structures of meanings..., they are provokers of meaning and pleasure, they are completed only when taken up by people and inserted into their everyday culture." Certainly people do not just soak up the forms of violence I am discussing in this chapter, but their power to shape behavior should not be underestimated. John Fiske, *Reading the Popular* (Boston: Unwin Hyman, 1989), 6.

8. My position here is a blend of two theories, symbolic interactionism and cognitive learning theory, which make the point that while people are capable of interpreting and even ignoring the messages and symbols of our society, one is not capable of totally acting outside the ways in which we are socialized. We are as much products of society as we are of our own free wills.

9. Eugene Provenzo, *Video Kids: Making Sense of Nintendo* (Cambridge: Harvard University Press, 1991).

10. Joan McCord,"Placing American Urban Violence in Context," in Joan McCord, ed., *Violence and Childhood in the Inner City* (Cambridge: Cambridge University Press, 1997), 87.

11. Between 1994 and 1996, the United States exported $67.3 billion dollars worth of armaments. This is 55% of global arms exports and is quadruple the share of its closest competitor.

12. While U.S. homicide rates are among the highest in the world, too often the focus on homicide shifts attention away from the equally dire problem of suicide. During most years, the number of suicides involving a handgun exceeds that of homicide. Each year there are about 18,000 suicides involving firearms, a few thousand more than homicides.

13. Franklin Zimring, "Firearms, Violence, and Public Policy," *Scientific American*, November (1991): 48–54.

14. Franklin Zimring, "Kids, Guns, and Homicide: Policy Notes on an Age-Specific Epidemic," *Law and Contemporary Problems* 59 (1996): 25–37.

15. Diana Zuckerman, "Media Violence, Gun Control, and Public Policy," *American Journal of Orthopsychiatry* 66 (1996): 383.

16. There exists research that shows no correlation between gun-control policy and decreased levels of violence. However, there are often faults with this research, which has been pointed out by Zuckerman (see previous note) and other researchers and writers on the topic. For example, some well known studies, which the NRA like to tout, showed that gun control laws of the 1980s did not reduce violence. However, the focus on state laws neglects to account for how easily guns from states where laws are lax enter states where there is some degree of gun-control policy. For example, many Washington, D.C., homicides are carried out with guns traced to Virginia where there are few restrictions on gun purchases. Also, laws are essentially weak, therefore it is quite possible that gun-control policy will not be effective given the huge loopholes that exist in the laws.

17. Mona Wright, Garen Wintemute, and Frederick Rivara, "Effectiveness of Denial of Handgun Purchase to Persons Believed to Be at High Risk of Firearm Violence," *American Journal of Public Health* 89 (1999): 88–90.

18. Reported in Zuckerman, "Media Violence," 386.

19. When the District of Columbia filed a lawsuit against 23 major gun manufacturers and two distributors in January 2000, it became the 30th local or county government to sue the industry. The district sought reimbursement of medical and other costs associated with shootings and also changes in gun distribution practices which would prevent guns from states where laws are lax from entering the district. Meanwhile the NRA had been largely successful working at local levels to persuade a number of other cities after Atlanta to pass legislation to prohibit law suits against gun manufacturers.

20. Michael Firestone, "Gun Lobby Begins a Concerted Attack on Cities' Lawsuits." *New York Times* (February 9, 1999), A13.

21. George Will, "Having Failed at Persuasion, Gun Opponents Try Litigation." *Washington Post* (January 24, 1999), A25.

22. Fox Butterfield, "To Rejuvenate Gun Sales, Critics Say, Industry Started Making More Powerful Pistols," *New York Times* (February 14, 1999), 16.

23. Michael Tonry, *Malign Neglect: Race, Crime, and Punishment in America* (New York: Oxford University Press, 1995), 201.

24. The privatization of prisons has been a boom business, especially for Capital Corrections Resources, a business which operates prisons in Texas. The violence and abuses that exist in federal and state prisons are as rampant in privately owned prisons. In Texas, guards were caught on videotape kicking and beating inmates at a prison owned by Capital Corrections Resources, which led to a lawsuit, which the inmates won. Missouri, which sent inmates to Texas, agreed to a five-year moratorium on sending prisoners to Texas or any prisons run by the company.

25. Peter Elikann, *Superpredators: The Demonization of Our Children by the Law* (New York: Plenum Publishing, 1999), 53.

26. This was an oft-cited conclusion of the most tragic school shooting to date in Littleton, Colorado. The two students who carried out the slaughter were avid players of *Doom* and *Quake*, two very violent video games, and were acting as if they were playing a video game as they shot down their school mates.

27. Daniel John Derksen and Victor C. Strasburger, "Media and Television Violence: Effects on Violence, Aggression, and Antisocial Behaviors on Children," in Allan M. Hoffman, ed., *Schools, Violence, and Society* (61–78) (Westport, CT: Praeger, 1996), 62.

28. Gini Sikes, *8 Ball Chicks: A Year in the Violent World of Girl Gangs* (New York: Dell Publishing Group, Inc., 1997), 99–100.

29. The V-chip is inexpensive micro-circuitry developed in the United States and Canada that enable television owners to block certain categories of television programming (based on a rating scheme by networks) on particular televisions. Some call the technology "C-chips," in reference to "choice" rather than "violence," which is a softer way of alluding to the censorship technology.

30. Scott Decker and Barrik Van Winkle, *Life in the Gang: Family, Friends, and Violence* (New York: Cambridge University Press, 1996), 88.

31. Margaret Reith, "Viewing of Crime Drama and Authoritarian Aggression: An Investigation of the Relationship Between Crime Viewing, Fear and Aggression," *Journal of Broadcasting and Electronic Media* 43 (1999): 211–21.

32. While in 1970 the Commission of Obscenity and Pornography found no evidence that pornography increases male aggression toward females other research has shown that when the media are sexually violent then such materials increases acceptance of sexual coercion and aggression. The effects of such media on youths (and adults) continues to be debated. In the 1980s, the Attorney General's Commission on Pornography, appointed by Edwin Meese, found that sexually violent pornography increased aggression. Meanwhile, the Workshop on Pornography and Public Health, organized by Surgeon General C. Everett Koop, found that adverse effects were revealed only when sexual aggression in the media was portrayed as pleasurable to the victim. Both commissions analyzed the same literature and came to two distinct conclusions. See Janet St. Lawrence and Doris Joyner, "The Effects of Sexually Violent Rock Music on Males' Acceptance of Violence Against Women," *Psychology of Women Quarterly* 15 (1991): 49–63.

33. Cameron McCarthy, Alicia P. Rodriguez, Ed Buendia, Shuaib Meacham, Stephen David, Heriberto Godina, K. E. Supriya, and Carrie Wilson-Brown, "Danger in the Safety Zone: Notes on Race, Resentment, and the Discourse of Crime, Violence, and Suburban Security," *Cultural Studies* 11 (1997): 275.

34. See Douglas M. McLeod, William Eveland, and Amy Nathanson, "Support for Censorship of Violent and Misogynic Rap Lyrics," *Communication Research* 24 (1997): 153–174.

35. The video-gaming of the United States has even shaped presentations of war since the first digitalized presentations of modern warfare that were the staples of CNN programming during the Gulf War.

36. Howard Zinn, *Declarations of Independence* (New York: HarperCollins, 1990).

37. Barbara Ehrenreich, *Blood Rites: Origins and History of the Passions of War* (New York: Henry Holt and Company, Inc., 1997).

38. See the article by Jack Gilroy in the *National Catholic Reporter*, "Time for Academics to Teach U.S. Youth to Wage Peace," November 12, 1999.

39. Linda Rennie Forcey and Ian Harris, *Peacebuilding for Adolescents: Strategies for Educators and Community Leaders* (New York: Peter Lang, 1999), 24.

40. Lewis A. Leavitt and Nathan A. Fox, *The Psychological Effects of War and Violence on Children* (Mahwah, NJ: Lawrence Erlbaum, 1993).

41. Eugene Carroll interview cited in Daniel Hallock, *Hell, Healing, and Resistance: Veterans Speak* (Farmington, PA: The Plough Publishing House, 1998), 25.

42. Cited in Hallock, *Hell, Healing, and Resistance*, 22.

43. Books on education by military leaders are a staple during times when politicians and the public recognize and declare a "crisis in education." After the launching of Sputnik in 1957 books such as *American Education—A National Failure* by Admiral H.G. Rickover were common. In more current times—faced again with a national crisis in education—books by such people as Major General John Stanford, who wrote *Victory in Our Schools* (New York: Bantam Books, 1999) after becoming superintendent of Seattle Public Schools, are endorsed by educators, generals, and CEOs.

44. John Van Maanen, "Observations on the Making of Policemen," *Human Organization* 32 (1973): 407–18.

45. But the flip side of this is that, like the military, police officers in school, including DARE teachers, were signs of future employment for students; in addition, they were often people who were sympathetic to students. At Brandon High, the school DARE officer was not only teacher, but a resource person for advice and information about child custody laws, judicial systems, parole, and other issues students wanted, and in some cases needed, to know about. He also provided information about police training and what the police academy was like. At Rosemont High, the black police officer, who had lived all his life in the city and

was a volunteer coach and PAL instructor, seemed to be one of the few adults in the school who interacted with students in the hallways and cafeteria in informal, friendly, and respectful ways. He knew students' names, knew handshakes, and bantered about music, social events, and sports.

Chapter 7. Where the Kids Are

1. Dave Grossman made the point that even in "good wars" a majority of soldiers do not fire their guns directly at the enemy. Citing one survey, as many as 85% of World War II soldiers did not fire directly at the enemy, but shot over their heads or refused to shoot at all, in *On Killing: The Psychological Cost of Learning to Kill in War and Society* (New York: Little, Brown and Company).

2. Chris Pipho, "Living with Zero Tolerance," *Phi Delta Kappan* (June 1998): 725.

3. Rebecca Jones, "Absolute Zero," *The American School Board Journal* 10 (October 1997): 29–31. See also Perry A. Zirkel and Ivan B. Gluckman, "Due Process in Student Suspensions and Expulsions," *Principal* 76 (March 1997): 62–63; Marlene Lozada, "Ground Zero," *Techniques* 73 (March 1998): 37–41.

4. Pedro A. Noguera, "Preventing and Producing Violence: A Critical Analysis of Responses to School Violence," *Harvard Educational Review* 65 (1995): 190.

5. In the Report on State Implementation of the Gun-Free Schools Act, issued in August 1999 by the U.S. Department of Education, it was reported that during the 1997–98 school year 3,399 students were expelled under zero tolerance policy. However, of that number, 1,485 (44%) had sentences shortened to less than one year, suggesting that a significant number of administrators as well may feel that the policy is too harsh.

6. Report by the Advancement Project and The Civil Rights Project. *Opportunities Suspended: The Devastating Consequences of Zero Tolerance and School Discipline Policies* (Cambridge, MA: Harvard University, 2000).

7. James Short, *Poverty, Ethnicity and Violent Crime* (Boulder, CO: Westview, 1997), 201

8. Michael Tonry, *Malign Neglect: Race, Crime, and Punishment in America* (New York: Oxford University Press, 1995), 13.

9. Bob Peterson, "The Struggle for Decent Schools," in William Ayers and Patricia

Ford, *City Kids, City Teachers: Reports from the Front Row* (152–169) (New York: The New Press, 1996), 155.

10. Linda Darling-Hammond, *The Right to Learn: A Blueprint for Creating Schools That Work* (San Francisco: Jossey-Bass Publishers, 1997), 335.

11. Deborah Meier, *The Power of Their Ideas: Lessons for America from a Small School in Harlem* (Boston: Beacon Press, 1995), 168.

Bibliography

Agnew, R. (2000). Strain theory and school crime. In S. Simpson, ed., *Of crime and criminality: The use of theory in everyday life* (159–178). Thousand Oaks, CA: Pine Forge Press.

American Association of University Women Educational Foundation and Louis Harris Associates. (1993). *Hostile hallways: The AAUW survey on sexual harassment in America's schools*. Louis Harris Associates: Washington, D.C..

Anderson, D. (1998). Curriculum, culture, and community: The challenge of school violence. In M.. Tonry and M Moore, eds., *Youth Violence* (317–64). Chicago: University of Chicago Press.

Anderson, E. (1999). *Code of the street: Decency, violence, and the moral life of the inner city*. New York: W.W. Norton.

Anderson, E. (1997). Violence and the inner-city street code. In J. McCord, ed., *Violence and childhood in the inner city* (pp.1–30). New York: Cambridge University Press.

Anderson, E. (1990). *Streetwise: Race, class, and change in an urban community*. Chicago: University of Chicago Press.

Anyon, J. (1997). *Ghetto schooling: A political economy of urban educational reform*. New York: Teachers College Press.

Artz, S. (1998). *Sex, power, and the violent school girl*. Toronto: Trifolium Books.

Arum, R. & Beattie, I. (1999). High school experience and the risk of adult incarceration. *Criminology*, 37, 515–39.

Astor, R., Meyer, H., & Behre, W. (1999). Unown places and times: Maps and interviews about violence in high schools. *American Educational Research Journal*, 36, 3–42

Athens, L. (1997). *Violent criminal acts and actors revisited*. Urbana and Chicago: University of Illinois Press.

Bandura, A. (1977). *Social learning theory*. Englewood Cliffs, NJ: Prentice-Hall, Inc..

Bandura, A. & Walters, R. (1963). *Social learning and personality development*. NY: Holt, Rinehart, and Winston.

Bandura, A. & Walters, R. (1959). *Adolescent aggression: A study of the influence of child-training practices and family interrelationships*. New York: The Ronald Press.

Becker, H. (1963). *Outsiders: Studies in the sociology of deviance*. New York: The Free Press.

Besag, V. (1989). *Bullies and victims in schools: A guide to understanding and management*. Milton Keynes: Open University Press.

Best, J. (1990). *Threatened children: Rhetoric and concern about child-victims*. Chicago: University of Chicago Press.

Biklen, D. (1992). *Schooling without labels: Parents, educators and inclusive education*. Philadelphia: Temple University Press.

Blair, F. (1999). Does zero tolerance work? *Principal*, 79, 36–37.

Block, A. (1997). *I'm only bleeding: Education as the practice of violence against children*. New York: Peter Lang Publishing.

Bogdan, R. & Biklen, S. K. (1998). *Qualitative research in education: An introduction to theory and practice* (3rd ed.). Boston: Allyn and Bacon.

Books, S. (1998). Speaking of and against youth. In S. Books, ed., *Invisible children in society and its schools* (183–99). Mahwah, NJ: Lawrence Erlbaum.

Bouffard, J., Exum, L., & Paternoster, R. (2000). Whither the beast? The role of emotions in a rational choice theory of crime. In S. Simpson, ed., *Of crime and criminality: The use of theory in everyday life* (159–178). Thousand Oaks, CA: Pine Forge Press.

Bourdieu, P. (1991). *Language and symbolic power*. Cambridge, MA: Harvard University Press.

Burstyn, J., Bender, G., Casella, R., Gordon, H., Guerra, D., Luschen, K., Stevens, R., & Williams, K. (2001). *Preventing violence in school: A challenge to American democracy*. Mahwah, NJ: Lawrence Erlbaum.

Bushweller, K. (1993). Guards with guns. *The American School Board Journal*, January, 180, 34–37.

Camras, L., & Rappaport, S. (1993). Conflict behaviors of maltreated and nonmaltreated children. *Child abuse and neglect*, 17, 455–64.

Casella, R. (2000). The benefits of peer mediation in the context of urban conflict and program status. *Urban Education*, 35, 326–357.

Casella, R. (1999). What are we doing when we are 'doing' cultural studies in education—and why? *Educational Theory*, 49, 107–123.

Cloward, R., & Ohlin, L. (1960). *Delinquency and opportunity: A theory of delinquent gangs*. New York: The Free Press.

Cohen, S. (1979). In the name of the prevention of neurosis: The search for a psychoanalytic pedagogy in Europe: 1905–1938. In B. Finkelstein, ed., *Regulated children/Liberated children: Education in psychohistorical perspective* (184–219). NY: Psychohistory Press.

Coleman, M. (1996). Victims of violence: Helping kids cope. In A. Hoffman, ed., *Schools, Violence, and Society* (199–224). Westport: Praeger.

Curwin, R., & Mendler, A. (1999). Zero tolerance for zero tolerance. *Phi Delta Kappan*, 81, 119–120.

Darling-Hammond, L. (1997). *The right to learn: A blueprint for creating schools that work*. San Francisco, CA: Jossey-Bass Publishers.

De Li, S. (1999). Social control, delinquency, and youth status achievement: A developmental approach. *Sociological Perspectives*, 42, 305–324.

Decker, S., & Van Winkle, B. (1996). *Life in the gang: Family, Friends, and violence*. New York: Cambridge University Press.

Derksen, D., & Strasburger, V. (1996). Media and television violence: Effects on violence, aggression, and antisocial behavior in children. In A. Hoffman, ed., *Schools, Violence, and Society* (61–78). Westport: Praeger.

Deutsch, M. (1993). Conflict resolution and cooperative learning in an alternative high school. *Cooperative Learning*, 13, 2–5.

Devine, J. (1996). *Maximum security: The culture of violence in inner-city schools*. Chicago: University of Chicago Press.

Dewey, J. (1980). *The school and society*. Carbondale: Southern Illinois University Press.

Dewey, J. (1916). *Democracy and education*. New York: The Free Press.

Dill, V., & Haberman, M. (1995). Building a gentler school. *Educational Leadership*, February, 69–71.

Durkheim, E. (1953). *The division of labor*. New York: The Free Press.

Economic Policy Institute. (2000). State income inequality continued to grow in most states in the 1990s. Center on Budget and Policy Priorities. Washington, D.C.: Author.

Ehrenreich, B. (1997). *Blood rites: Origins and history of the passions of war*. New York: Henry Holt & Co., Inc..

Elikann, P. (1999). *Superpredators: The demonization of our children by the law*. New York: Plenum Publishing.

Elliott, J. (1999). Social isolation and labor market insulation: Network and neighborhood effects on less-educated urban workers. *The Sociological Quarterly*, 40, 199–216.

Epp, J.R. (1996). Schools, complicity, and sources of violence. In J.R. Epp & A.M. Watkinson, eds., *Systemic violence: How schools hurt children* (pp. 1–23). Washington, D.C.: The Falmer Press.

Fagan, J., & Wilkinson, D. (1998). Social contexts and functions of adolescent violence. In D. Elliot, B. Hamburg, & K.Williams, eds., *Violence in American Schools* (55–93). Cambridge: Cambridge University Press.

Featherstone, M. (1995). *Undoing culture: globalization, post-modernism and identity*. London: Sage Publications.

Feld, B. (1999). *Bad kids: Race and the transformation of the juvenile court*. Oxford: Oxford University Press.

Finders, M. (1996). *Just girls: Hidden literacies and life in junior high*. New York: Teachers College Press.

Fine, M. (1991). *Framing dropouts: Notes on the politics of an urban public high school*. Albany: University of New York Press.

Finkelstein, B. (1979). Reading, writing, and the acquisition of identity in the United States: 1790–1860. In B. Finkelstein, ed., *Regulated children/liberated children: Education in psychohistorical perspective* (114–139). New York: Psychohistory Press.

Fishman, S. (1979). The double-vision of education in the nineteenth-century: The romantic and the grotesque. In B. Finkelstein, ed., *Regulated children/liberated children: Education in psychohistorical perspective* (96–113). New York: Psychohistory Press.

Fiske, J. (1989). *Reading the popular*. Boston: Unwin Hyman.

Foley, D. (1990). *Learning capitalist culture*. Philadelphia: University of Pennsylvania Press.

Forcey, L. R., & Harris, I. (1999). *Peacebuilding for adolescents: Strategies for educators and community leaders*. New York: Peter Lang Publishing.

Fordham, S. (1996). *Blacked out: Dilemmas of race, identity, and success at Capital High*. Chicago: University of Chicago Press.

Foucault, M. (1975; 1995). *Discipline and punish: The birth of the prison*. New York: Vintage Books.

Foucault, M. (1980). *Power/knowledge: Selected interviews and other writings*. New York: Pantheon Books.

Fox, J. (1996). *Trends in juvenile justice: A report to the United States Attorney General on current and future rates of juvenile offending*. Washington, D.C.: Bureau of Justice Statistics.

Fox, K. (1999). Reproducing criminal types: Cognitive treatment for violent offenders in prison. *The Sociological Quarterly*, 40, 435–453.

Freire, P. (1970). *Pedagogy of the oppressed*. New York: Continuum.

Fry, D. (1993). The intergenerational transmission of disciplinary practices and approaches to conflict. *Human Organization*, 52, 176–185.

Gluckman, I. (1996). Legal and policy issues of school violence. In A. Hoffman, *Schools, Violence and Society* (79–100). Westport: Praeger.

Goffman, E. (1963). *Stigma: Notes on the management of spoiled identity*. New York: Simon and Schuster.

Goldstein, A. (1994). *The ecology of aggression*. New York: Plenum Press.

Gottfredson, G., & Gottfredson, D. (1985). *Victimization in School*. New York: Plenum Press.

Grant, G. (1988). *The world we created at Hamilton High*. Cambridge, MA: Harvard University Press.

Green, D. (1985). Veins of resemblance: Photography and eugenics. *The Oxford Art Journal*, 7, 3–16.

Grossman, D. (1996). *On killing: The psychological cost of learning to kill in war and society*. New York: Little Brown & Co..

Hall, G. S. (1905). *Adolescence: Its psychology and its relations to physiology, anthropology, sociology, sex, crime, religion, and education*, (2 vols.). New York: D. Appleton.

Hallock, D. (1998). *Hell, healing, and resistance*. Farmington, PA: The Plough Publishing House.

Harwayne, S. (1999). *Going public: Priorities and practice at the Manhattan New School*. Portsmouth, NH: Heinemann.

Haugaard, J., & Feerick, M. (1996). The influence of child abuse and family violence on violence in the schools. In A. Hoffman, ed., *Schools, violence, and society* (79–100). Westport: Praeger.

Hawkin, D., Farrington, D., & Catalano, R. (1998). Reducing violence through the schools. In D. Elliot, B. Hamburg, & K.Williams, eds., *Violence in American Schools* (188–216). Cambridge: Cambridge University Press.

Hirschi, T. (1969). *Causes of delinquency*. Berkeley: University of California Press.

Hudson, K. (1999). No shortage of nonstandard jobs. Washington, D.C.: Economic Policy Institute, Briefing Paper.

Jackson, P., Boostrom, R., & Hansen, D. (1998). *The moral life of schools*. San Francisco: Jossey-Bass Publishers.

Jacobs, B. (1999). *Dealing crack: The social world of streetcorner selling*. Boston: Northeastern University Press.

Jacobs, J. (1961). *The death and life of great American cities*. New York: Vintage Books.

Jargowsky, P. (1997). *Poverty and place: Ghettos, barrios, and the American city*. New York: Russell Sage Foundation.

Johnson, D., & Johnson, R. (1995). *Reducing school violence through conflict resolution*. Alexandria, VA: Association for Supervision and Curriculum.

Jones, J. (1995). Back to the future with *The Bell Curve*: Jim Crow, slavery, and *G*. In S. Fraser, ed., *The bell curve wars: Race, intelligence, and the future of America*. New York: Basic Books.

Jones, R. (1997). Absolute zero. *The American School Board Journal*, 10, 29–31.

Katz, J. (1995). Reconstructing masculinity in the locker room: The mentors in violence prevention project. *Harvard Educational Review*, 65, 163–188.

Katz, M. (1995). *Improving poor people: The welfare state, the underclass, and urban schools as history*. Princeton: Princeton University Press.

Katz, M. (1989). *The undeserving poor: From the war on poverty to the war on welfare*. New York: Pantheon Books.

Kennedy, D., Piehl, A., & Braga, A. (1996). Youth violence in Boston: Gun markets, serious youth offenders, and a use-reduction strategy. *Law and Contemporary Problems*, 59, 147–196.

Kett, J. (1977). *Rites of passage: Adolescence in America 1790 to present*. New York: Basic Books.

Kingery, P., Coggeshall, M., & Alford, A. (1999). Weapon carrying by youth: Risk factors and prevention. *Education and Urban Society*, 31, 309–333.

Kivel, P. (1999). *Boys will be men: Raising our sons for courage, caring and community*. British Columbia, Canada: New Society Publishers.

Lasch, C. (1977). *Haven in a heartless world: The family besieged*. New York: Basic Books.

Laub, J., & Lauritsen, J. (1998). The interdependence of school violence with neighborhood and family conditions. In D. Elliot, B. Hamburg, & K. Williams, eds., *Violence in American Schools* (127–158). Cambridge: Cambridge University Press.

Lawrence, J., & Joyner, D. (1991). The effects of sexually violent rock music on males' acceptance of violence against women. *Psychology of Women Quarterly*, 15, 49–63.

Lawrence, R. (1998). *School crime and juvenile justice*. New York and Oxford: Oxford University Press.

Leavitt, L., & Fox, N. (1993). *The psychological effects of war and violence on children*. Mahwah, NJ: Lawrence Erlbaum.

Lee, P. (1999). In their own voices: An ethnographic study of low-achieving students within the context of school reform. *Urban Education*, 34, 214–244.

Lesko, N. (1996). Past, present, and future conceptions of adolescence. *Educational Theory*, 46, 453–472.

Levinson, B., Foley, D., & Holland, D. (1996). *The cultural production of the educated person: Critical ethnographies of schooling and local practice*. Albany: State University of New York Press.

Lozada, M. (1998). Ground zero. *Techniques*, 73, 37–41.

Mackey, W., Fredericks, J., & Fredericks, M. (1993). *Urbanism as delinquency: Compromising the agenda for social change*. Lanham, MD: University Press of America.

MacLeod, J. (1987). *Ain't no makin' it: Aspirations and attainment in a low-income neighborhood*. Boulder: Westview Press.

Mariarty, L., Grant, P., & Hague, J. (1998). Victims and the church: Model approaches to building support. In L. Moriarty & R. Jerin, eds., *Current issues in victimology research* (153–162). Durham, NC: Carolina Academic Press.

McCarthy, C., Rodriguez, A., Buendia, E., Meacham, S., David, S., Godina, H., Supriya, G., & Wilson-Brown, C. (1997). Danger in the safety zone: Notes on race, resentment, and the discourse of crime, violence, and suburban security. *Cultural Studies*, 1997, 274–95.

McCord, J. (1997). Placing American urban violence in context. In J. McCord, ed., *Violence and childhood in the inner city* (78–115). New York: Cambridge University Press.

McQuillan, P. (1998). *Educational opportunity in an urban American high school: A cultural analysis*. Albany: State University of New York Press.

Meier, D. (1995). *The power of their ideas: Lessons for America from a small school in Harlem*. Boston: Beacon Press.

Miller, J. (1998). *Last one over the wall: The Massachusetts Experiment in closing reform schools*. Columbus: Ohio State University Press.

Moffitt, T. (1993). Adolescence-limited and life-course-persistent antisocial behavior: A developmental taxonomy. *Psychological Review*, 100, 674–701.

Muscat, B. (1998). Sexual harassment: A new look at an old issue. In L. Moriarty & R. Jerin, eds., *Current issues in victimology research* (195–208). Durham, NC: Carolina Academic Press.

National Center for Education Statistics. (1998). *Indicators of School Crime and Safety*. Washington D.C.: U.S. Department of Education.

Noddings, N. (1992). *The challenge to care in schools: An alternative approach to education*. New York: Teachers College Press.

Noguera, P. (1995). Preventing and producing violence: A critical analysis of responses to school violence. *Harvard Educational Review*, 65, 189-212.

Oakes, J. (1995). Two cities' tracking and within-school segregation. *Teachers College Record*, 96, 681–690.

Oakes, J. (1985). *Keeping track: How schools structure inequality*. New Haven, CT: Yale University Press.

Oakes, J., & Stuart Wells, A. (1998). Detracking for high school achievement. *Educational Leadership*, March, 38–41.

Oakes, J., & Guiton, G. (1995). Matchmaking: The dynamics of high school tracking decisions. *American Educational Research Journal*, 32, 3–33.

Oliver, M., Johnson, J., & Farrell, W. (1993). Anatomy of a rebellion: A political-economic analysis. In R. Gooding-Williams, ed., *Reading Rodney King, Reading Urban Uprising*. New York: Routledge.

Pallone, N., & Hennessy, J. (1993). Tinderbox criminal violence: Neurogenic impulsivity, risk-taking, and the phenomenology of rational choice. In R.V. Clarke & M. Felson, eds., *Routine activity and rational choice: Advances in criminological theory*, vol. 5 (New Brunswick, NJ: Transaction Publishers.

Pattillo-McCoy, M. (1999). *Black picket fences: Privilege and peril among the black middle class*. Chicago: University of Chicago Press.

Perlstein, D. (1998). Saying the unsaid: Girl killing and the curriculum. *Journal of Curriculum and Supervision*, 14, 88–104.

Peterson, B. (1996). The struggle for decent schools. In W. Ayers & P. Ford, eds., *City kids, city teachers: Reports from the front row* (152–169). New York: The New Press.

Petersen, G., Pietrzak, D., Speaker, K. (1998). The enemy within: A national study on school violence and prevention. *Urban Education*, 33, 331–359.

Pinderhughes, H. (1997). *Race in the hood: Conflict and violence among urban youth*. Minneapolis: University of Minnesota Press.

Pipho, C. (1998). Living with zero tolerance. *Phi Delta Kappan*, June, 725–726.

Plotz, J. (1977). The perpetual messiah: Romanticism, childhood, and the paradoxes of human development. In B. Finkelstein, ed., *Regulated children/liberated children: Education in psychohistorical perspective* (63–95). NY: Psychohistory Press.

Prothrow-Stith, D., with M. Weissman. (1991). *Deadly consequences: How violence is destroying our teenage population and a plan to begin solving the problem*. New York: HarperCollins.

Provenzo, E. (1991). *Video kids: Making sense of nintendo*. Cambridge, MA: Harvard University Press.

Public Law 103-382. (1994). *Safe and Drug-Free Schools and Communities Act*. SEC. 4001, 20 USC 7101.

Public Law 103-227. (1994). *Safe Schools Act*. SEC. 701, 20 USC 5961.

Public Law 103-227. (1994). *Gun-Free Schools Act*. SEC 1031, 20 USC 2701.

Public Law 101-647. (1990). *Gun-Free School Zones Act*. SEC 1702, 18 USC 921.

Rabinowitz, P. (1994). *They must be represented: The politics of documentary*. London: Verso.

Reith, M. (1999). Viewing of crime drama and authoritarian aggression: An investigation of the relationship between crime viewing, fear and aggression. *Journal of Broadcasting and Electronic Media*, 43, 211–21.

Report by the Advancement Project and The Civil Rights Project (2000). *Opportunities Suspended: The Devastating Consequences of Zero Tolerance and School Discipline Policies*. Cambridge: Harvard University.

Rist, R. (1970). Student social class and teacher expectations: The self-fulfilling prophecy in ghetto education. *Harvard Educational Review*, 40, 411–451.

Rosenbaum, J., DeLuca, S., Miller, S., & Roy, K. (1999). Pathways into work: Short- and long-term effects of personal and institutional ties. *Sociology of Education*, 72, 179–196.

Rubin, L. (1976). *Worlds of pain: Life in the working-class family*. New York: Basic Books.

Sabol, W., & Lynch, J. (1997). *Crime policy report: Did getting tough on crime pay?* Washington, D.C.: The Urban Institute.

Sampson, R. (1997). The embeddedness of child and adolescent development: A community-level perspective on urban violence. In J. McCord, ed., *Violence and childhood in the inner city* (31–77). New York: Cambridge University Press.

Sampson, R. & Laub, J. (1993). *Crime in the making: Pathways and turning points through life*. Cambridge: Harvard University Press.

Scheurich, J. (1993). Policy archaeology: A new policy studies methodology. *Journal of Education Policy*, 9, 297–316.

Shaw, C. (1966). *The jack-roller: A delinquent boy's own story*. Chicago: University of Chicago Press.

Shaw, C., & McKay, H. (1942). *Juvenile delinquency and urban areas*. Chicago: University of Chicago Press.

226 *Bibliography*

Sheley, J., & Wright, J. (1998). *High school youths, weapons, and violence: A national survey*. Washington, DC: National Institute of Justice.

Short, J. (1997). *Poverty, ethnicity and violent crime*. Boulder, CO: Westview.

Sikes, G. (1997). *8 ball chicks: A year in the violent world of girl gangs*. New York: Dell Publishing Group.

Sinclair, B., Hamilton, J., Gutmann, B., Daft, J., & Bolcik, D. (1998). *Report on State Implementation of the Gun-Free Schools Act*. Washington: U.S. Department of Education.

Skiba, R., & Peterson, R. (1999). The dark side of zero tolerance: Can punishment lead to safe schools? *Phi Delta Kappan*, 80, 372–382.

Skinner, B. F. (1938). *The behavior of organisms: An experimental analysis*. NY: Appleton-Century-Crofts, Inc..

Soriano, M., Soriano, F., & Jimenez, E. (1994). School violence among culturally diverse populations: Sociocultural and institutional considerations, *School Psychology Review*, 23, 216–235.

Stein, N. (1995). Sexual harassment in school: The public performance of gendered violence. *Harvard Educational Review*, 65, 145–188.

Stevahn, L., Johnson, D., Johnson, R., Laginski, A., & O'Coin, I. (1996). Effects on high school students of integrating conflict resolution and peer mediation training into an academic curriculum. *Mediation Quarterly*, 14, 21–36.

Strauss, A. (1993). *Qualitative analysis for social scientists*. Cambridge: Cambridge University Press.

Stumbo, C. (1989). Teachers and teaching. *Harvard Educational Review*, 49, 87–97.

Thrasher, F. (1927). *The gang: A study of 1,313 gangs in Chicago*. Chicago: University of Chicago Press.

Toby, J. (1994). The politics of school violence. *Public Interest*, 116, 34–56.

Toby, J. (1993). Everyday school violence: How disorder fuels it. *American Educator*, Winter, 4–9.

Tonry, M. (1999). Why are U.S. incarceration rates so high? *Crime and Delinquency*, 45, 419–437.

Tonry, M. (1995). *Malign neglect: Race, crime, and punishment in America*. New York and Oxford: Oxford University Press.

Tyack, D. (1994). *The one best system: A history of American urban education*. Cambridge, MA: Harvard University Press.

Tyack, D., & Cuban, L. (1995). *Tinkering toward utopia: A century of public school reform*. Cambridge: Harvard University Press.

Tyler, T., & Boeckmann, R. (1997). Three strikes and you're out, but why? *Law and Society Review*, 31, 237–65.

Van Maanen, J. (1973). Observations on the making of policemen. *Human Organization*, 32, 407–18.

Vestermark, S. D. (1996). Critical decisions, critical elements in an effective school security program. In A.M. Hoffman, ed., *Schools, violence, and society* (101–122). Westport, CT: Praeger.

Vigil, J. D. (1999). Streets and schools: How educators can help Chicano marginalized gang youth. *Harvard Educational Review*, 69, 270–288.

Ward, J. (1995). Cultivating a morality of care in African-American adolescents: A culture-based model of violence prevention. *Harvard Educational Review*, 65, 175–188.

Warner, B., Weist, M., & Krulak, A. (1999). Risk factors for school violence. *Urban Education*, 34, 52–68.

Willis, P. (1977). *Learning to labor: How working class kids get working class jobs*. New York: Teachers College Press.

Wilson, W. J. (1996). *When work disappears: The world of the new urban poor*. New York: Knopf.

Wilson, W. J. (1987). *The truly disadvantaged: The inner city, the underclass, and public policy*. Chicago: University of Chicago Press.

Wright, M., Wintermute, G., & Rivara, F. (1999). Effectiveness of denial of handgun purchase to persons believed to be a high risk for firearm violence. *American Journal of Public Health*, 1999, 88–90.

Yeakey, C., & Bennett, C. (1990). Race, schooling, and class in American society. *Journal of Negro Education*, 59, 3–18.

Zimring, F. (1991). Firearms, violence, and public policy. *Scientific American*, November, 48–54.

Zinn, H. (1990). *Declarations of Independence*. New York: HarperCollins.

Zirkel, P. (1999). Zero tolerance expulsions. *NASSP Bulletin*, 83, 101–105.

Zirkel, P. & Gluckman, I. (1997). Due process in student suspensions and expulsions. *Principal*, 76, 62–63.

Zuckerman, D. (1996). Media violence, gun control, and public policy. *American Journal of Orthopsychiatry*, 66, 378–389.

Index